Fort Greene, U.S.A.

Fort Greene, U. S. A.

by Barbara Habenstreit

The Bobbs-Merrill Company, Inc.
Indianapolis / New York

Published by the Bobbs-Merrill Company, Inc.
Indianapolis   New York

ISBN 0–672–51832–5
Library of Congress catalog card number 74–3886
Designed by Paula Wiener
Manufactured in the United States of America
First printing

For Abe, David and Shelly

Contents

Introduction

IN ALMOST every city across the country, the conditions under which the urban poor live are very much the same. From the Watts ghetto in Los Angeles to the tenements of Harlem in New York City, poor people everywhere experience similar deprivations and hardships, and consequently the patterns of their everyday lives are fairly similar. Frequent unemployment, poor schooling, inadequate health care, a high rate of welfare dependency, drug addiction, crime and juvenile delinquency are familiar aspects of life in every urban poverty area, so that if a poor person were suddenly transplanted from the slums of Chicago to the slums of Boston or Washington, he would scarcely recognize the difference; his living conditions would not have been altered in any significant way.

This is not to imply that all poverty areas look alike on the surface. For example, Watts, which was shattered by riots in the summer of 1965, hardly looks like a typical slum. With its neat one- and two-story houses set back on trim lawns, Watts could pass for a modest working-class neighborhood. But its relatively pleasant facade belies a poverty that is as cruel and severe as that of any decayed, overcrowded, vermin-filled ghetto, and life in Watts is basically no different from life in any other place where large numbers of poor people are concentrated.

In focusing on one particular poverty area—the Fort Greene section of Brooklyn, New York—I am trying to present a portrait not of a poor neighborhood that is unique in any way, but rather of one that is fairly typical. What is happening in Fort Greene is likely to be happening in most poor urban communities around the country; the way people live there is very much the same as the way poor people live in other cities. In short, to study Fort Greene is to study the problems of urban poverty in microcosm.

The only way that Fort Greene may be a little different from other poverty areas is that most of its poor are clustered in massive public housing developments rather than crumbling tenements. But here, too, Fort Greene is not really unusual, because in every major city, slum housing is gradually being replaced by high-rise public housing units. This type of housing is now becoming as characteristic of poor urban neighborhoods as are the long-familiar tenement structures.

I chose Fort Greene for this study of poverty simply because I have lived in the neighborhood for the past eight years and have gotten to know many of the people who live and work there. I first moved to the area in 1965 when my husband was working at the Brooklyn Center of Long Island University, which is located in the heart of Fort Greene. At that time, L.I.U. was attempting to become an integral part of the surrounding black community rather than to remain an alien institution that had no connection with its neighborhood. The idea was that the school and the community could join forces and work together to improve social conditions and to uplift the quality of life in the area. But the attempt never really got very far, and today L.I.U. still has as little beneficial impact on the people of Fort Greene as Columbia

University has on the people of Harlem or the University of Chicago on its South Side neighbors. In general, it would seem that the presence of such prominent high-level institutions really makes very little difference in the everyday lives of the people who live in the surrounding poor communities.

The institutions that acutely affect the lives of the poor are the most basic ones—the public schools, the hospitals, the welfare centers, and all the other places that provide fundamental public services. To a great extent, the quality of life in poor urban neighborhoods depends on the availability of such services and the benevolence of the government, for the poor are far less able than the middle class to provide for their own essential needs.

This extreme dependency on government services is just one of the basic problems of urban poverty, and it exists wherever large numbers of poor people exist, whether in Fort Greene or anywhere else. Fort Greene is far from unique, and when we look at this community, we might just as well be looking at any poor city neighborhood in the United States.

Fort Greene, U.S.A.

The Pratt Institute Center for Community and Environmental Development

1. Farragut housing project area
2. Fort Greene housing project area
3. Downtown Brooklyn shopping area
4. Brooklyn Heights
5. Middle-income development (University Towers, Kingsview Cooperative)
6a. Willoughby Walk ⎫
  b. St. James Towers ⎬ middle income developments
7a, b. Brownstone renovation areas

1

The Neighborhood

UNTIL a few years ago, the ancient Myrtle Avenue El that wound through Fort Greene, Brooklyn, had the distinction of being the only train in New York City with wooden cars. The shaky old relic used to groan and shudder along its run, leading passengers to fear that it might topple right off its tracks. Yet when heavy snows fell and practically all the subways in the city were immobilized, the old el could still be seen hobbling steadfastly along. It was a freak and a curiosity, and the people of Fort Greene were almost fond of it, except that its noise invariably drowned out their television programs at crucial moments.

Finally the city decided to tear down the old el before it crumbled, and for the first time since 1888 sunshine hit Myrtle Avenue. The result was unexpectedly dismal—nobody had quite realized how filthy the street was until the benevolent shadow of the el was stripped away and the street lay naked in all its grime. To make things worse, the demolition job was suspended for a time, and for several months the hollow stumps of the el's pillars still remained, overflowing with the trash and debris that people had stuffed into them over the years.

Eventually the stumps were removed; the avenue was cleaned up a little, and it acquired the look that it has today —a shabby, glass-strewn street lined with an assortment of unkempt stores and a few boarded-up shops.

This dreary but busy avenue is the heart of the Fort Greene community—one of twenty-six communities in New York City that have been officially designated as "poverty areas." To qualify as a poverty area, according to criteria set by the city's Council Against Poverty, a neighborhood must have a high rate of juvenile delinquency, a large percentage of residents on welfare, and a high percentage of families with annual incomes under four thousand dollars. In these respects, Fort Greene is eminently qualified as a poverty area. Over the past fifteen years it has consistently had one of the highest juvenile delinquency rates in New York City, along with Harlem, the South Bronx, Bedford-Stuyvesant, and Brownsville. Over twenty-five percent of the families living in Fort Greene's vast public housing projects are supported by welfare; more than sixty percent of the project's residents are poor enough to qualify for the welfare department's food stamp program; and more than half of the children in the community's public schools come from families with incomes under four thousand dollars, which is below the federal poverty level.

The neighborhood is more than seventy percent black and Puerto Rican, with many of the black families concentrated in the low-income projects and the Puerto Ricans living mainly in the decayed brownstones and rooming houses that fan out from historic Fort Greene Park.

Despite years of neglect and abuse, the thirty-acre park is still a majestic sight from afar. It is built on a hill that soars steeply from the street, and at its peak, towering above the flatlands of Brooklyn, is a monument to the prison ship martyrs of the American Revolution. The monument honors 11,500 American soldiers and sailors who died in British prison ships anchored in Brooklyn's harbor during the War for Independence. The martyrs' remains were actually buried in the park in 1873, a hundred years after they died. The park itself was designed in the late 1860s by Frederick Law Olmsted and Calvert Vaux, the famed landscape architects who also designed Central Park in Manhattan and Brooklyn's Prospect Park.

In its earlier years, Fort Greene Park was renowned for its beauty and its historic significance. But as the surrounding neighborhood declined, the park was virtually forgotten. Now, when you enter the park, you can see that the hills are eroding, many trees are dead and dying, and the once lush meadows are scarred with barren patches where no grass grows. Broken glass and empty beer cans are strewn all over, graffiti is scrawled on benches and walls, and the winding paved walkways are cracked in many places.

The section of the park that faces the sprawling Fort Greene housing projects has large, well-equipped playgrounds that are inhabited mainly by derelicts, winos, and junkies. Mothers are usually afraid to take their children there. But sometimes in the winter, when a thick snowfall covers the park's steep hills, hundreds of children converge on the slopes to enjoy some of the best sledding anywhere in New York City.

The park tends to divide Fort Greene into two sections. West of the park, lying just across the river from Manhattan, is the part of Fort Greene that contains huge public housing projects, a few dozen ancient factories that employ surprisingly large numbers of people, a small cluster of high-rise middle-income buildings, and the Brooklyn Center of Long Island University. Most of the housing here has been built since the 1940s as part of a mammoth slum clearance effort. Old tenements, shacks, and shanties once stood on these sites, but even though they have long since been razed, the poverty still remains. The 1970 federal census showed that the median income of families in the various census tracts around here hovered at about fifty-five hundred dollars. This meant that half the families had incomes above that level and half below it. The median family income for the nation as a whole in 1970 was more than ten thousand dollars.

The neighborhood east of Fort Greene Park is somewhat more affluent than its western counterpart and bears little physical resemblance to it. Here, the tree-shaded streets are lined with old brownstones that once were very elegant. But over the decades their wealthy and middle-class occupants moved away and deterioration began. Today, many of these fine old structures have been carved up into dreary rooming houses and crammed with far more occupants than they were ever meant to hold.

The proudest and most costly of these houses, actually small mansions, were built along Clinton Avenue, so that the area around there acquired a name of its own—Clinton Hill, or just "the Hill." It was here that Charles Pratt, the millionaire oil merchant and founder of Pratt Institute, built an elaborate townhouse for himself in 1875. Later he built equally grand homes across the street for each of his three sons. Pratt's original mansion now houses St. Joseph's College for Women, while one of his sons' mansions serves as the residence of the Roman Catholic Archbishop of Brooklyn. Because so many of the mansions along Clinton Avenue have been preserved by educational and religious institutions, the street is still one of the most beautiful in the city—an oasis of nineteenth-century elegance surrounded by mid-twentieth-century urban decay.

About eight blocks east of Fort Greene Park, just off Myrtle Avenue, is Pratt Institute. It is around this area that the most affluent residents of Fort Greene live today, elbow to elbow with their poorer neighbors but far removed from them in income and life-styles. In the census tract immediately adjoining the institute, the median family income in 1970 was

$12,084. Only six percent of the families there had incomes below the poverty level, whereas in other areas of Fort Greene, both east and west of the park, between twenty-five and forty percent of the families were living below the poverty level.

With a total population of about 73,600, Fort Greene is a fairly small community. According to boundaries established by the city's Community Planning Board, Fort Greene is the smallest community planning district in Brooklyn. It is bounded on the north by the Brooklyn Navy Yard and the East River; on the east by the huge Bedford-Stuyvesant ghetto; on the west by the downtown Brooklyn business and civic area, and just beyond that by posh upper-middle-income Brooklyn Heights. On the south, Fort Greene merges into the Atlantic Avenue railroad terminal area where a multimillion-dollar urban renewal job is taking place.

In the decades before World War II the neighborhood was largely Italian, but there were enough Irish, Jews, and blacks living there to make it a multiethnic interracial community. The small stores that lined Myrtle Avenue were owned mainly by Italians and Jews who lived around there, but in the years following the war they began to move away—just as the wealthy mansion owners had moved away before them. The Italians and Jews still continued to own most of the stores, however, even though their customers were now predominantly black and Puerto Rican. In more recent years these aging store owners began selling out if they could, but if they were unable to find any buyers—and increasingly this was the case—they simply closed up shop. In the 1960s many of these empty stores were taken over by various antipoverty and social welfare agencies that offered such services as job training, drug rehabilitation, activities for teenagers, career counseling, etc. There was such a proliferation of these agencies along Myrtle Avenue that people could get just about any kind of social help they needed—but they were finding it increasingly difficult to buy a bottle of aspirin or a newspaper. If they shopped on Myrtle Avenue west of the park, they no longer had a drug store, a candy store, a shoe store, a TV repair shop, a bakery, a hardware store, or a shoe repair shop. All these small businesses were gone, driven out by rising crime rates, vandalism, and fear.

The bodegas—small Puerto Rican grocery stores—remained, and eventually a few black families also opened up stores along Myrtle Avenue.

Today, if you drive over the Manhattan Bridge into Fort Greene, the first store you'll see on the corner of Myrtle and Flatbush is the Shabazz Steak 'n Take, a small, well-scrubbed Muslim restaurant that offers quick over-the-counter meals. A large dry-cleaning store is also owned by Muslims, and there are other clear indications that Muslim economic strength is on the rise. Muslim food products bearing the Shabazz label are carried in several stores along Myrtle Avenue, including the two large supermarkets—A&P and Finast —and advertisements for Shabazz products are plastered in store windows.

It is not easy for businesses to survive on Myrtle Avenue. About two years ago Kentucky Fried Chicken opened up a small take-out place that was protected by elaborate security measures. Although the shop was no bigger than twelve by twelve feet, a closed-circuit television camera monitored the premises. Clerks worked behind a floor-to-ceiling partition with tiny glass windows that were more like slits, and they spoke to customers through an intercom system. But despite the precautions, people were reluctant to go there, because all too often they would be waylaid right outside the door by teenagers who would try to steal their chicken. It was almost like a game on the part of the chicken thieves, and after just one year Kentucky Fried Chicken closed.

John's Bargain Store—a large low-priced variety store— also didn't last long. There was so much pilferage that more of the store's merchandise was being hawked by the pilferers out on the street than was being sold in the store itself.

Flink's Drug Store had been in business for a long time, but about five years ago Mr. Flink decided he had had enough. He used to complain that the teenagers he had known from infancy and had watched grow up were now robbing him into bankruptcy. Despite offers from community groups to subsidize him if he would remain open, he closed his doors for good. After that, the people in the Fort Greene projects had to walk about ten blocks to the nearest pharmacy.

As with so many of the other stores, Flink's Drug Store was replaced by an agency rather than a business. The Willoughby House Settlement opened an after-school center for the children of working mothers. Next door, where a shoe repair shop had once stood, the Fort Greene Youth Patrol was set up with antipoverty funds. This was an organization of teenagers who were paid to help patrol the housing projects and to escort people home from the subways and the surrounding factories late at night.

Among the old-time storekeepers who are still hanging on today is Jack, owner of a Myrtle Avenue fish market. Jack is an Italian who grew up in Fort Greene in the pre-World War II days. He remembers the neighborhood before the housing projects went up and has been selling fish there for over thirty years. Nowadays, Jack lives out in Massapequa, Long Island, and if it didn't take so long to commute he would move even farther away from Brooklyn.

As the familiar old businesses leave, new-style operations come in. One of the newest is a storefront medical center called the Fort Greene Family Health Group. Signs in Spanish and English announce that the center has a dentist, a physician, a pediatrician, an obstetrician, a gynecologist, an eye specialist, a surgeon, X rays, a dermatologist, and a podiatrist. A tiny pharmacy is also part of this setup, but it is open only at irregular hours. The Family Health Group deals almost entirely with patients who are on Medicaid and Medicare. Before these medical plans came into being, it simply wasn't lucrative enough for private doctors and dentists to practice in poor neighborhoods like Fort Greene. Except for old Dr. Vitelli, who has had an office across the street from the projects for more than a quarter of a century, there were practically no doctors or dentists in the area. But now, with Medicaid and Medicare to pay the bills, storefront medical centers like the Family Health Group have been springing up in poor neighborhoods all across the city. Whether these doctors have come with the intention of performing vitally needed health services or whether they are there mainly for the purpose of ripping off Medicaid remains to be seen. Many people in the neighborhood still don't trust these doctors and prefer to go to the hospital clinics.

There are two large supermarkets on Myrtle Avenue that serve the people in the projects, A&P and Finast. Although the prices in both are about the same, the stores are regarded very differently by the people, who have been virtually at war with the A&P, which is always much emptier than Finast.

Hostility among ghetto residents toward the A&P chain dates back many years, and in the late 1960s Operation Breadbasket started a boycott against the chain to protest the low quality and high prices of its merchandise in ghetto areas and its failure to hire black managers or supervisors. One specific charge was that A&P frequently raised its prices on the days when people got their welfare checks.

The Fort Greene community did not actually organize against the A&P until after a tragic incident occurred. Early one evening a man walked into the store with a five-pound bag of potatoes. He claimed that he had bought the potatoes in the store, but that many of them were rotten, and he wanted to exchange his bag for another bag. The A&P manager insisted that the potatoes had not come from his store in the first place, and a loud argument ensued. Finally, the irate customer simply walked over to the produce counter, helped himself to a different bag of potatoes, and started to leave. At this moment an A&P guard emerged from a rear storage room with a gun, took one shot, and killed the man.

Although the guard was arrested at once, this episode set off a remarkably potent neighborhood boycott against the Myrtle Avenue A&P—remarkable because the community as a whole had never mobilized itself before for effective social action. Hardly anyone set foot in the A&P for months, and finally the manager and several of his assistants were removed and a new managerial crew brought in. Chris, the black produce manager, was promoted to acting manager of the entire store; restitution was promised to the family of the slain man; other issues were thrashed out between the chain and the community leaders; and eventually the boycott was halted. But a lot of the bitterness still remained, and the A&P was never able to recapture all its old customers. Its volume is still low compared to Finast's, and there are rumors that A&P is not planning to renew its lease when it runs out.

The A&P is burglarized or vandalized a little more frequently than the other stores along Myrtle Avenue, and even its steel gates don't provide much protection. In a recent burglary in July 1973, the gates were simply bent backwards, the front window was broken, and the thieves ran off with a cache of cigarettes and Motown records that the store had been featuring as a special.

Right next to the A&P on Myrtle Avenue is an alley where most of the neighborhood winos and unemployed men hang out. Anyone who lives in Fort Greene doesn't have to pick up the newspaper to find out whether the unemployment rate is up or down; he can just walk along Myrtle Avenue and count the number of jobless men out on the street.

Many of the men who lounge around the alley tend to work sporadically at odd jobs for short periods of time. Ranging in age from the late twenties up to the forties or fifties, they are mostly unskilled or semiskilled black and Puerto Ricans, and they can seldom count on long-term employment. Contrary to what many of the people in the neighborhood think, most of the alley men are not on welfare. Except for the hard-core alcoholics who may qualify for welfare under the "disabled" category, a lot of these men somehow manage to get by on a few months' work here and there, and some have wives or girlfriends who work regularly and support them. Others may have part-time jobs at odd hours which leave them plenty of time for hanging around the streets.

The alley is like a social club, and even men who have moved away from the neighborhood frequently come back just to see what's doing in the alley. Winter or summer, the men shoot craps, stand around drinking cheap wine and booze from bottles in brown paper bags, and even hold birthday parties. Many of them show up at the alley as early as seven o'clock in the morning, as promptly and regularly as if they were reporting for work. In snow or rain they huddle in doorways, so that whatever the weather, there is always a small army of men loitering about Myrtle Avenue.

Many of the people—particularly the white residents—who live in the middle-income buildings just around the corner are afraid to walk down Myrtle Avenue because of the presence of these men. The police of the Eighty-fourth Precinct say that they repeatedly get calls from people in the two middle-income complexes—Kingsview Cooperative Houses and University Towers—demanding that they "get the bums off the avenue." But the police are reluctant to do this for fear of angering the black residents in the low-income projects, who are likely to know many of the loiterers and do not object to having them hang around the streets.

Actually, the police feel that the men's presence in the street tends to cut down on the amount of crime. "When they're not around, that alley is a haven for purse snatchers and muggers," a spokesman for the Eighty-fourth Precinct said. "But when the men are there, it's pretty safe. They themselves are harmless, and they stand there all day long just talking and drinking, and they watch everything that's going on. You'd be surprised. It deters a lot of crime."

Nevertheless, many of the middle-class residents of Fort Greene—both black and white—seldom set foot on Myrtle Avenue even though it is just around the corner from where they live. They prefer to get into their cars and go elsewhere to do their marketing. In a sense they are not part of the neighborhood at all, and most of them have no contact whatsoever with the people in the low-income projects. The fact that their buildings are clearly branded "middle income," while the people on the other side of Myrtle Avenue live in buildings clearly branded "low income," is a very divisive factor—more divisive than race. When the black and white middle-income residents bemoan all the crime committed by "them," they both mean the people in the projects. "Them" is the poor; "us" is the middle class. It is a schism based on economics.

When the middle-income buildings first went up, pressure was exerted to have the children from these buildings zoned into P.S. 20, a school that lay on the other side of Fort Greene Park and was about a ten-block walk away. A much more convenient school would have been P.S. 67—located in the projects—which was only about a block away. But the middle-income parents preferred P.S. 20 because that was where the more affluent families who lived around Pratt sent their children. Their efforts succeeded, and as a result the residents of the far-flung middle-income "pockets" in Fort Greene developed more contacts with each other through P.S. 20 than with their poorer neighbors who lived right across the street.

There haven't been any racial clashes in Fort Greene in recent memory, not even during the turbulent sixties. However, Myrtle Avenue acquired a definite black power ambiance during that period, with militant blacks standing on street corners handing out protest leaflets or addressing passersby over loudspeaker systems. At times the speeches became abrasively antiwhite, so that any white shoppers who happened to be passing by would get a little nervous; they would usually avert their eyes and try to pretend they didn't see or hear anything. As it turned out, they needn't have worried, because there were no actual incidents. In Fort Greene, at any rate, revolutionary fervor seemed to be directed against the concept of a far-off, anonymous, omnipotent "Whitey" who was oppressing the poor, not the flesh-and-blood whitey who lived around the corner.

Such political activity was even more widespread along Fulton Street, the hub of the downtown Brooklyn shopping center, which is just a few blocks west of Fort Greene. Despite the deterioration of much of the surrounding residential area, the downtown Brooklyn shopping area is still flourishing. It is the city's second most important regional shopping center, right behind the 34th Street area in Manhattan, and it attracts more than two hundred thousand shoppers in an average business day. The annual sales volume of these downtown Brooklyn stores is more than three hundred million dollars. Abraham & Straus, Korvette's, Martin's and Mays are the major department stores lining Fulton Street.

The sidewalk in front of A&S is almost always a whirlwind of political activity, and during the late 1960s the Black Panthers, the Black Muslims, the Young Lords, the Progressive Labor Party, the Students for a Democratic Society, and the Student Non-Violent Coordinating Committee were usually out in full force, so that shoppers had to run a gauntlet of leaflets, petitions, newspapers, and contribution cans. (It wasn't a completely political scene, however; the radical groups had to vie for sidewalk space with the Salvation Army, Jehovah's Witnesses, Hare Krishna, and sometimes a nun or two.)

Of all the radical groups that flourished on Fulton Street

during the 1960s, only one is still there on a regular basis—the Black Muslims. It's easy to spot the Muslims, because they dress far more dapperly than the average Fulton Street habitué. Even in the hottest weather they stand around in their immaculate suits, starched white shirts, and bow ties, politely trying to persuade people to buy their newspaper, *Muhammed Speaks*. While other radical groups have come and gone, making only a fleeting impact on the black and the poor of the city, the Muslims seem to have worked their way more deeply into the fabric of ghetto life. But in Fort Greene, at least, their influence appears limited almost entirely to the economic sphere. Politically they do not seem to be much of a factor at all.

Myrtle Avenue, too, is quiet now, and in a political sense the whole neighborhood is very much the same as it was before the tumult of the sixties began—inert and sluggish. The only visible changes that have emerged from all the strife involve the growth of black pride and self-esteem. Most black people in the neighborhood no longer straighten their hair, and hardly anyone uses skin bleaches or lighteners anymore. The theme "black is beautiful" has had a strong impact.

But Fort Greene is as poor now as it ever was, at least in the area around the public housing projects. The stores are just as shabby, and there is just as much dirt and broken glass littering the streets. Large numbers of people are still dependent on welfare, and so are the stores along Myrtle Avenue; if the people didn't have welfare money to spend, the stores couldn't stay in business very long. In this sense, Fort Greene as a whole couldn't survive without those welfare checks.

Most of the people cash their checks in the Myrtle Avenue supermarkets or in a Manufacturers Hanover Bank on Flatbush Avenue a few blocks away. Before the bank moved to larger quarters, the police had to put up barricades on the sidewalk to handle the mobs of people that jammed in on the first and sixteenth of the month—welfare check days. Joe, the manager of the Finast supermarket on Myrtle Avenue, says that most of his customers are on welfare and that he always anticipates a big crush on check days.

Unlike the A&P, Finast has had a fairly good relationship with the people in Fort Greene. This may be due more to Joe, who has been in that store for sixteen years, than to any policies set down by the chain itself. Joe knows most of his customers personally, and although he is white and almost all the supervisory personnel in the store are white, the community has not made an issue of this as it has with A&P— possibly because the old A&P manager was aloof and unfriendly, while Joe has always been pleasant to everyone and is popular with his customers. From his vantage point on Myrtle Avenue, Joe has gotten to know the neighborhood pretty well and has become something of an expert on what it is like to run a business in a poverty area.

2

Joe

"I'LL NEVER forget the week when the city first started giving out food stamps to people on welfare. Business in this store hit an all-time high. People were buying like there was a war on. Nobody guessed what an impact it would have. We did over eighty thousand dollars in business that week, when normally we do around fifty-five or sixty thousand. The old people especially were buying things like roast beef and steak, and they were telling me, 'You know how long I haven't eaten roast beef?'

"You see, the old people were getting a special bonus with the stamps that time—they paid one-third and they got two-thirds free. So if they paid thirty dollars or so, they could get enough stamps to buy ninety dollars' worth of food. The sixty-dollar difference was like found money. But they knew they could only spend the money for food, so they were stocking up. They were buying pounds of butter at a time, eight or nine or ten pounds.

"Even in normal times, people around here buy large orders of food. In these kinds of areas, people love to eat. People on welfare. They haven't got anything else to look forward to—let's put it that way—so their stomachs come first.

A person with a big family on welfare doesn't think any-thing about buying three or four big boxes of cornflakes at a time, or eight large cans of tuna fish. That's how you get these big orders. In a middle-class area like where I used to work it's different. The people there do a lot more eating out and they have smaller families, so when they go into a super-market they buy smaller portions. You think they buy five pounds of potatoes? They're looking for maybe two pounds. Or they're looking for half a pound of onions, maybe just one onion. That's the difference in shopping habits.

"Here, the welfare mothers with the big families buy things mostly in the large sizes where they're getting the most for their dollar. On the whole, with the money they get, I think they do the right thing by it. It's hard today even for middle-class people to make ends meet, as far as food prices go. Chopped chuck today is up to $1.09 a pound. It's ridicu-lous! Last year it was 69¢ a pound. And these people have to make do on the same welfare money they were getting last year and the year before. So they wind up eating meat only twice a week or so. They buy a lot of eggs, a lot of tuna fish. You can feed a family of six or seven with two or three large cans of tuna fish, some mayonnaise and celery, and a couple of loaves of bread.

"Even though the people can't afford much meat because the prices are so high, they don't try to do anything about it. They don't put up a fight. Remember when there was that big meat boycott a while ago? Well, it hardly affected our meat sales here at all. These people were not willing to give up whatever meat they were buying, even for a week. But our stores out in Long Island, in the middle-class neighborhoods, their meat sales were down more than forty percent.

"But the people here don't waste their money either. They don't go in too much for the frilly items. The biggest con-venience food that we sell is those little Banquet dinners with the meat in the bag that you boil. Those are for quick lunches, and they're very inexpensive—just a quarter each. When the welfare mothers cash their checks they stock up mainly on a lot of canned merchandise, enough to last them the two weeks until the next check comes. They buy the big cans of spaghetti and meatballs, ravioli, and macaroni and cheese. In between they come in every few days or so for their perishables, like bread and milk.

"Buying the food and paying the rent—that's the first two things on people's minds when they cash those welfare checks. They take care of those things first, and then they do the best they can with whatever money is left. I would say that over sixty percent of our customers use food stamps, and an awful lot also are on welfare. They live mainly in the Fort Greene projects and in the Farragut projects, and we cash their checks for them. In an average check week—the first or sixteenth of the month—we cash between forty and fifty thousand dollars' worth of welfare checks. And since our volume is about sixty thousand dollars a week, you can see how much of our business depends on welfare money. If we were cashing only about twenty thousand dollars' worth of checks and doing fifty thousand dollars' worth of business, it would mean that there were a lot more working people in the area.

"Cashing all those checks creates some problems for us, but it's better than it used to be. Up to about two years ago we used to take a loss of about five percent because of all the checks we cashed that turned out to be stolen or duplicates. You see, the city won't reimburse us for these. What would happen was, someone would get their check and cash it in our store. Then they'd go to the welfare center and say they never got their check, or that it was stolen. So the center would give them a duplicate check and they'd come back to our store and cash that one too. We didn't keep records then, so we had no way of knowing that the person had just cashed another welfare check a few days earlier. Then we would send off all our checks to the city for reimbursement. But if there was trouble with a check—if it had been reported stolen—it would take almost a year before the city would send that check back to us with 'no payment' stamped on it. By that time the person who had cashed the check had either moved or we never saw him anymore, so there was no way we could collect on that check.

"But about two years ago the city started sending these bad checks back to us much faster. We get them back in about two weeks now, so we can usually catch the people who cashed them. A lot of the times they promise to make it up to us out of their own pockets—and they do, too, 'cause they know they've done something wrong. Also, we've got our own record system now. There's a girl working in the office here, and she records every check that's cashed. Plus we have a camera set up, so anytime a person cashes a check his picture is taken. This way we have a foolproof way of knowing who cashed a check in the first place, and we can usually catch people who are trying to cash duplicate checks. Now our losses from bad checks are much less than they used to be.

"There are quite a few middle-class people in this neighborhood, too. They're right around the back, in the Kingsview houses and University Towers. But a lot of them don't shop here because they don't want to come onto Myrtle Avenue. They're afraid. The main thing is fear—they're afraid of muggings and this and that. They feel they can't handle themselves around here. So they get in their cars and they go someplace else to shop, like Brooklyn Heights. Now, I feel my store is a good place to shop in. Pricewise, we're competitive with everybody. But there's been a lot of crime in the area, and the middle-class people just don't want to come here.

"In my company, Finast, they call this a 'ghetto' store. It's not an official label, but like, if I go to a managers' meeting and we're all sitting around a table and someone'll ask, 'Where are you from?' and I say, 'Myrtle Avenue,' right away they say, 'Oh, the ghetto area.' They don't realize there might be a lot of middle-class people here. They don't realize that Long Island University is right around the corner. They call it 'ghetto area,' and it becomes bad by reputation. Word gets around.

"To give you an example, a manager out in Elmont, Long Island, needed some register tapes a few weeks ago. We have the same kind of cash registers, so he was going to send someone over here to pick up the tapes from me. We're really not very far from him. Maybe a half-hour drive away. Well, he asked three or four people from his store to come here and get the tapes, but none of them would come. His help just wouldn't come down here because of the reputation of the area. They were afraid they'd be mugged or their cars would be stolen. All they know about this area is what they hear, and from the outside looking in it's a completely different picture. I know better. I work here every day, and I'm still alive. I've been in this store for sixteen years, and I know that the number of incidents that happen here compared to the number of people who live here is really very small.

"But you do have a lot of incidents inside the store, with pickpockets and pilferage and things like that. We don't have purse-snatchings, because you never see women carrying purses here. They're afraid to. They keep their money in their pockets. But while a woman is looking over the meat or vegetables and her attention is taken away, it's very easy for a guy to lift her wallet right out of her pocket. I've seen it happen, and most of these pickpockets are just young kids.

"There's a lot of pilferage, too. At the end of a busy day we find a lot of empty packages of toothpaste and other drug items, or open cookies and cold cuts. You'll get a lot of people who'll steal a quarter pound of butter, or they might steal a box of dates, maybe a package of bologna. When they take things like this, it's for themselves. Maybe they can't make ends meet. You get shoplifting in middle-class stores also, but it's pretty negligible compared to what goes on in a poor area, because the need is greater here. The families are bigger, more food is needed, more money is needed.

"But the main thing—the thing that hurts us the most—is not this kind of petty pilferage. It's the real big pilferage that's done for profit, mainly with meats. More meats are stolen in a supermarket than anything else because they're a highly saleable item. A guy can get rid of meat quick. I've caught guys with seventy or eighty dollars' worth of meat. They stuff it into shopping bags or under their coats. Women carry it under their skirts, anywhere. Meat has a high resale value. Anybody will buy meat—and this isn't only now because of the high prices. This is all the time. If you take ten round steaks and go down to one of the bars a few blocks away and sell them to the bar, they'll serve them for lunch. A bar will buy them—anything that's cheap, that they can make a buck on, they're going to buy it. This is the kind of area it is.

"It's mostly teenagers who are doing this heavy stealing. They also go for things like cigarettes, shrimp or lobster meat, stuff that they can sell. They're not doing it because they're hungry. Most of them live with their mothers, and even though they're usually on welfare, the kids are well fed. There's no reason for them to steal food, not because of hunger, anyhow. I know most of the mothers—I have a whole list of phone numbers in my pocket—but when I talk to them about their kids, they just can't do anything. They can't control them. Their families are so large. They know what their kids are doing, because most of them have had to go to court in the middle of the night when their kids got caught. How many mothers have I faced in night court when we got their sons for breaking into the store or for stealing steaks or robbing from the trucks in the back?

"They start very young, too. I see little kids, really little, and they curse me out like they're eighteen or nineteen, screaming, 'You white no good - - -!' And I think, 'How could they be saying that? They're only four years old, five years old.' But you hear it. And you find them stealing M&M's

and things like that, sticking them inside their belts, and so you have to throw them out.

"Our main problem right now is kids. Mostly kids. The aggravation of running the store with these kids around is terrible. They come in, eight or ten at a time, and they try to raid the place. Really, that's what it comes down to. They're up and down the aisles, and you got to go chasing after them. They're mainly after snacks and candy, that type of stuff. It's rare that they go in the back to steal meats—unless they're told to by the older guys. That happens also. The older ones will have their little brothers do the stealing for them.

"I remember one day I was looking out the window and I see this guy—a well-known thief that I threw out of here a hundred times. He was about fourteen or fifteen years old. I see him waiting outside and I knew there must be something up. So what happens? Ten minutes later I see this little kid—he must've been six years old—walking out the door with a bag. I stopped the kid and I took the bag. I see he has a whole load of candy, cold cuts, a TV dinner, and a bottle of soda. 'Where's your receipt?' I asked him. 'Oh, that girl over there checked me out, and she didn't give me no receipt,' he says. He's six years old, and he's telling me a story. So I asked the girl and she said she never saw him. Then I put two and two together. The guy outside was the little kid's brother. He told him to go in and what to take.

"Sometimes a guy will send in a girl to steal. The girls today, they're starting to get worse than the fellows. But still, you don't seem to watch out for the girls as much, even though you should. They carry these big shoulder bags—they look like duffel bags—and they load them up with meats. Those bags are so big a girl can stuff in forty cans of tuna fish or ten jars of coffee.

"When we catch shoplifters, sometimes we report them and sometimes we let them go. If the same guy is stealing from you day after day, you report him. But the problem is, he's usually out of court quicker than I am, plus the judge keeps the evidence. One time I caught this guy stealing a big eight-pound ham. I took him to court, and afterwards, when the hearing was over, I said, 'Let me have the ham, judge.' He says, 'No. I got to keep it here for evidence.' Well, I never saw that ham anymore.

"But you have to press charges sometimes, because you want the word to get around that there's no playing around in your store. Stores get reputations, you know. Guys will say, 'Let's go over here. It's easy.' They know the easy spots, where to hit. And if your store gets a reputation for being an easy spot, you're in for a lot of trouble. Take the bodegas around here. They'll cut a guy's head off before they'll let him get away with stealing. They're rougher than we are. They'll handle the problem right on the street, and I don't think they have too much trouble with shoplifting.

"The bodegas do most of their business toward the end of the month, or just before the welfare checks come. You see, people can buy on credit there, but they can't here. That's why the end of the month is usually our slowest time. The bodegas are a lot more expensive than we are. If we're selling an item for 49¢, they'll probably get 59¢ for it. But the people on welfare have no choice. If they have no money left they have to buy on credit at the bodega's prices.

"We've only had one holdup in the daytime here. That was a long time ago when I was the produce manager. Of course, we've had lots of nighttime burglaries and break-ins. Plenty of times I got called down here at night because somebody broke in. I remember one summer when I got called three times in one week because guys kept breaking in. They just ripped down the gates and broke the windows. The A&P got hit, too. A lot of these break-ins happen in the summer. Even if the guys don't get anything, a lot of it is just a matter of letting out steam.

"There was a time six or seven years ago when we didn't even have gates or an alarm system. A lot of the other stores were unprotected, too. But then things got worse and we had to put in the gates and the alarm, and we even changed our windows so only the upper half is glass. The lower part is steel. Some of the other stores around here have put on these solid metal curtains that come down over the whole front of the store. They're the best, but they're very expensive. Also, guys can still get in through the back and through the roof.

"We'll have trouble with the same kids stealing from us the whole time they're growing up, but by the time they're eighteen or so they usually stop hanging around the markets. They sort of drift away. They go into other things. Sometimes they get a job and they settle down. I knew guys who used to come in here and really bust our chops, but they grew up and some of them turned out good. Others just went on to bigger crimes—armed robberies, holding up banks, assaults. A lot of them are in prison now.

"Some become junkies. I see them as little kids, I watch them grow up, and then I see the switch—I start seeing that they're on it. And pretty soon they're coming in and trying to sell me stuff. These junkies are all over the place. They're on the hustle. They have to be out making a buck, and they hit the department stores on Fulton Street all the time. A lot of these addicts are on welfare now. They have to report in to a welfare center to pick up their checks, and they have to be in a methadone program or some other drug program to get their welfare money. It's like they're being paid by the city to keep them out of trouble and get them off heroin.

"From what I understand, the methadone program is working out pretty good. That's what I hear from a lot of the people around here, and from a lot of the addicts also. They feel they can operate better, perform better, even hold a job. And a lot of them do. With heroin, there's a stigma. But when you say methadone, it doesn't sound as bad as heroin, even though it's just another form of addiction.

"The addicts talk to me a little about these programs they're in. I can talk to practically anybody, only I don't get much of a chance for long conversations here. Like, I'll be at the checkout working a register, and I'll see someone and say, 'Hi. How ya been? Where ya been?' and they'll say, 'I been away' or 'I'm on methadone now, and it's working for me.' So this way I pick up bits of information. They don't have any embarrassment in telling me, because there's plenty of times they came in saying to me, 'Joe, I need a dollar for this' or 'I need two more dollars to get a bag.' And I could see them, like rubbing their noses and showing all the symptoms that they needed a fix. So I would give them a dollar or two if I had it.

"When you work in this kind of area, you have to work with the people. If a guy wants to borrow a dollar, you loan him a dollar. You know you're probably never going to see that dollar again, but you've got to get involved with people's problems. You can't just act like you don't want to know them. You do get involved whether you like it or not. You don't survive unless you do.

"These guys, the addicts and winos, they don't make it a habit of coming in here every day for a loan 'cause I stop that right away. You can't let it become an everyday thing. But if I see a guy once a month or so, well, that's okay. I have feelings, too. When I see a guy needs a fix, and he might go out and do something to get the money, I feel for him. I seen so much of it. I've known a lot of guys who died from overdoses, who used to come into the store. And every time I hear about it, I feel a little twinge of guilt. How many times did he ask me for a dollar? And you wonder what happened the last time. Maybe he went for a bigger dose, or whatever. But somehow, you feel involved.

"Even though I've been in this area for so long, I don't know everything that's going on. I guess I don't know ninety percent of what's going on, because people keep to themselves. But if a guy needs a fix, or if someone gets busted, or someone takes an overdose, the word gets around."

3

In the Welfare Centers

IN STUDYING a poverty area, one of the first things you realize is that whether the number of residents on welfare is increasing or decreasing has little to do with the general economic picture or the amount of unemployment. It is a political question, for if politics demands a shrinking of the welfare rolls, they will shrink, regardless of other circumstances.

For example, in the 1960s the prevailing political mood was one of benevolence toward the poor. It was an affluent era, and the country was generous. Antipoverty programs were launched amid great fanfare, and the poor were encouraged by various legal and welfare rights groups to assert themselves and get all they could. In New York City, at least, easier policies toward welfare eligibility were put into practice, and the welfare rolls swelled to bursting.

Then a political backlash set in, coincidental with a nationwide economic belt-tightening. Caught in an inflationary squeeze and pressed for money, working-class and middle-class Americans grew increasingly resentful of welfare recipients who, they felt, were getting a free ride. The political pressure was on to reduce welfare spending, and by 1973 the number of people on welfare in New York City began to drop sharply. This was not because more poor people were working or enjoying a higher living standard, but because welfare eligibility standards were being tightened so that many new applicants could not get on the rolls, and many previous recipients were dropped. This was not just a matter of flushing out welfare cheats, but of making it tougher for *anyone* to get welfare. Even though the inflationary pressure was hurting the poor as much as anyone else—and more of them probably needed welfare aid—fewer of them were getting it.

Actually, even in badly blighted low-income areas there never have been as many of the poor on welfare as people seem to believe. Of all the people living below the poverty level in Fort Greene, for example, only about half are supported by welfare. This is due partly to the fact that the welfare eligibility level in New York State is below the poverty level as defined by the federal government,[1] so that even though people are very poor, they may not be poor enough to qualify for welfare. Whereas the federal poverty level for a nonfarm family of four in 1972 was $4,275, the state of New York would only allow a welfare grant of $2,496 plus rent to a family of four. Assuming that the family's rent was about $100 a month (the average for a four-member welfare family as of January 1972), the New York family would receive a maximum cash grant of $3,696 a year—or $579 *below* the minimum standard of need. Welfare grants were due to go up ten percent as of January 1, 1974, but since the cost of living has also gone up a great deal in the last year or two, nothing will really change.

[1] At the core of this definition of poverty is a nutritionally adequate food plan —an "economy" plan—designed by the Department of Agriculture for "emergency" or "temporary" use when funds are low. The "poverty level" depends on the cost of this food plan, as well as the overall cost of living as reflected in the Consumer Price Index. Thus, the poverty level changes as the cost of living changes. Families with incomes below the poverty level are classified as poverty families.

It is not only the people living below the poverty level who are poor. Families earning $5,000 or $6,000 a year must also be considered poor in a city where a "moderate" standard of living for a family of four requires a gross annual income of $11,880. Then there are people who are barely managing to survive on their pensions or Social Security allotments. They too are part of the nonwelfare poor.

All of these low-income people are simply not eligible for welfare, despite their poverty. In addition, there are many others who might be eligible but have never applied for a variety of reasons. Either they are too proud to admit they are in need; they dislike the loss of privacy that would result if they came under the scrutiny of the Department of Social Services; or they have steady jobs, and though these jobs pay very little (under $3,696 net per year for a family of four, for example), the workers are just not aware that they may be eligible for supplementary welfare money. People with very low Social Security benefits or miniscule pensions may also be eligible for supplementary welfare aid without realizing it.

All together, then, there are many desperately poor families in Fort Greene who somehow manage to scrape by without any welfare help at all. The same is true in other poverty areas throughout the city which reveal similar ratios—only about half the people with incomes below the poverty level receive welfare checks.[2] When people assume that just about all of New York City's poor are living on welfare, they are quite wrong. In fact, a study by New York's Rand Institute showed that there are about 480,000 poor people in the city who are eligible for welfare but are not on the rolls.

[2] 1970 federal census. Although the census has undoubtedly undercounted the total number of people in poverty areas, as well as the numbers of those with incomes below the poverty level and those receiving welfare—undercounted them by as much as forty percent, according to New York City's Rand Institute —people who work in the various welfare centers believe that the census *proportions* of welfare poor to nonwelfare poor are fairly accurate.

In Fort Greene, as elsewhere, those most in need of welfare help are women and children. According to the city's Department of Social Services, 78.7 percent of the entire welfare caseload in 1970 consisted of children and the adults who were caring for them—that is, a total of 685,303 children and 231,697 adults, mostly women. Disabled adults accounted for 10.3 percent of the welfare load; people over sixty-five years of age accounted for 6.3 percent; and employed people whose earnings were so low that they needed supplementary welfare aid accounted for 2.5 percent of the caseload. Only 2.2 percent of all welfare cases were considered "employable."

The welfare population of Fort Greene is handled by several welfare centers, each of which also handles portions of other neighborhoods as well. For example, the Fort Greene Income Maintenance Center actually handles only a small corner of Fort Greene, plus parts of Prospect Heights and Coney Island. Furthermore, the center does not handle any cases involving the aged, disabled, and blind; nor does it handle drug addicts who are receiving welfare, or recent Vietnam veterans who can't find jobs. All these groups are assigned to special welfare centers. Thus, it is impossible to isolate the precise number of welfare people in any particular neighborhood, because welfare statistics are not broken down that way; they are broken down according to the type of case rather than the locale.

Turning to Fort Greene, it is estimated that out of nearly 18,300 people living in the public housing projects, about twenty-five percent are on welfare. But perhaps as many as sixty percent are poor enough to receive some type of public assistance benefits, such as supplementary welfare aid, Medicaid or food stamps. (A family of four is eligible for food stamps if its gross annual income does not exceed six thousand dollars. By buying these stamps, low-income people can increase their food-purchasing power by about thirty percent without spending any extra money. Total Medicaid coverage is also available to low-income people who are not on welfare, provided their gross annual income does not exceed forty-five hundred dollars for a family of four.)

Outside the projects, in the rundown brownstones and rooming houses that sprawl throughout Fort Greene, it is harder to estimate the number of welfare recipients. One thing is certain, however: their number has been decreasing in recent years, because they are being forced out of the neighborhood by young middle-class families who are buying and renovating the brownstones. Many of these evicted welfare tenants eventually find other housing in neighboring Bedford-Stuyvesant.

Since Fort Greene is so conveniently located near the downtown Brooklyn business and civic area, it is just a short distance from almost all the welfare centers in Brooklyn. The welfare center for drug addicts and single unattached persons and the welfare center for Vietnam veterans are both located right off Myrtle Avenue, which means that hundreds of addicts and jobless veterans converge on the neighborhood daily. The regular family welfare centers are located around here as well, so that there are always a lot of bewildered people wandering around Fort Greene asking for directions to "the Linden Welfare Center" or "the Fulton Center" or "the Wyckoff Center."

Inside these different centers, the scene is very much the same. When they first apply for welfare, people are told to come very early in the morning, even before the centers open, to make sure they are seen that day. Some people have said they were told to come as early as 8:30 A.M., even though the centers don't open until 9:00. Once there, they line up on the sidewalk and wait. Also in the early-morning lines are people who are already on welfare but are having special problems—perhaps their last check was stolen or it never arrived, or they just received an eviction notice. These people know from past dealings with the Department of Social Services that they *must* arrive early. All the welfare centers are woefully under-staffed, and a visit to a center can be an all-day hassle.

Ann Rosenhaft, director of the Fort Greene Income Maintenance Center, estimates that her staff is thirty percent below quota. "And actually we're in a better position staffwise than almost every other center in the city," she says. "I think the major problem in running a welfare center is insufficient staff. No job can be done properly if you don't have enough people to do it. That's one of the reasons for the long periods of time people have to wait."

But some of the welfare clients have other explanations for the long delays. As one woman wrote in the January 1973 issue of a newsletter put out by welfare clients:

> On November 30, I went to the Linden Center to apply for Public Assistance. I was told to return on December 1. On December 1, I arrived at the Center at 8:30 A.M. I made out an application and was sent to the fourth floor. There I was to wait to be interviewed. I waited and I noted strange things around me. At one desk there were three people sitting, not working, just talking. At a second desk there were four people sitting, just talking, not working. At the third desk, one lady sat from 10:30 A.M. to 12:30 P.M. She wasn't working, just sitting, talking and smoking. All around me people were waiting to be helped. Children were crying, but the workers were just sitting and talking. They weren't concerned with the people that needed help. They were too busy talking.
>
> —Name Withheld

Another letter in the same issue of the newsletter offered this account:

> The doors of the Employment Center at 330 Jay Street, Brooklyn [a new welfare center for single, em-

ployable people, including addicts] were closed on November 2. Staff told people trying to get in that they couldn't take any more people for appointments. But I was there and I know that they only had nine appointments for the day. They only saw five of these and told the remaining four to return on November 8. I think somebody should look into this situation. At the "New Applicants" desk, the workers even refuse to disclose their names.

—Katie Wilder, Fort Greene

Visits to several welfare centers confirmed the fact that there are workers who sit around for long periods of time doing nothing, and many who linger over two-hour lunches. At the same time there are other workers who seem overburdened and harassed, working the whole day at a feverish pace. Such inefficiency and uneven distribution of work are obviously important factors in the long waits that clients are subjected to at the welfare centers.

Many women who are applying for welfare have to bring their young children with them to the centers, so that wailing infants and high-spirited toddlers who dash around the crowded rooms are always a part of the welfare center scene. Aside from the children, however, most of the clients appear subdued. They seem to have an infinite capacity for waiting, and only a few actually make a fuss over the long amount of time they have to spend there. It is as if they are afraid to show they are angry for fear of being denied public assistance.

"The poor don't really cause much trouble," said Yvonne Powell, a welfare supervisor from the Greenwood Center. "It's the clients from middle-class backgrounds who really drive you crazy. Before we became a special center for the aged, disabled, and blind, our center used to cover some pretty affluent white neighborhoods, like along Ocean Avenue, Ocean Parkway, and Shore Parkway. If you're familiar with Brooklyn, you know it's all beautiful homes around there, and beautiful modern high-rise buildings. These are houses with patios and twenty-four-hour doorman service, saunas, swimming pools, and garages—places that I couldn't afford to live in. But there are people there who are receiving public assistance. Sometimes I used to think that all of Ocean Parkway was on public assistance. Our center was handling about twenty thousand cases, and they were mostly people from neighborhoods like this.

"We would get these women coming in here with Vuitton handbags and expensive alligator shoes, telling us they'd lost their jobs or their husbands were out of work. They had used up all their savings and they expected welfare to pay their bills and their rent, which might have been $250 or $350. Now, what they said was usually legitimate—they had all the documentary proof of how they'd been living off their savings for the last few months or so, and by now they just had nothing left. They were flat broke. But they really demanded a lot and they made a big scene over everything.

"And what happened was, a lot of times they did wind up getting more money than a poor client because their basic expenses were higher, their rent was higher. You couldn't just tell them to get out of their apartments right away, because where were they going to go so fast? And anyway, we would have had to pay their moving costs. Besides, they figured their troubles were only temporary, and they were very stubborn and difficult about moving. So a lot of times we wound up having to get special clearance to budget them for a much higher rent than we normally allow. And still they weren't satisfied. If we pressured them to borrow from relatives or friends so they could at least pay part of their rent themselves, they were really furious.

"The real problem was that they were just not used to hard times, to adversity, and they didn't know how to cope with it.

It threw them into a panic, and they wanted welfare to solve all their problems for them. But with the poor it's different. They're accustomed to poverty; they're already living at a low level because they were never able to earn very much in the first place, and they don't expect or demand so much. They can deal with hard times better."

On one fairly typical day inside a welfare center near Myrtle Avenue, there were between thirty and forty clients or applicants waiting in the ground floor reception room. Almost all of them were black or Puerto Rican, except for a disheveled-looking young white couple who were sitting off by themselves and reading the book, *On Chanting Hare Krishna*.

A young Puerto Rican named Mario was working at the reception desk behind a low partition. He was slim and neatly dressed and wore his hair in a big Afro. A medallion with the flag of Puerto Rico on it hung from his neck. Mario would call out a number, and someone from the waiting throng would get up and approach him. No chair was provided for the client, who would usually wind up draped over the partition while talking to Mario. This preliminary interview could last as long as twenty minutes or half an hour, and its purpose was to determine if the applicant was in the right center and had a reasonable chance of qualifying for welfare. If so, the applicant was given a twelve-page form to take home and fill out; a list of the documents and papers that he would be required to give to the Department of Social Services, such as birth certificates, old pay stubs, and rent receipts; and an appointment to come back in a week or two to see a caseworker.

One middle-aged woman, after going through a prolonged reception procedure, came away muttering, "You don't mind sitting down with someone and telling him your troubles, but here you got to lean over a counter and talk about all these personal things. They could at least let you sit down."

Most of the people who were applying for welfare on this particular day were women and children. Their stories were all depressingly similar. One young woman of about twenty, with a three-year-old child clinging to her dungarees, told Mario that her husband had just deserted her and that she had another child—an infant—at home. She had no idea where her husband had gone off to, and she was destitute. She couldn't go out to work because she had no one to watch her children on a full-time basis.

Mario gave her an appointment to see a caseworker the following week and told her that at that time she must bring her children's birth certificates, her rent receipts, papers showing where her husband had worked and how much he earned, her own Social Security card, and various other documents. He also gave her the twelve-page application for welfare, which she was supposed to fill out and bring back at the time of her appointment.

This young woman was followed by another girl, perhaps slightly younger, who was obviously in her last months of pregnancy. She too said that her husband had vanished, and she had used up all the money she had. She asked for emergency assistance, but Mario told her the local centers did not give out emergency checks anymore. However, he said he would try to help her by squeezing her in for an appointment in just three days. He also instructed her to fill out the lengthy form and bring back the required documents.

While this was going on, a short, heavy-set woman emerged from the elevator, her eyes red from crying. She said that her case had been rejected because the Department of Social Services claimed she had a bank account. Although she insisted she had no money in the account, the department said she would have to produce her bank book to prove it.

Another woman was telling Mario that her husband had been injured on his job some time ago and that his disability benefits had run out. Their savings were also gone and he was still unable to work, so she had to stay home and take care of him.

A man of about twenty-five, dressed in a green raincoat, black knit hat, and dungarees, told Mario that he had just gotten out of prison the previous week and had to have some welfare help until he could find a job. Another man, about forty-five or fifty years old, had the shabby, tattered look of a derelict. He had been waiting for about an hour and a half and was finally told he was in the wrong center. A tall, neatly dressed man who was hobbling about on crutches was given an appointment for the following week.

All of these welfare applicants were being put through a much more arduous process than they would have encountered if they had applied a year or two ago. The whole welfare eligibility procedure has been tightened up, so that it is now much more difficult to get accepted. The twelve-page application form alone is a big hurdle, and the demand for various documents, receipts, and bills discourages many people from ever coming back to keep their appointments. This is all part of a deliberate effort to reduce the bulging welfare rolls, with little regard for actual need.

Under the new, more rigorous procedures, people who were already receiving welfare had to go back to their centers for face-to-face recertification. If they didn't show up, they were dropped. They also had to show the same documents and papers required of new applicants. As a result, large numbers of recipients were sliced off the rolls, and fewer new clients were added.

The city also has begun using a computer system designed to merge data on welfare, Medicaid, food stamp, employment, and social service clients. Once this system is fully in operation, the city expects a savings of two hundred million dollars a year because of reductions in ineligibility and fewer errors in welfare and Medicaid payments. Workers in the welfare centers will have instantaneous data on clients and the payments for which they are eligible, as well as a central index of the estimated total of twenty-six thousand narcotics addicts who receive welfare benefits.

The tightening-up process first began to show results in October 1972 when a decrease in the welfare rolls was recorded. The downward trend continued, and by May 1973 the caseload level had fallen to 1,207,869—a drop of more than 68,000 recipients in seven months. But the total cost of welfare programs in New York City rose by five million dollars during the same period, due mainly to the rising cost of rents that the Department of Social Services had to pay for welfare clients. Rents have been on the climb since the city decontrolled them several years ago. In addition, a 7.5 percent rent increase was authorized under the maximum-base rent program in January 1973, and the effect of this was reflected at once in added welfare costs.

The changes currently taking place in New York City's welfare system are part of a complete overhaul that was begun several years ago and has been breeding chaos and confusion ever since. The system used to be organized so that each applicant was assigned to a particular caseworker who had to visit the applicant's home, see all the documentation, and determine whether or not to accept the case. Once a case was accepted, the worker had to make periodic visits to the client's house. The client, in turn, took all his problems to that particular caseworker.

This system came under repeated attack over the years because of the enormous load of cases assigned to each caseworker, the invasion of privacy that was involved in visits to the welfare recipients' homes, and the close supervision of their personal affairs by the caseworkers. Welfare rights groups and other social welfare organizations called the system "dehumanizing" and demanded a change.

During the politically active sixties, these groups tried to organize welfare recipients so they would have some influence over the policy decisions that affected them. They staged sit-ins and demonstrations at the centers, informed people of all the benefits available to them that they might not be aware of, and helped people get special welfare grants for clothing and furniture.

Partly in response to this unrest, a number of changes were made. For a start, visits to the clients' homes were eliminated. Next, the need for documentation was dropped, and the Department of Social Services went on an "affidavit" system based simply on the client's declaration that he was in need of help. Finally, the idea of each caseworker's being responsible for a specific group of clients was abandoned. Under the new setup, any client's problems could be handled by any worker, so that a client could wind up dealing with someone new each time he came into the center or telephoned.

While these changes were being instituted, the welfare rolls shot up beyond all expectations. They had been rising steadily throughout the sixties but took several big leaps toward the end of the decade, as can be seen in the charts on the following pages.

The welfare rolls continued to rise in the early 1970s, and by September 1972 the total had swelled to over 1,275,800. An angry backlash ensued, and the pressure to get the totals down became enormous. Welfare workers complained that they were getting constant commands from city hall to "shave the caseload," while city hall, in turn, was being pressured by Albany to reduce welfare spending.

Consequently, procedures were tightened up considerably. All special grants were eliminated, and there was a renewed requirement for documentary proof that financial aid was desperately needed. In short, many of the policies that the welfare rights groups had fought for and won were discarded.

Commenting on the short-lived affidavit system, one case-worker said, "It was really abused. Anyone could just walk

Distribution of Persons Receiving Public Assistance, by Type of Person,
New York City: December 1960, 1964, and 1970

Type of person	Number of persons			Percent distribution		
	1960	1964	1970	1960	1964	1970
Total	329,651	483,121	1,165,583	100.0	100.0	100.0
Children *	183,732	282,118	685,303	55.8	58.4	58.8
Adults caring for children	50,747	81,849	231,697	15.4	16.9	19.9
Disabled adults (social and physical)	41,666	45,329	120,577	12.6	9.4	10.3
Aged adults (over 65 years)	39,351	47,223	73,184	11.9	9.8	6.3
Employables	6,956	18,306	25,111	2.1	3.8	2.2
Employed persons receiving supplementary assistance	7,199	8,296	29,711	2.2	1.7	2.5

* Children under 18 years in 1960 and 1964, and under 21 years in 1970. Figures do not include the following numbers of children receiving foster care: 19,915 in 1960; 22,432 in 1964; and 27,895 in 1970.

Source: For 1960 and 1964, based on data published in *The Welfare* (City of New York, Department of Social Services), issues of April 1961 and April 1965; figures for 1970 are unpublished.

Bureau of Community Statistical Services Research Department
Community Council of Greater New York
August 6, 1971

Recipients of Aid to Dependent Children,
United States and New York City,
December 1960-70
(in thousands)

Year	New York City	Percent change from previous year	United States	Percent change from previous year	New York City ADC recipients as percent of U.S.
December 1960	200.1	—	3,073	—	6.5
December 1961	235.8	18	3,566	16	6.6
December 1962	251.1	6	3,789	6	6.6
December 1963	294.3	17	3,930	4	7.5
December 1964	338.5	15	4,219	7	8.0
December 1965	388.5	15	4,396	4	8.8
December 1966	458.0	18	4,666	6	9.8
December 1967	582.9	27	5,309	14	11.0
December 1968	722.8	24	6,086	15	11.9
December 1969	769.3	6	7,313	20	10.5
December 1970	863.7	12	9,660	32	8.9

* Includes temporary ADC to unemployed parent.

ADC Recipients and Population*

(in thousands)

	1960	1970
New York City	7,782	7,896
Percent ADC recipients	2.6	10.9
United States	179,323	203,166
Percent ADC recipients	1.7	4.8

* Population as of April 1; ADC recipients as of December.

Sources: U.S. Department of Health, Education, and Welfare; New York City Department of Social Services; Bureau of the Census.

into a welfare center and say, 'I'm hungry, my husband left me yesterday, and I have five kids to feed,' and the case would be accepted that day. We didn't ask for any proof that the woman really had five children. It was strictly an honor system. We took the clients' word for anything they said.

"As a result, there were many duplicate cases. A client would come into one welfare center and apply for public assistance, then go to another and another. In some instances the same person would be receiving public assistance from ten different welfare centers under different names. As long as he had an address that the check could be sent to, that's all he needed—and if he had friends here and there, he could come up with a lot of different addresses.

"It was the drug addicts in particular who abused this system. Also, the single, unattached people who were on home relief. With the families, there were really very few duplicate cases. The main fraud there was that some people would claim to have three or four children in the household, and those children just did not exist. Or maybe the woman had one child and claimed to have three or four to get a larger grant."

Although the stringent requirement for documentation has weeded out many of the ineligibles and the cheats, it has also intimidated others who really are in need. The system also has drawbacks that can result in extreme cruelty at times. For example, in one case a seventeen-year-old mother of a five-day-old baby could not get emergency assistance to buy the child's formula because written proof was required that her parents in Puerto Rico no longer supported her. A few days later the infant was admitted to a hospital suffering from malnutrition. The city had to pay the hospital bill.

In another case, a man who had recovered from tuberculosis could not be released from the hospital because emergency welfare assistance was not available for his food and medical needs. While the formal twelve-page application was being approved, the man had to remain in the hospital. The unnecessary additional time he spent there cost the city $1,240.

Ex-convicts who have just been released—with no money, job or home—are also frequently denied emergency assistance even though they are supposed to receive it. Many of them find they have to go through the lengthy application process before they can get any financial help, and frequently they resort to crimes to support themselves during this crucial period.

Such incidents are the result of a system where welfare workers either adhere too rigidly to fixed procedures, or simply ignore procedures they should follow. The whole system is arbitrary and capricious, and many times cases are decided on the basis of whether or not a particular welfare worker is sympathetic to a client.

Some inequities are built right into the system itself—inequities that can work against the very poor and benefit those who are a little more affluent. Consider the case histories of two welfare applicants, both of whom lived in Fort Greene, and both of whom worked but needed supplementary welfare assistance.

Alice was married and had two children under six years of age. Her husband was an alcoholic who went on periodic binges. Even though his salary was $3.50 an hour, he seldom put in a full work week because of his drinking problem, so Alice had to work full-time even though the children were very young. The family lived in a small two-bedroom apartment that rented for $190, and Alice paid $65 a week to a baby sitter. As long as the family was together, they could just about get by on their combined incomes.

But in January 1973 Alice's husband went on another binge and disappeared, apparently for good. Alice continued working, but by herself she could not afford the $190 rent plus the $65-a-week baby-sitting expense. Without some sort of help she would have had to quit her job to stay home with her children, and the family would have been entirely dependent on welfare. Instead, Alice applied for supplementary welfare aid under the Employment Incentive Program.

This program is aimed mainly at mothers who have young children and are the sole support of their families. It was designed to encourage these women to work by providing them with public assistance to help defray their baby-sitting expenses and by allowing them to keep a large percentage of their earnings besides. Other types of work incentive programs are open to people who are already on welfare, including families and home relief cases.

Alice's net earnings were $210 semimonthly, which meant that she had a net annual income of $5,040. Normally, a family of three—an adult and two children—would not be eligible for welfare with that kind of income, but under the Employment Incentive Plan for working mothers they become eligible if they can show that they have a serious and legitimate budget deficit that would actually force them to stop working. Alice's high working expenses—$65 for a baby sitter, plus carfare, lunch money, and clothes—as well as her rent of $190 gave her a gaping budget deficit. When an allowance was computed for her under the standard Work Incentive Program formula, Alice was granted $154 semimonthly, with only $32 deducted from her salary, leaving her a net income of $332 semimonthly—or almost $8,000 per year, net. This was the equivalent of a gross salary of about $9,500 per year. In addition, as a welfare recipient Alice was automatically entitled to food stamps and Medicaid—the combined value of which was estimated at another $1,500 per year—so that she wound up with a package that was worth about $11,000 in cash and benefits.

"This case really hurt my heart," said the welfare supervisor in charge of the application division. "Alice is really better off than I am now, because she gets Medicaid and food stamps, which I don't have. After the workers in my department figured out her allowance, they kept saying, 'Oh, my god! That's ridiculous, that's ridiculous.' But if you look at it more closely, it really isn't. After all, Alice is paying someone else a full-time salary of $65 a week out of that money. Plus she has two growing children to take care of and other working expenses, so she does need that money to live on.

Also, welfare is only paying her $2,928 in cash. The rest is benefits plus money she earns herself. If she quit her job, welfare would be paying her $161 per month plus rent—a cash total of $4,212. So under Work Incentive we actually come out ahead, and so does Alice. That's the whole idea of this program.

"This was the first case we'd had where the Employment Incentive allowance came out so high. Most welfare mothers who work are earning a much lower salary than Alice was. Not that a net of $210 semimonthly is so high, but most of the mothers only manage to get little neighborhood jobs, or jobs that pay sixty or seventy dollars a week gross. When these mothers get welfare under Work Incentive, it doesn't add up to so much."

In contrast to Alice was the case of Juan, a widower with two sons who was earning only $88 a week net, or $4,576 a year. Juan and his two sons, together with Juan's mother, lived in what was actually a one-room apartment. Juan gave his mother about ten dollars a week toward the rent. There were no baby-sitting expenses since Juan's mother took care of the children after school.

In November 1972 Juan came into a welfare office to apply for supplementary public assistance. He brought a letter from the guidance counselor in the school his sons attended saying that the family's living quarters were "deplorable" and that the boys would be better able to concentrate on their schoolwork if they didn't have to live under such cramped conditions. Juan had found a two-bedroom apartment where the rent was about $150 a month, but he couldn't afford the moving expenses or the two months' security that the landlord was asking. Also, he would have needed continued supplemental assistance to pay the new rent.

But under the welfare department's formula Juan was not eligible for any public assistance, because he could not show an acceptable budget deficit at the time he applied. He was paying only about forty dollars in rent a month and he had no baby-sitting expenses, so according to welfare standards his salary of eighty-eight dollars per week was sufficient.

As one welfare worker pointed out, "If Juan had somehow been able to move into that $150 apartment *first,* and then had come to us with the letter from the guidance counselor and shown us he had a budget deficit, he would have been eligible for some supplementary assistance. As it was, he wasn't eligible for a cent. My heart really went out to him— to deny him—but that's the way the system works sometimes. You stay at the level you're at when you apply. If you're living in a little flophouse in Bedford-Stuyvesant someplace and you have to go on welfare, they'd never allow you to move into a $250 rental on Shore Parkway afterward. They wouldn't approve such a rental. But if you were already living on Shore Parkway and applied for public assistance, they wouldn't make you move into a Bedford-Stuyvesant flophouse either. That's why those who are better off to begin with can benefit more from the system."

Sometimes it turns out that those who do not work at all— those who are totally dependent on welfare—actually wind up with a higher standard of living than the working poor who do not receive any supplemental assistance. In July 1973 a congressional subcommittee[3] reported that in New York City a working family paying taxes and work expenses would have to earn a gross annual income of nearly $7,000—about $135 per week—to match the standard of living of a welfare family of four.

The report said that the combined benefits of various federal, state, and city programs such as food stamps, free school

[3] Subcommittee on Fiscal Policy of the Joint Economic Committee, Congress of the United States, "Income-Tested Social Benefits in New York: Adequacy, Incentives and Equity," by Blanche Bernstein with Anne N. Shkuda and Eveline M. Burns, consultant.

lunches, Medicaid, dental care, day-care for children, and homemaker services, as well as the welfare grants themselves, "can make it extraordinarily unprofitable to work," especially at jobs that pay less than $7,000 per year. In New York City there are many jobs that pay below $7,000 annually. About thirty percent of the jobs pay less than $90 a week, or under $4,680 annually, and there is just no incentive for a man with a family to work at such a low-paying job, because he and his dependents would remain impoverished anyhow. The family would be better off financially if he deserted them (or pretended to) and they became eligible for cash assistance and the benefits available to them under the Aid to Dependent Children program.

Representative Martha Griffiths, Democrat of Michigan, whose subcommittee released the report, said, "It makes a compelling case for some type of reform," because the welfare programs "are shot through with disincentives and inequities" and represent "an overly complex administrative nightmare."

The study noted that the fear of losing Medicaid benefits, in particular, was "the greatest impediment to efforts to increase income on the part of the welfare recipients," and on the part of the working poor as well. A working family of four is eligible for free, *total* Medicaid coverage only if its net annual income is four thousand dollars or less (which is a gross income of about forty-five hundred dollars). A family receiving cash assistance from welfare—no matter how small the amount—automatically gets full Medicaid coverage.

The study concluded that a New York City family of four would have to earn over eight thousand dollars before it achieved any "significant" gains in living standards over and above the welfare family.

All of this is not meant to suggest that welfare families receive too much, but that nonwelfare low-income working families should be eligible for more social welfare benefits than they now enjoy and should remain eligible for some of them, such as Medicaid—perhaps for a small sliding fee—at least until their income rises to the point where they enjoy a "moderate" standard of living. This would be a type of income maintenance or income assistance plan to benefit the working poor so that they can live above the welfare level and have some advantages to show for their labor. Such an incentive would also help make low-paying jobs more attractive to those on welfare. This is an important factor, because the main problem does not appear to be a lack of *any* jobs, but rather a lack of jobs that pay a living wage to unskilled, undereducated people.

According to the Community Council of Greater New York, a family of four needed a gross annual income of $11,880 "to live at a moderate level" in New York City in 1972. By "moderate," the study meant a family who lived in rent-controlled housing, averaging about $182 per month for rent, utilities, and the purchase of household furnishings. The family had no car. The man used public transportation to get to work and ate his lunch at an inexpensive counter-type restaurant. The family spent about sixty dollars a week for food, and their appliances included a black-and-white television set but no washing machine or dryer. That is a "moderate" standard of living in New York, and it certainly is modest enough.

The current welfare standard of living—despite all the public benefits—is far, far more austere. The welfare family of four is budgeted at $2,496 annually, plus rent. This allows about thirty-nine dollars a week for food (including the value of the food stamps), based on the U.S. Department of Agriculture's Economy Food Plan—the cheapest, rock-bottom, minimal food budget developed by the department.

The Community Council of Greater New York points out that "besides struggling to make the available money cover the purchase of the necessities of life, the family must do without many of the commonplace goods and services. . . ."

The family that lives according to the welfare department's budget "must do without television, magazines, books, movies, radios, newspapers, stationery, postage, pets, cigarettes, ice cream cones, Christmas trees, and birthday cards. This is the family that never exceeds fifty message units a month and that never makes a long distance phone call. This is a family that reads its newspapers and magazines in the library. This is a family that never buys a hot dog from a corner vendor.

"It may be no hardship for American families to do without a few of these items, but a family that must endure the loss of all of them while at the same time waging a daily struggle to purchase the bare necessities of life is manifestly deprived."

Seen in this light, even though a welfare family of four may be better off in some ways than a nonwelfare working family that earns less than seven thousand dollars a year, both groups are still exceedingly poor.

Turning to Fort Greene, the 1970 census revealed that the median income of families in sixteen census tracts throughout the neighborhood ranged from a low of $4,327 to a high of $6,893, with an average of about $5,600.[4] This means that the great majority of families in the community have an abysmally low standard of living—whether or not they are on welfare—and chances are that at some time in their lives they will have to apply for welfare assistance. The welfare rolls are not made up of a steady group of people who stay on welfare forever. There is a high turnover (particularly in the home relief category of single, employable adults) amounting to close to fifty percent annually, according to the Rand Institute. Each year large numbers of welfare recipients drop off the rolls and new recipients come on. Those who tend to stay on for the longest periods of time without interruption are

[4] This excludes three census tracts around Pratt University, where the median income was much higher.

the aged, disabled, and blind. (The federal government took over all payments to this group as of January 1974.) Welfare mothers often remain on the rolls as long as their children are young, but as the children grow older, many of the mothers gradually enter the job market. However, their earning capacities are usually so low that even when they are working they cannot escape the poverty trap, and they are scarcely better off than before. In their old age, many of them will have to turn to public assistance again.

Thus, the working poor and the welfare poor are often interchangeable, with people shifting back and forth from one category to the other. This periodic need for welfare help is a commonly accepted fact of life in a poverty area like Fort Greene, and the great majority of residents have probably visited the local welfare centers at one time or another.

Where is the welfare system heading now? In a group discussion Ann Rosenhaft, director of the Fort Greene Income Maintenance Center; Arlene Beesing, community consultant for the Human Resources Administration's Department of Community Affairs; and Isidore Cooper, senior case supervisor in the Fort Greene Center, evaluated the many changes that are taking place.

MS. BEESING: There is a misconception in the welfare system now that somehow you can put everybody's life on a piece of paper and throw it into a computer, and all problems will be solved. But you cannot solve problems like that. There are a million and one exceptions to everything that don't fit on those punch cards. You see, what they want to do now is computerize everything. That means that individuality—individual problems—will no longer exist. It's the Social Security approach. You're either accepted or rejected. You get your check once a month If you don't get your check, you fill out the form and in a couple of months you may get the check replaced.

MS. ROSENHAFT: Except that Social Security had a back-up—
us.

MS. BEESING: That's right, because if a Social Security check
didn't come for some reason, people could come on
public assistance or get temporary help from us while
waiting. Social Security isn't interested in people's problems. They only send out checks. That's all. They don't
do anything else. That's not their function.

MS. ROSENHAFT: This is the philosophy behind the changes
that have taken place in our operations over the last
years. The old system—where individual caseworkers
were responsible for a certain number of cases and visited
the families—has been discarded. I think it's a distinct
change for the worse.

MS. BEESING: I'll agree with that. Now the caseworker doesn't
know anybody; he doesn't know what's going on with the
client; he doesn't have any idea of where anyone is or
what they're doing.

MS. ROSENHAFT: This is not to say that the former system was
good. It was falling apart. It was in severe need of change
or modification of some kind. But the concept that anybody at any time can work on any case—with no individual accountability—I think is wrong.

MR. COOPER: From the viewpoint of the client, under the old
system he had a personal relationship with his caseworker. They knew each other as two people who could
talk to each other as people. The client could talk over
his problems and so forth, whether they were financial or
not. I know, because lots of clients talked over all kinds
of problems with me. Now there is no caseworker, and
the depersonalization is even more complete. The clients
feel lost. They complain about it all the time.

MS. ROSENHAFT: The clients keep asking, "Who is my caseworker? I want to know *who* my caseworker is."

MR. COOPER: Or they'll say, "I want someone to talk to."
That's almost as great a need as money.

MS. ROSENHAFT: The system was changed partly because of the demands of the welfare rights organizations who felt that there was an invasion of privacy. Personally I think this is another case where a liberal principle was picked up and used for conservative purposes. I suppose it could happen the other way around, too. But what I'm saying is, something that was presented by welfare rights groups as a humanizing idea has been built into a less humanized system—and actually increased its dehumanization in a way.

MS. BEESING: This is clear to everybody who works with people. It's clear to our clients.

MS. ROSENHAFT: I think we're going into an era now of every man for himself.

MS. BEESING: If you can't pull yourself up by your own bootstraps, you're going to suffer. If you need someone to help you pull on your bootstraps a little, you're not going to get it. This is what we're going into, and I think we're going to have to live with it for quite a few years. We've gradually swung that way in the last five years. The welfare rights organizations are practically defunct now, although they keep telling me they're going to reorganize.

MS. ROSENHAFT: My own feeling is that when the welfare rights groups were at the peak of their power, they missed their chance to organize.

MS. BEESING: They were at their peak for only two or three years.

MS. ROSENHAFT: Then the reaction against them set in. One of the reactions was to buy off some of the leadership by giving them jobs in the antipoverty programs. Another was the punitive regulations, like the elimination of special grants that the Department of Social Services used to give out to clients. Also, welfare families and home relief cases got a ten percent cut a few years ago. This was the time when the welfare rights groups should have strengthened their organization, and apparently they weren't able to. Apparently too much of their appeal had been on the basis that "we can get you a special check," and when they couldn't get that check anymore, they lost support.

MS. BEESING: They will probably never resurrect themselves, because all their leaders, even on the lower levels, have been pulled into the community social services. Many of them are now working for the Department of Social Services. They have really been co-opted, because now they can't work against the department. So the welfare rights groups are leaderless.

MR. COOPER: Except for one thing. Once the Office of Economic Opportunity is abolished and a lot of the antipoverty programs are ended, these people will lose their jobs and go back into the community.

MS. ROSENHAFT: But at that point, I think they'll be in the position of having to start from scratch all over again.

MS. BEESING: Yes, because by now a lot of people are really dissatisfied with the welfare rights organizations because they haven't been doing anything. People are not so blind that they can't see that their old leaders were all working for the antipoverty agencies, and they all had good jobs, and that's why they weren't doing anything. So it's going to be very hard for these old leaders to go back into the community and convince everyone to take up where they left off. People are going to see right away that they're doing it because they don't have a job now, and it's going to be very hard for them to become a viable group again.

4

The "Workfare" Program

AS PART of the general crackdown on welfare recipients, New York State passed a law in 1971 ordering all able-bodied relief recipients to take jobs or get off the rolls. The lawmakers casually assumed that there were jobs for them to take and that employers would be willing to hire them despite the fact that most had few skills, a low educational level, and a sporadic work history. Mothers of young children were also included in the go-to-work edict, although there were not nearly enough day-care centers in either the state or the city to accommodate the large numbers of preschool-age children on the welfare rolls.

Under the law, welfare recipients were required to pick up their semimonthly checks at state employment offices and be available for jobs or job training. Those not placed in regular jobs within thirty days were to be given part-time public work jobs—without extra pay—to work off the value of their relief checks. At the same time, they were supposed to continue looking for regular employment.

Recipients were also required every two weeks to file a certification from their state employment office that no suitable jobs were available for them: that they had reported for required job interviews; that they had told state employment officials the results of these interviews; and that they had not failed to report for any job that was available.

If they did not comply with all these requirements of the law, they would be dropped from the public assistance rolls.

The law was challenged in the courts almost immediately, and in 1972 a three-man district court in Buffalo ruled that recipients in the aid to families of dependent children category—that is, mainly welfare mothers—were exempt from the law. The court held that these recipients got a large portion of their welfare funds from the federal government, under provisions of the federal Social Security Act. As long as they were deemed eligible under *that* act, the state could "not impose additional conditions of eligibility."

So welfare mothers were not bound by the new law at first—not until the district court's ruling was overturned by the Supreme Court in June 1973. But with regard to other welfare recipients in New York, the work law was upheld from the start.

Welfare workers in New York City were very doubtful that such a law could be effective in reducing the number of people on welfare, especially during a period when the unemployment rate in New York City was up to seven percent. They also pointed out that the majority of the people who received public assistance in New York City were children; in 1970 they accounted for almost fifty-nine percent of the welfare caseload. Their parents—or, in most cases, just mothers—accounted for almost twenty percent. The aged, disabled, and blind, and those who were already employed, took up another 19.1 percent of the caseload. This meant that the new law could apply only to the relative handful of welfare recipients who were considered potentially employable—2.2 percent of the entire New York City caseload, or about forty thousand people. In the end, only twelve to fifteen thousand of these were deemed medically fit to work.

Nevertheless, state and city officials began to enforce the law with gusto, in response to the public's demand to "put all those lazy welfare cheats to work." But the effect of the new edict on a poor urban community like Fort Greene was practically nil—there were really very few welfare recipients in the neighborhood who qualified as "employable." Alcoholics and drug addicts were listed in the "disabled" category, and they were not forced to work. This left only those in the small home-relief category, which consisted mainly of unemployed, single, able-bodied men and women, and some fathers whose families were not eligible for aid under the ADC program. Putting them to work would not save the city very much money because they got such small grants to begin with. A single person on home relief in New York gets a base grant of only nineteen dollars a week (not including rent money) to cover food, clothing, and other personal needs.

Among those affected by the new law was Reuben V., who was married and the father of four children. He had been out of work for some time and was receiving welfare payments for himself and his family. Even before the law was passed he had been reporting to the New York State Employment Office regularly, but the agency was unable to find a job for him in any private business or industry. (As it turned out, this was not at all unusual. In 92.8 percent of the cases, welfare recipients were unable to find jobs through the New York State Employment Agency within thirty days, as the new law required.)

So Reuben was placed in a public works job for the Department of Parks solely for the purpose of working off his welfare check. He was assigned to a park in Brooklyn where he worked eight hours a day, five days a week, doing custodial chores such as cleaning boilers. Most people in the Public Work Program were required to work only about two days a week, but Reuben had to work off a welfare grant that covered six people. He worked alongside thirteen regular civil service employees and sixteen other welfare workers like himself. They all did exactly the same job.

But Reuben was paid $2.57 an hour—just enough to pay off his welfare check over the course of a full work week—while the regular civil service workers earned $5.43 an hour. Also, Reuben was not covered by workmen's compensation or entitled to vacation time and health insurance, as they were. Nor could he list the work as experience on job references.

With the aid of the New York Civil Liberties Union, Reuben filed suit stating that he would like to keep working at his job, but that he felt he was entitled to the same wages that the civil service workers were getting. "Equal pay for equal work," was his demand. Otherwise his job amounted to "peonage."

The Civil Liberties Union pointed out that Reuben could not get his job by taking a civil service test, because even if he passed it the city had a job freeze at that time that prevented new hiring. The NYCLU charged: "As civil service employees retire or otherwise vacate their jobs, they are replaced by welfare recipients whom the city refuses to employ but who are forced to work at less than half the wages they are entitled to. . . . The state can't have it both ways. If it wants to force employable welfare recipients to work, it has to pay them regular wages, permit them to join unions and to derive all the benefits of employment. . . . New York's forced work program is simply a resurrection of slavery."

But the State Supreme Court rejected the argument, stating, "However difficult the loss of home relief is, a person is not held in a state of peonage when the only sanction for his refusing to work is that he will not receive payments currently." The court also held that the welfare recipients were not entitled to civil service benefits because they were not civil service employees. "The legal situation is not altered because the work they do is similar to that done by civil service employees."

It would hardly be surprising if welfare recipients ex-
pressed deep resentment at the moral—if not legal—injustice
of having to work for less than half the pay their co-workers
receive. What is surprising is that so many of them do *not*
appear resentful. On the whole they tend to enjoy their work
and seem almost indifferent to the unequal pay rates. In
fact, it is as if they do not really connect their jobs with their
welfare checks and feel as if they are doing volunteer work.
Some of them say that their public work jobs are more interesting than any other kind of work they were able to get
before, and the fact that they are working enhances their self-
esteem.

Many of these welfare recipients are assigned to jobs in the
welfare centers themselves. Ann Rosenhaft observed that the
public work jobs actually seem to benefit the welfare recipients psychologically. "The jobs tend to break that cycle of
inertia and despair and the sense of isolation that develops
in all of us if we're out of work for a long period of time,"
she said. "You just wind down in a way unless you have some
sort of work. Many of the PWP people referred to us have
indicated that they're pleased to be active, in a work
situation."

Mario, the young Puerto Rican who was working at a reception desk in one of the welfare centers near Myrtle Avenue, was actually a welfare recipient himself. He was enrolled
in the Public Work Program and was working off a biweekly
grant of $97.15 (which covered his rent as well as all other
expenses, and was a little larger than the normal home relief
grant because it included a little extra money for furniture).

Mario lived in a one-and-a-half room apartment in an old
brownstone not far from Fort Greene Park. He had originally
been sent to the welfare center to act as an interpreter for
Spanish-speaking welfare clients, but the center was so under-
staffed and Mario was such a quick learner that they started
putting him to work as a receptionist—a job that normally

requires two years of college. Mario could not have gotten such a job through the usual civil service channels, because he had completed only the tenth grade.

How was it that this apparently healthy and obviously intelligent young man had wound up on the welfare rolls? His story is not unlike that of many unskilled, undereducated blacks and Puerto Ricans in New York.

MARIO

"I was put into the Public Work Program in December 1972. Before that I was on welfare for about six months. I had tried looking for a job, but the best I could get was a job for eighty dollars a week. I tried it out for about a month, but in those types of jobs the work is just too heavy for me. You see, the doctor put limits on the kind of work I can do. I'm not supposed to stand up too much, and I finally had to quit this job because I was getting pains.

"My trouble is, I have some bullet wounds. A couple of them I got in Vietnam, but those don't really bother me. They were just flesh wounds. But after I came home from Vietnam I started working for the Youth Services Agency up in the South Bronx. I was working with those gangs up there, and I got shot worse than in Vietnam. I almost died.

"The way I got that job was that I had grown up in the South Bronx and I knew the president of one of the gangs. I knew this guy since he was real small. He was a friend of mine. Then I had some other friends who were already youth workers, and they helped me get a job with the agency. Normally, I couldn't have gotten that job so fast because there was a waiting list, but since I was a veteran and also I knew people, they took me right away.

"This gang leader who was a friend of mine—he's the head

of the Royal Javelins—he showed me around, and through him I got to know a lot of the gangs. It's hard to be a youth worker up there, because a lot of gang members don't like the sight of any youth worker, unless they seen that he was really trying to help them. There was a lot of youth workers who didn't really try. They'd just be there, just for the job. You see, it's the kind of job where there isn't much to do, really, unless you want to. You can just hang around the clubhouses, dance, do the same things the members do. And the members don't like youth workers who act like this.

"But if they see you're putting out your part to help them, it's different. They'll accept a youth worker who helps them get things, like storefronts, money to get equipment, guitars, stereos, basketballs, things like that. If you serve them this way, they'll accept you.

"But even then there can be trouble. Last year, one youth worker was killed trying to avoid a rumble between two gangs. This was by Roosevelt High School. There was another youth worker who was shot in the face. He's lucky to be alive. The bullet didn't go through. It just traveled through the front of his face. He was one of the head youth workers who had been trying to get different gangs together, organizing them into one group. They would all take trips to places like Washington, D.C., to see about getting funds for projects. It was effective until they started fighting against each other.

"The gangs now are a lot more violent than the gangs of the old days. The biggest thing they had in those days was zip guns. Now they even get their hands on M-16s. They find a contact—maybe a veteran who brought back weapons from overseas—they get their hands on them and they buy them. Everything goes for a price.

"Most of the kids in these gangs need a lot of help, but they just don't want to listen to advice. They think what they're doing is the best thing for them. There are a lot of gangs up in the Bronx. There are some gangs here in Fort Greene, too, but it seems to me that most of the gangs here know how to use their minds better than the kids in the Bronx. Up there, they just go crazy. They buy guns and everything. They have to prove that their gang is tougher than the other gang. They start all kinds of fights for no reason.

"But most of these gangs are against drugs. Like, for instance, the Royal Javelins were totally against it. They had a punishment for anyone caught with any possession or use of it. It was an awful sight, but they really got their message across. They would whip the person across the back with a belt—twenty-five lashes. It was effective for a lot of them. But there were also some who were hard-headed and kept on using stuff anyhow.

"My friend who is the leader of the Javelins, he knows how to use his head. He's pretty bright, but he can't always control the actions of the members. One time there was a get-together at the clubhouse, everyone was having a party, and then all of a sudden a brawl started and one of the guys got stabbed. The next night I was in there, in the clubhouse working with the kids, and some members of another gang came in shooting. I got caught in the fire. Me and about three gang members got hit. I was the only worker that got caught in there. Nobody got killed, but I was the one that was stricken the worst. I was in critical condition for about a week. After that, I just didn't want to work there anymore. I wanted to work with the kids 'cause I like the job of helping people, but I was afraid.

"I don't go back up to the South Bronx much anymore. Even though I lived there most of the time when I was growing up, we also lived in Brooklyn for a couple of years. So I just moved back here. My sister lives around here, too, right near me. I have my own apartment and I like being on my own. I want to show people, like my mother, that I can be on my own.

"I was born in Puerto Rico, but I came here at the age of

three. I only been back there once, so I don't know too much about Puerto Rico. My mother hasn't been back in Puerto Rico in years, and my little sister never even seen Puerto Rico, only in pictures.

"We all went to school here, in the Bronx, but the only time I ever had a teacher take a lot of interest in me was when I was in junior high school. She thought I had an art talent, and she wanted me to build it up. But I didn't think too much about school then. All I wanted to do was go out and play. I used to love to play handball and basketball.

"When I started going to Morris High School, my interest in school left me completely. I didn't feel I was learning too much there, and there was a lot of drug traffic. I was with a lot of friends who used drugs, so I tried it. I was on smack, but I was only using it on the skin—skin-popping. I used it for about three months, and then I seen that everybody, all my friends, were starting to shoot it into the vein. They were getting hooked and having pains and everything. So I told myself I have to cut it loose. I just didn't want to see myself being thrown away like that. For one thing, I ain't got the talent to be going around stealing or casting myself inside a jail cell. So I tried to leave it. Then one of my friends caught hepatitis and I caught it from him. I was in the hospital for six months. From then on, I just stayed away from drugs.

"Meanwhile, I wasn't doing too good in school because I had been messing around with drugs, and then because I was in the hospital. So I left high school in the tenth grade.

"Three days after my seventeenth birthday, I joined the marines. That was in 1969. I was having problems with my mother, and I wanted to get away from the city. I just wanted to get away from everything for a while. My mother was on welfare at the time, and that's another reason I went into the service. I just didn't like the whole welfare thing. I mean for myself. For a person who really does need it, I could see it. But for myself, I couldn't see it. So I went into the service to avoid being on welfare. I thought I could do something for myself that way. I figured I could get to be an officer or something, but things didn't work out that way. The marines are a very strict branch, but they are the best, as far as I can see.

"When I was in Vietnam, it wasn't so bad anymore. The fighting was slowing down. I seen a lot of ground fights, but the veterans who were there before me saw a lot worse.

"Aside from Vietnam, I was also in Panama, and I even got to take a trip to Puerto Rico. Since I had relatives there, they gave me a five-day pass and I went by boat. I saw the neighborhood where I was born, and I really enjoyed it. I already knew some of my relatives from when they had come up here, but there was a lot that I had never met before.

"You know, I don't agree with the Puerto Rican liberation movement. They say Puerto Rico should be free from the United States, but I think it's one of the worst mistakes Puerto Rico could do, 'cause if they do get liberated they'll just turn to communism. Russia or one of the other Communist countries will move in. That's what I think. Puerto Rico is too small and it doesn't have enough money to support all the Puerto Ricans that are on the island.

"When you're in the marines, you meet a lot of people who just can't stand Puerto Ricans and blacks. I found a lot of prejudice, a lot of people who didn't want to get along with you because of the way you looked. When I was in Panama, especially, a lot of marines there had a bad opinion of Puerto Ricans.

"One time I had a fight. I had just got married with this Panamanian girl, and there was this one marine who was always talking about Panamanians. I had said to him, 'If you don't like a person, or a certain breed of people, you should keep it to yourself.' Then he told me, 'You Puerto Ricans ain't good for nothing, neither.' So me and him had a fight. We were both lance corporals, and he got busted for the fight. They didn't do nothing to me except give me some extra work to do. I met this guy again in Charleston, South Carolina, just about the time I was getting out. I had been made a corporal by then. Well, this guy tried to get back at me by telling my commanding officer that I was a user of marijuana, so I got into another fight with him. This time I got busted. They busted me back to lance corporal. But he had no more stripes on his sleeve, so they couldn't do nothing to him except put him on extra duty.

"As for my Panamanian wife, I just got divorced from her here, through the mail.

"While I was in the service in Panama, I did some studying and went to classes, and I got my high school equivalency diploma. I kept that diploma in with my things, but by the time I got back here to the states, I couldn't find it anymore. That was the only proof I had that I ever got the degree, so I didn't know what to do. I really wanted to make something of myself, be something besides a marine. At about the time I was applying for that Youth Services Agency job, I thought I would also try for the transit police. When I told my old friends in the Bronx about it, they said, 'You going to be a pig? You'll go around arresting kids? You pig!' I got the application anyway, but since I had nothing to prove that I had got my equivalency diploma, I let it go.

"A lot of my old friends are on drugs now. Some of them are trying to do something for themselves. They're on methadone and so forth. But there's a lot of them who aren't. When I first got out of the service I tried to help them. I got them off drugs for a while. But being that I couldn't spend all my time with them, they would get together with somebody else —one of their other friends who was on drugs—and they would just go back to it. So there was nothing I could do, and I just gave up on them. They had no will power. If you have a strong will power, you could see it all around you and just walk by it. You could throw it out and burn it.

"You know, of all the friends that I grew up with—of all the ones who lived in the same neighborhood with me ever since we were small—there are only two who *never* touched drugs. One of them is the leader of the Royal Javelins. He's married now and his wife just had a baby, but he's out of work. He doesn't even try anymore. He doesn't have too much going for him.

"The other friend is someone who I consider like my brother. My mother's just crazy about him, and he's been like one of us. He's doing pretty good. He's going to aviation school, and he's really building himself up. He's about the only one I see who's trying for himself.

"Anyhow, after I got shot, I couldn't really work at anything except a desk job, and I couldn't get that. So I had to go on public assistance. There was no way I could get any income by myself. If I had been shot in Vietnam the way I was shot in the Bronx, I would have been entitled to benefits. The service only gives you benefits if you've been disabled or if any part of your body was removed, and nothing like that happened to me over there. Just flesh wounds.

"Since I got put into the Public Work Program, I work two days a week at the welfare center. I enjoy it very much. From any other place that I worked, I think this center is the best place where I've found a lot of friends. I get along a lot better than I have at other places. And I think the people that work here are very interesting people. I never had too much contact with the people who worked in the office at the Youth Services Agency. They were pleasant, but I never really got to know them. Here it's different.

"There are other people in the center who are in PWP also. Most of them are doing good, but there was this one guy—I think they had to throw him out. I haven't seen him for a while. Now there are about seven others besides myself.

"I was supposed to be an interpreter at first. But after about two days, just by watching, I caught on to reception. So now when I come to work here, they put me on reception.

"There's a lot of Spanish who come in here. Some of them bring along a person who knows how to speak English, but most of them don't, and they don't know any English at all. So I help them 'cause I can do all the reception work in Spanish.

"I really like this work. It's a lot of headaches, but as far as being able to help a person that's really in need, I think it's worth getting a headache for.

"The most common thing you hear is women coming in and saying their husbands have abandoned them, or women who are pregnant and the father of the child just don't want to know nothing about them. A lot of the time these are just young girls, like sixteen or seventeen, and as far as welfare is concerned, they're supposed to be with their parents. But either they've left their parents or their parents don't care about them, and now that they're pregnant they don't know what to do. I try to help them because I can see their need. They have a child coming in, and nobody to support them.

"Now the government has been making it harder for people to get welfare. Like, they used to give out emergency checks, but they don't do that anymore unless it's really an emergency, like the house burned down or a person's coming out of an institution. But if a person comes in and says she don't have money for food, she's told she'll have to borrow from her friends or relatives until her case is accepted.

"After I started working at this center, the people here told me about a Post Office training program that I should enroll in. I'm in it now. I go to classes, and at the end I have to pass a test. If I do, I get put on a waiting list. Whoever gets the highest score gets on top of the list. If you get a real low score you don't have too much chance of getting called, because they tear up the lists after a while and start all over again. They're starting a new list now. So far I have fifteen points going for me because I'm a veteran. It's a bonus they give us.

"What I'd really like to do is go to college somehow, but because I can't find that equivalency diploma, I'd have to take those high school classes all over again. A lot of my friends— my new friends, who I met since I got out of the service— they've started going to college. Some of them are on scholarships to Long Island University, which is a few blocks from here, and the others are in New York City Community College. That's near here, too. You see, we all like music and we formed this little band. Sometimes I go to school with them just to see what's going on. I really want to go to school. I wouldn't mind how far I'd have to travel as long as I could get myself a real good education. I'd go as far as I can for it."

Mario did not remain in the Public Work Program very long. Through his co-workers at the welfare center he found out about a special veterans' program that was being offered by Staten Island Community College (a branch of the City University). Under this program, any veteran who wanted to go to college—whether he had a high school diploma or not— could enroll in a four-month pre-college remedial course. If he completed the course, he would automatically be admitted to Staten Island Community College as a full-fledged, matriculated student. All those in the program were to receive a stipend from the Veterans Administration.

Mario was accepted in the program, and because his stipend was a little larger than his welfare check, he was able to get off the welfare rolls. When last heard from, he had successfully completed the course and had entered Staten Island Community College as a regular student in September 1973.

Mario was far more fortunate than many of the others in the Public Work Program, but his case was not totally unique. Just the fact of being in a work situation and mingling with other working people helps open up opportunities that welfare recipients might never find out about otherwise. It also seems to give many of them more of an incentive to continue job hunting on their own.

Nevertheless, the Public Work Program cannot be called a success. A study by the Rand Institute in conjunction with the Department of Social Services showed that neither PWP nor two other job training and referral programs for welfare recipients—Manpower and Career Development and the New York State Employment Agency check pick-up program—had much effect in getting people *real* jobs (as opposed to jobs that just involved working off a welfare grant). After welfare mothers were subjected to the job requirement as a result of the Supreme Court ruling, over 170,000 "potential employables" should have become involved in the various work programs. But in fact only 55,700 were enrolled in any training or job program operated by the city or state.

Furthermore, less than eight percent of the thirty thousand welfare clients who had to report to the State Employment Service to pick up their relief checks were referred to and placed in jobs. This particular program, the study said, "appears to have directed far fewer people into the labor market than the cost and scale of the operation merits."

Human Resources Administrator Jule M. Sugarman said the Rand Institute study showed the "futility of following manpower policies which simply train people but pay little or no attention to providing real jobs at the end of that training."

The study emphasized that the participants in each program were actively interested in work, but that low wages and short-term jobs made it necessary for them to resort periodically to welfare "as a back-up source of income to help meet family needs."

The median wage for those placed in jobs by the program was $2.24 an hour, or $340 a month for a full-time job. The study pointed out that in most instances such earnings—after subtracting work-related expenses and taxes—were "less than or equal to what could be received from public assistance."

At least twenty-three percent of the participants from the Manpower and Career Development Agency and the Public Work Program who held jobs at any time from January 1970 to July 1973 received less than the minimum wage of $1.85 an hour. In other words, they worked full-time for less than $64.75 gross per week.

In another, separate study, about 110,000 mothers were interviewed by the Department of Social Services to determine their eligibility for the Work Incentive Program, and 40,000 were referred to the State Employment Service for placement. The outcome: only about 2,000 got jobs, and 1,500 were enrolled in some form of vocational training. However, most of the jobs lasted less than five weeks.

At present, New York City has begun another experiment —the Work Relief Employment Program (WREP)—which is designed to replace the Public Work Program. The new plan will provide regular part-time municipal jobs for welfare clients and will eliminate some of the injustices of the old system. These municipal jobs will all be entry-level positions not covered by civil service, and no educational background will be necessary. The jobs will range from janitorial work to nurses' aides or clerks.

The number of days each client will be working under the new program is determined by his individual welfare budget. His pay check is to equal the amount he has been receiving in support payments plus the added costs of carfare and lunches. The full-time salaries of the jobs range from fifty-two hundred dollars a year to six thousand dollars, but in almost all cases the clients will be working half-time for half-pay.

Unlike the old setup, clients will be able to join unions, they will be covered by workmen's compensation and health insurance, and they will be entitled to vacation time. However, they will be docked for each day of work they miss, whereas under the old program they received their regular stipend even if they missed days.

As soon as the program was announced, it ran into opposition from the civil service unions. Victor Gotbaum, executive director of District Council 37 of the American Federation of State, County, and Municipal Employees, stated that "whatever the intentions, the program as constituted involves discriminatory hiring in civil service." He added that the city had a hiring freeze, and the new program could be used to circumvent it.

Perhaps a greater threat to the program comes from the fact that more than one hundred thousand welfare mothers may have to be added to it now. The whole concept of WREP was based on the idea that it would involve relatively small numbers of people on home relief—no more than twelve to fifteen thousand recipients. "If all these mothers are added to the program we'll be swamped," said Lucille Rose, deputy administrator of the Human Resources Administration in charge of employment programs. "Where will we ever find the jobs?"

It is now up to the state to determine whether the welfare mothers *must* be included in the city's new municipal job program—and city officials are hoping they will not be.

5

Pounding the Pavements
in Fort Greene

JUST across the street from the Fort Greene housing projects on Myrtle Avenue is a Manpower Neighborhood Employment Center. Wedged in between the A&P and a dry cleaning store, the Manpower center occupies a large storefront whose grimy windows are always papered with hand-lettered announcements and job offerings. But anyone who passes by regularly knows that, except for the few people who work there, the center is always nearly empty.

That's why in the summer of 1973 it was startling to see large mobs of people piling into the storefront each day, with the overflow lined up on the sidewalk outside. It looked as if the Manpower center must be giving out jobs by the hundreds, but in fact this was hardly the case. The center had started distributing free packaged lunches to anyone in the neighborhood who wanted them.

Judging from the signs in the window, Manpower had far more food available than jobs. Most of its listings were for federal positions, such as:

Nursing asst.—psychiatry—G.S. 2—$100 a week
G.S. 3—$110 a week

> Clerical—$5,432 a year
> $6,128 a year
> Key punch—$5,432 a year
> $6,128 a year

But such jobs require civil service tests, and many of the chronically unemployed in Fort Greene do not have sufficient education or sharp enough skills to do well in a competitive examination. Jobs with private companies seemed to be in very short supply, with only a few listings, such as:

> Exper. spray painter, $3.90 per hour.
> Apprentice carpenter, $4.90 per hr. Complete 10th grade.
> Maintenance position open.

One listing seemed almost absurdly out of place on Myrtle Avenue: "Hospital controller—$20,000+." Anyone from the neighborhood who was likely to wander into the Manpower office was wholly unlikely to have the qualifications needed for such a job, and after four months had gone by, the listing was still in the window.

The Manpower storefront on Myrtle Avenue is a branch of the Fort Greene Manpower Training and Development Center, whose main office is on Fulton Street. Funded by the Office of Economic Opportunity in Washington, D.C., Manpower is designed to provide job training and placement services for low-income people. It is closely affiliated with federally funded antipoverty organizations such as the Fort Greene Community Corporation.

The main Manpower center in Fort Greene is far busier than its Myrtle Avenue branch. The branches were intended to be "outreach" posts. That is, the workers in these offices were supposed to go right into the community—knocking on people's doors, talking to people in the streets—to round up all those who might be in need of services. The theory was that if the people who needed help wouldn't come to Manpower, Manpower would go to them. But the branches have always been too understaffed for the workers to go out and thoroughly canvass the community, so the "outreach" concept has had little success.

In contrast, there is always a flutter of activity in the main Manpower office, which functions like a regular employment agency and is an educational center as well. Located next to a boarded-up movie theater on the fringe of the downtown Brooklyn shopping hub, the central Manpower office in Fort Greene serves people from that community only and is usually packed with job-seekers on Mondays and Tuesdays. The crowds dwindle thereafter, and by Friday the office is practically empty.

Many of the neighborhood people who come to Manpower have already exhausted other means of finding work. They have been to the New York State Employment Agency, and they have fruitlessly explored whatever leads they were given by friends and relatives. By the time they reach Manpower they may have been out of work for six months or more, and they exude an air of weary resignation as they sit quietly in the Manpower waiting room.

On the whole, these people have few skills or are totally unskilled—leaving them at the bottom of the heap in terms of employability in a tight job market. The unemployment rate in New York City averaged 7 percent in 1972—quite a bit higher than the nationwide jobless rate of 5.6 percent. The unemployment rate for blacks throughout the country was 10 percent, and for black teenagers it reached a staggering 33.5 percent.

To make matters worse, New York City keeps losing jobs as more and more businesses transfer their operations to the suburbs or to other states. Between May 1972 and May 1973 the city lost 28,400 jobs. Thus, the city is facing a serious problem of declining employment and high unemployment—and the people most affected by it are those who are already at the bottom of the economic ladder. Ann Rosenhaft noted that it was increasingly difficult to find jobs for people on welfare, despite all the pressure being applied by the state government in Albany. "Our rate of placement of employable people is extremely low," she said.

A random sampling of the people sitting in the Manpower waiting room on a Tuesday morning in March 1973 revealed that most were *not* on welfare, even though they were out of work. They ranged in age from the late teens to the mid-twenties, and many of them were still being supported by their families.

Aside from their generally low skills, they also seemed to lack knowledge of how to go about finding a job on their own. They tended to rely very heavily on public agencies to find jobs for them and, to a lesser extent, on tips from people they knew. None of them were in the habit of looking through the want ads in newspapers every day, and most of them seemed to share one girl's outspoken belief that the ads in *The New York Times* were "only for college people and secretaries." (In reality, this girl, Grace, who had some typing and switchboard skills, might very well have qualified for a number of jobs advertised in *The Times*'s "clerical" or "receptionist" categories, but she was totally unaware of it.)

Many of the people in the waiting room could probably have benefited from a course on the techniques of job-hunting, for their lack of sophistication in this regard may have been a contributing factor in the prolonged joblessness of those who had some office skills, although it probably made little difference with the unskilled.

The majority of the people there tended to stick fairly close to home in their search for work, so that the number of jobs available in or around the Fort Greene community was an important factor. Jobs in the area declined over the years as the fortunes of the Brooklyn Navy Yard declined. At one time the Navy Yard was the largest employer in Fort Greene, with seventy thousand workers on the federal payroll. But by the time the Yard closed as a government facility in 1967, only ten thousand people were still employed there. The Yard is now being turned into an industrial park. To date, twenty-three companies have moved into the 265-acre facility, and they employ 3,729 people, many of them from Fort Greene, Bedford-Stuyvesant, and Williamsburg.

The Navy Yard is now operated by a nonprofit organization, the Commerce, Labor, and Industry Corporation of the County of Kings, commonly known as CLICK. The anticipated development of the Navy Yard has been slow, for CLICK has had a hard time finding commercial tenants. Thus, the large pool of jobs that the Yard's development was expected to provide has not yet materialized. Far more employment is provided by the many small antiquated factories that exist near the waterfront between the Manhattan and Brooklyn Bridges. Many people from the projects work there, and they can just walk to their jobs.

Random sampling of the people who drifted in and out of the Manpower office that day showed that quite a few of them had been victimized in some way while looking for work. A number of them said they had been hired for jobs they thought were permanent, only to be told after a week or two that they were just temporarily replacing people who had been sick or were on vacation. Others reported going to private employment agencies and being told they had to pay a fee regardless of whether the agency actually got them a job. None of them were aware that this practice was illegal—that the agencies were just taking advantage of them because they were unsophisticated and vulnerable and badly in need of jobs.

A few of those in the waiting room said they had been

through a Manpower training program of one type or another and had picked up some new skills. Yet they were having just as much trouble finding jobs as before.

According to the statistics, 435 clients came to the Fort Greene Manpower Center during the month of March 1973. Of these, 192 had been to the agency before and were either still unemployed or had gotten jobs but the jobs had ended. The other 243 clients were newcomers to the agency.

Over the course of the month, 184 of these clients were tested by the Manpower psychometrician for general intelligence and English and math skills to determine their aptitude for some of the more difficult training programs. About ten percent failed the test. They were told to bone up on their studies, and then to come back and take the test again. Usually, about three or four percent of those who fail the first time manage to pass the retest. But even if they fail, they can still enroll in the easier training programs.

Altogether, 126 clients were sent to the various Manpower training programs during the month of March. About fifteen clients were sent to supportive agencies for help, such as Catholic Charities or the Department of Social Services. Those needing welfare were given a letter from a Manpower counselor requesting emergency assistance.

Of all these clients, how many actually got jobs? That is impossible to say. A figure of fifty or one hundred placements in March would be meaningless unless a follow-up study was done to determine how many of these jobs actually lasted for a substantial length of time. Many Manpower clients either quit their jobs after a few weeks, or they get laid off—thus reappearing almost at once among the ranks of the jobless. As noted earlier, a study of employment among welfare mothers under the Work Incentive Program showed that most of their jobs lasted no more than five weeks. A similar pattern may be true among many of the unemployed who go to the Manpower agency for help.

Among the clients who were in the Manpower office that Tuesday in March, quite a few mentioned jobs that had only lasted a few weeks. Their job-hunting histories tended to be similar, and those who spoke up related experiences that were familiar to almost everyone else in the room.

ALBERTA

(An attractive, neatly dressed young woman of about twenty-two with a West Indian accent, who was wearing one of the curly black wigs that have become so popular.)

"I been looking for a job for six months now. What I would like to do is clerical work, but every place I go they say to me, 'We want someone with four or five years' experience.' There are no jobs for a person like me, without any experience.

"I first came to Manpower in 1971. Before that I was working in a factory for a little while, but I didn't like that and the pay was very low, so I left. At Manpower they tested me and they said I did very well. They told me I shouldn't waste my time with factory work, and they sent me to training classes where I learned all kinds of clerical work, like typing and filing. I enjoyed it very much and I hoped I would get a job doing this. Manpower sent me out on lots of interviews, but there were no office jobs for me. They all wanted experience.

"So I took a job as a domestic, but that ended six months ago. I didn't like it anyhow, and I don't want that kind of job again—only nobody wants to hire me for an office job. Maybe I just don't have good luck. Last year I knew a lot of people who were out of work, but most of them have jobs now. Except me. So I keep coming here every week to see if I can find something. I have some skills. I don't see why I should have to work in a factory or do domestic work anymore."

AL

(A quiet, soft-spoken young man with a small mustache and a thick Afro.)

"It's the same thing with me. Everywhere I go they only want someone with experience. I haven't worked in five months. Before that I had a job in a factory that I got through New York State Employment. But I only worked there for about two or three weeks, and then I got laid off.

"I'd take anything I could get. Like, I could be a general helper in a store or something. Manpower sent me out to two places so far. The first time was for a job as a guard. I would have liked that, but the trouble was I would have had to pay for the uniform myself, out of my own money, before I could start work. I didn't have no money to buy the uniform, so I couldn't get that job.

"The second place they sent me was also for a job as a security guard. At this place they told me I had to be over twenty-one, but I'm only nineteen, so I couldn't get that job either. You know, Manpower didn't even say that those guards had to be over twenty-one, but they must have known it. The man who interviewed me for the guard job said he had told that to the agency and he wanted to know why they had sent me over in the first place.

"My friends are having the same problem finding jobs that I am. The other day I filled out a form at the New York State Employment office for some kind of training program for auto mechanics. If I get myself a skill like that, I should be able to get a job."

GRACE

(A slim, beautiful, and vivacious girl who wore
her hair in a close-cropped Afro.)

"Oh, I been looking for work a *long* time—over a year and a half. I know four different kinds of switchboards, and I can type and work an adding machine and a mimeograph machine. I been to lots of places to see about a job, but when I get there they usually say they already hired someone. Or else they want someone who has at least six months' experience. It seems like they don't even want to give you a chance.

"Another problem is I never actually finished high school. I was going to John Jay, and there was some kind of mix-up. I hadn't taken all the credits I needed, and by the time I should have graduated it turned out I was one credit short. But I never got a chance to go back and make it up 'cause right after that I had my baby. Then I had some trouble with my high blood pressure, so I just sort of forgot about school.

"I'm nineteen now, and in the last year and a half I only worked about a month or two. One time my father got me a job in a factory. It was really hard. You punched in at eight in the morning, and aside from lunch, you only got one ten-minute break. Also, you had to stand on your feet the whole day. Well, I couldn't take that more than a month before my high blood pressure started causing trouble again. I almost passed out at work one day, and I quit.

"Anyhow, I never wanted no factory job. It was a real disappointment to me—going to school all those years—to end up in a factory.

"The other job I had was in Methodist Hospital. I had filed an application for a job there back in 1970, but I didn't hear nothing from them so I forgot all about it. Then in 1972 they suddenly called me up for a job. It was only a temporary job, but they didn't tell me that when they hired me. All they wanted was for me to replace somebody who worked in the dietary department until she got over being sick. But I thought the job was really mine. I liked it, too. I used to bring the food up to the patients and fix up the silverware. It was only part-time—three hours a day, six days a week—but the pay was pretty good. And I was just getting used to it when this other woman came back, and I was out of a job again.

"What I would really like is to be an airline stewardess or a model. Somebody told me about this model agency in Manhattan, and I went there. They told me they thought I would make a good model, but I would need a portfolio to show people. That would cost eighty-nine dollars, and they told me I had to use *their* photographer. I didn't have any money, so I had to ask my mother for it. But she thought the whole thing was a trick, and she wouldn't lend me anything. She may have been right, too.

"My mother's been taking care of my baby for me—the baby lives with her—because she knows I'm not well enough to raise a child by myself. Not with my blood pressure.

"I've been to a lot of employment agencies, like New York State and the Search agency, but I haven't had any luck. At one job they sent me to I had to take a typing test on an electric typewriter. I never used one of those things before. In my class in high school we only had regular typewriters. So I tried this electric thing—I pushed a letter and it went rrrrrrrrrrrrr—it just kept repeating and I couldn't stop it. It was crazy. I got to practice a little before the test, and really, I didn't do too bad. I did about sixty words a minute. But the girl next to me did sixty-one, and she got the job.

"People have been telling me that if I went to a private agency it would be better. So I called up this one agency that had an ad in the *Daily News,* and they told me over the phone that when I came in for an interview I should bring in twenty-five dollars. They said that after I paid them, they would send me out for lots of different jobs. But that didn't do me no good because I didn't have twenty-five dollars.

"Mostly I run around to places that my friends or family

tell me about. Like this morning, a friend told me she thought they might be doing some hiring at a factory a few blocks from here, so I went over. But she was wrong 'cause it's very slow there and they're not hiring anyone; they're laying off people. On the way home I happened to notice this Manpower place, so I just stopped off. Maybe they can do something for me here.

"About a month ago I went over to the welfare center. I figured if I could get welfare, I could lay on that for a while. That would be okay. I would get Medicaid that way, too. I would really like to have that, because I don't have any kind of medical coverage now. When I get sick, the only place for me to go is a city hospital.

"At the welfare center they asked me how I had been getting by without working, and I told them the truth. I told them my boyfriend has been helping me out, but he wasn't able to give me very much. (This boyfriend is not the father of my child.) So they said to me, 'Well, just keep on doing what you're doing,' and they tore up my application. They wouldn't help me get a job or nothing.

"When my girlfriend went to them, she lied—she said she didn't have no money and she was out in the streets hustling. They put her on welfare right away. But later on they found out she was lying, that she was living in a nice apartment and just needed a little help in paying the rent. So they cut her off.

"I don't want to lie. I really don't even want no public assistance. I just want a nice job I can stick with."

EDITH

(A tall, outspoken woman who appeared to be
in her mid-twenties.)

"I just had a job. I got it about two weeks ago for this jewelry manufacturing place. It was nice and I liked it quite a lot. I did a little typing, a little switchboard work, some other stuff. It wasn't just the same thing all day long. So I was enjoying myself for these two weeks and getting used to everything. I thought I was really set.

"Then I walked in yesterday morning and there's this woman sitting at my desk who I never saw before. So I went to the people who hired me and I said, 'What's going on?' And they said to me, 'Oh, didn't we tell you? Your job was just temporary. We needed someone to fill in 'cause this other woman was sick for a while.' I said, 'No. You never told me nothing like that,' and I just marched out of there. I was so mad!

"So now I got to look for a job all over again. But you got to be careful because people can really take advantage of you sometimes. They make you think it's permanent so you'll take the job, and then when they don't need you anymore they just drop you—after you've spent all that time trying to learn the routine. It's just plain mean."

STAN

*(A weary-looking man in a leather jacket and
a knitted cap who was slouching in a chair
by the wall.)*

"I guess I'm just looking for work as a general laborer. I've been looking now for about seven months, and I did get two factory jobs in that time. They each paid me two dollars an hour. One was on Broadway in Manhattan, and the other was on Nostrand Avenue in Brooklyn. I guess I worked about three weeks at each place. But the cost of living is just too high to work at jobs that pay so little.

"My big problem is that I just got out of the pen. I was in Auburn for eight years. I went in when I was seventeen, and I never had a steady job before then. So here I am, twenty-six years old, and I never really had a job outside of prison. A lot of the friends I grew up with have good jobs now—at least the friends that didn't go to jail. But for me now, the gap is just too big. I don't feel I can ever catch up. I'm really discouraged, and there's no telling what might happen.

"When I go for job interviews, they give me these forms to fill out, and there's usually something on it about whether I have any past convictions. Usually I tell the truth. Once or twice I put down 'no,' but that didn't help either, because then they wanted to know what I'd been doing for the past eight years, what kinds of jobs I'd had, any references—and I didn't know what to tell them. So even if I try to lie about being in jail, I get caught.

"In Auburn I took up barbering, but an ex-con can't get a job as a barber very easily, at least not in New York. You got to go through some special kind of process to get an apprentice license, and if you're an ex-con they may not give it to you. Then you got to work for a master barber for a few years before you can be a real barber yourself. Anyway, I'm not really interested in barbering. I don't know why I studied it.

"They had a pretty good school program in Auburn. Anyway, it seemed a lot better than the high school I went to on the outside, Metropolitan Vocational. At Auburn they got a machine shop and welding classes, or you could study to be a dental technician. They even had some college courses.

"When I was in prison I used to work as a presser—you know, in the laundry, ironing uniforms. So when I got out I applied for a pressing job at this place in Brooklyn, and they said they'd try me out. But all the machinery was different from what I had worked on in Auburn. Also, in jail you only press one thing—uniforms—while in this place they gave me all kinds of clothes, like women's clothes and kids' clothes. I was very slow 'cause everything was new to me, and after two days they let me go.

"This is the second time I've come to the Manpower agency. The first time they sent me to this factory where there was a job for $1.85 an hour. That's even less than I made on the other factory jobs, and I just didn't want it. I don't want to kill myself for no $1.85 an hour. That's only about seventy-five dollars a week.

"My parole officer's been pressuring me to get a job, or at least to get into some kind of a training program. He gave me some places to try. What I would like is to get into a tractor-trailer training program where you learn while you're on the job. When I went to New York State Employment they told me they couldn't put me in a training program because I never worked steady. At that agency they don't really have your interests at heart. There's so many people they have to see each day—how can they care what happens to this one or that one? My counselor here at Manpower seems more interested than the people at New York State Employment, but still she hasn't had nothing for me.

"I'm not going to go to one of those private agencies because I can't see buying a job, paying twenty-five or thirty dollars for a job that only pays two dollars an hour. I never was to a private agency, but I hear that's what they charge you just for sending you out to different places, even if you don't ever get a job out of it."

There are many unskilled ex-convicts like Stan drifting around Fort Greene, and the problems they face in seeking jobs often seem insurmountable. Most of them come out of prison after several years totally lacking useful skills, even though they are supposed to receive vocational training in jail. Their lack of skills combined with their prison records make it just about impossible for them to get decent paying jobs. Yet many of them, particularly if they are in their mid-twenties or older, seem to feel it is demeaning to work full time at a job that pays as little as $1.85 or $2.00 an hour. They regard such jobs not as stepping stones to better positions but as dead ends—and often they're right.

A study commissioned by the Department of Labor of more than one thousand low-wage earners in Detroit showed that their jobs paid so little and had such a limited future that the workers would probably be mired in poverty for the rest of their lives. It is mainly jobs like these—dead-end jobs—that are available to ex-convicts like Stan who, not surprisingly, are reluctant to take them. Thus, the biggest problem is not really a lack of jobs per se, but a lack of jobs that pay enough to pull a man out of poverty or at least offer him some hope for a better future.

Long Island University, located just a few blocks away from the Manpower center, found itself involved in the employment problems of ex-convicts when it agreed to serve as a halfway house beginning in the fall of 1971. Each term since then, about twenty ex-convicts have been sent to live in the L.I.U. dormitory and to attend classes under the supervision of parole officer Clifford Watterson. The university has tried to help them find jobs but has found it extremely difficult because of the widespread resistance to hiring ex-convicts—plus the attitude of some of the ex-convicts themselves. In a number of cases they just casually left their jobs after a few weeks—to the exasperation of school officials who had put in a lot of effort to find work for them in the first place. Interviews with three of the parolees showed they were just not willing to work at jobs that didn't pay a respectable wage, even if nothing else was available at the moment.

MICKEY

(Twenty-five years old.)

"I went out and got a job at Chock Full O' Nuts, but I terminated it myself today. I was only working there five days, and it was a hassle. I made no money down there. I know that I can't start making three or four hundred dollars a week right now. I know I'll have to start at a minimum wage, but at that place it was like below minimum. I was talking to some of the other fellows who'd been there a couple of months, and they told me that with tips, with a full salary for a full eight-hour day, five days a week, their check before taxes would be anywhere from ninety to ninety-five dollars. And that's ridiculous, 'cause what happens if you get no tips? You make maybe seventy dollars.

"Then there's the job itself. I couldn't take it for that kind of money. The harassment you get from those customers. I'd like to mush them with some pie."

(Mickey was one of the few parolees who had picked up a marketable skill in prison. He had become a good machinist in Walkill, and after several months of persistent and intrepid job-hunting he finally managed to get a job in a small machine shop in Brooklyn. He worked there for a while and then went on to take a better-paying job elsewhere, also as a machinist.)

MARC

(Twenty-five years old.)

"I'm looking for a job too. You see, my wife and kids have been on welfare for two years, so I need a good job. I could've gotten fourteen jobs already if I was willing to work for, say, two dollars an hour. The parole officers keep sending us out for dumb jobs like these. Like the two guys I room with here, they're working at two-dollar jobs in Manhattan. They're twenty, twenty-two years old, something like that. For them it's all right. But I can't work for two dollars an hour anymore. I'm better than that."

(Marc eventually settled for a job that paid only a little more than two dollars an hour, which he got with the help of a relative.)

MOE

(Twenty-three years old.)

"Until a few weeks ago I was working part-time at a Davega store in Manhattan. Nobody got the job for me. I just made the rounds myself, went to employment agencies and finally got work. Afterwards Mr. Watterson asked me to explain to the rest of the fellows in the program how I went about getting my job, because most of them don't seem to know what to do, or else they're afraid to try. They wait for the L.I.U. Placement Office or Mr. Watterson to get jobs for them.

"Anyhow, I finally quit that job because it really didn't pay enough. It was only part-time, and after I finished paying for carfare and lunches, it seemed I was losing more than I was making." (Moe wound up back in jail.)

Such attitudes are not confined to ex-convicts. They are prevalent among many people and reflect the values of a society that places a high premium on material goods and tends to judge people according to how much money they make. Americans have high expectations of life—higher than those of people in most other societies. Their "work ethic" is geared to the notion that honest labor eventually brings material rewards (as well as being good for the soul). A man who works hard but earns very little is generally regarded, by himself as well as others, as a failure in this society.

Nevertheless, most low-income people still do adhere to the "work ethic" and prefer even a dead-end job to no job. But for others it seems to be a matter of pride not to work at all—to try to rip off society somehow—rather than work at a menial job, since a menial job is equated with failure.

The special dilemma of ex-convicts is that their prison record often prevents them from getting anything but a menial job, no matter what their capabilities. Their predicament is shared by many of the city's poorly educated unskilled laborers, particularly members of minority groups.

This does not mean that unemployed able-bodied men necessarily go on welfare if they can't get decent paying jobs. Crime, not welfare, is the big rip-off. It is the main alternative to legitimate employment in New York, according to a study by Columbia University's Conservation of Human Resources Staff titled, "New York Is Very Much Alive." The study showed that opportunities in the underworld sector of the economy—in drugs, prostitution, gambling and other illegal activities—are far more lucrative than welfare payments or jobs for the unskilled. Edited by Eli Ginzberg, the study estimated that 250,000 people derived a regular income from illegal sources in New York.

Ironically, then, this would suggest that the relatively small number of unemployed men who *are* on welfare are more likely to be honest than are the chronically unemployed men who are *not* on welfare. As Mario said when he was on the welfare rolls, "I ain't got the talent to be going around stealing or casting myself in a jail cell."

New York City was faced with a major unemployment problem at the start of 1973, when large numbers of Vietnam veterans began returning home. About thirty thousand Vietnam veterans live in New York, and it was estimated that in low-income areas like Fort Greene one out of four could not find work. In the city as a whole about seventy-five hundred veterans had no choice but to go on public assistance.

In March 1973 a special welfare center exclusively for Vietnam veterans with honorable discharges was opened on Myrtle Avenue about two blocks away from the Fort Greene housing projects. (Veterans with less-than-honorable discharges, which are often drug-related, must apply for welfare in the regular city centers.) In the special center, veterans have to go through the same painstaking procedure as other welfare recipients. They have to show as many as eight different documents, including identification papers, past pay stubs, rent receipts, cancelled bank books, utility shut-off notices, and birth certificates for any dependents. Those who qualify are allotted about thirty-eight dollars bimonthly for subsistence, plus a rent allowance.

All able-bodied veterans must show up at the center in person twice each month to collect their checks. They must also be available for possible employment. But for them, too, the jobs available are mainly low paying. One veteran, Lewis Delano, complained, "The kind of jobs they show you are hellhole sweatshop jobs, like working in a laundry for eighty dollars a week. It's like they're encouraging you to stay on welfare. It's like this kind of economy doesn't have any jobs for you."

Although regular veterans' benefits are available to former servicemen with honorable or general discharges, they are not given to those with dishonorable discharges. Estimates of the number of veterans with bad discharges in New York City range anywhere from six thousand to eighteen thousand. About seventy-five percent of these less-than-honorable discharges were issued to blacks and other members of minority groups—and it is these men who are having the hardest time finding work.

Some veterans are especially bitter about their joblessness because they had expected a better homecoming; they had expected to get some kind of special consideration for having served their country, but instead they find that only P.O.W.s are treated like heroes. Because it was an unpopular war, even the veterans are not especially popular.

One veteran who was a radio operator with the 173rd Airborne Brigade said that he had come home after fourteen months in Vietnam with a Bronze Star—and an addiction to heroin. "They didn't take any of the good things I did into consideration," he said. "They just gave me an undesirable discharge, and now I'm on welfare."

Resentment and frustration on the part of the jobless veterans led to several minor outbursts in the welfare centers. Charles Morris, deputy administrator for income maintenance of the Human Resources Administration, explained: "They're not the usual welfare population. They're young men and usually healthy. They haven't found a job. Many picked up some drug addiction over there. The more recent veterans came back with a disenchantment about the war. They are among our more hostile welfare clients.

"It's very plain that they don't want to be on welfare," he continued. "They want a job, or, if they have a drug problem, they want treatment. When they come to the welfare center, it takes a real adjustment in self-image to walk through that door. It means they've failed and the system has failed."

Resentment against welfare recipients—particularly against the veterans and other able-bodied men—is probably strongest among those who work at relatively low-income jobs themselves. They believe, rightly or wrongly, that there are plenty of jobs available (jobs very much like their own), but that the welfare recipients just don't want them.

For example, many of the security guards who work at the

veterans' welfare center on Myrtle Avenue can scarcely disguise their contempt for men on public assistance. The guards themselves are mainly black and unskilled, and they feel that if they are managing to stay afloat without welfare, so can everyone else. They are particularly bitter that the welfare recipients get free benefits such as Medicaid while they themselves constantly have to worry about medical bills. Such resentment creates a class antagonism that is frightening.

One guard, looking around at all the clients in the welfare center with obvious distaste, launched into an angry diatribe against the jobless veterans. "I came from the same type of background as a lot of these guys here, but I've always been able to get a job," he said. "I've worked for ninety dollars a week and even less. You just got to go through those ads in the paper, go from one agency to another, and keep on pounding the pavement. You'll get something after a while. Anyone could if he tried. Even if the job is very low paying—like pushing a broom or something—well, you don't figure you'll stay in it forever. You take it just to be working, and meanwhile you look around for something that pays more or has more of a future. Anyhow, that's what you do if you have some ambition and drive. You gradually work yourself up. But you don't just refuse jobs 'cause you think they're not good enough for you, and then sit around collecting welfare checks. A lot of these guys here, they could be working if they really wanted to. It wouldn't be ten thousand dollars a year maybe, but at least it would pay them until something better came along.

"Just look at that guy over there. Look at that leather jacket he's got on. That cost at least $150. And his shoes. They're expensive, too. I can't afford shoes like that, or a $150 jacket. You can't tell me that guy needs welfare. But he's getting it anyhow. It's probably a racket with him, and with a lot of those other guys, too."

The starting salary for a welfare policeman is $7,800, in

contrast to a regular New York City policeman who starts at $11,200. Although this puts a welfare guard substantially above the official poverty level if he supports a family of four, it also leaves him substantially below the $11,880 that is needed for a moderate standard of living in New York. In short, it leaves him absolutely *nowhere*—he can't qualify for any of the benefits that the poor receive, but neither does he earn enough for the amenities he thinks he deserves for having upheld the "work ethic." He feels cheated, and his frustration is vented against those who, in his view, get almost as much as he does without working for it. Such are the grievances that pit group against group and set off the tensions that permeate the city.

6

Mothers on Welfare

IF YOU walk along the winding pathways of the Fort Greene housing projects on a sunny spring or fall afternoon, you may see a group of young girls—children, really—clustered around the benches in front of 90 St. Edwards Street. The girls appear to be no more than twelve or fourteen years old, and they behave like most other youngsters of their age. They talk and giggle in loud, high-pitched voices, their laughter interspersed with a little horseplay and rough-housing. But when they stand up to go back inside the building, you realize with a shock that all of these children are pregnant.

These are the girls of Project Teen-Aid, a high school for pregnant adolescents located on the ground floor of one of the buildings in the Fort Greene projects. Most of the girls are not quite so young as they look, with the majority being about sixteen. But there have been girls as young as twelve in the program, plus quite a few fourteen- and fifteen-year-olds who came to Project Teen-Aid from the local junior high schools, Sands and Rothschild.

More than ninety girls currently attend Project Teen-Aid, and according to the program's director, Marie Swearer, about ninety percent of them come from welfare families. "The rest are maybe one hundred dollars above what they call the poverty line," Ms. Swearer added. Many of these girls have grown up in one-parent homes, with their mothers receiving welfare money for their support under the Aid to Dependent Children program. Now these girls themselves are becoming mothers, and they too may have to rely on welfare to support their children. And so the poverty cycle perpetuates itself.

One of the basic goals of Project Teen-Aid is to equip these pregnant adolescents with something their mothers probably never had— a high school diploma plus marketable skills such as bookkeeping, typing, and stenography. Thus armed, it is hoped they will be able to break out of the welfare trap despite the fact that they are becoming mothers at such a young age.

The overwhelming majority of the people on the welfare rolls in New York City are mothers and children. According to a study by Lawrence Podell, "Families on Welfare in New York City," about twenty percent of these women are unmarried. Another forty percent have no husband—through separation or desertion (in most cases the separation came *after* the family went on welfare, not before, indicating that the husband could not support the family even while he was living with them); five percent are divorced; and five percent are widows. There is a husband in residence in only about a quarter of all the families on welfare in the city.

The Podell study also showed that about fifteen percent of the mothers on welfare had never worked, mainly because they had become pregnant while still teenagers. About half of all mothers on welfare became pregnant before the age of nineteen, and another twenty-five percent first became pregnant when they were sixteen or younger. These women tend to rely on welfare off and on—not necessarily continuously—during their childbearing years and while their youngest children are still at home. But after the age of forty there is a very sharp drop in the number of women on welfare, indicating that many of them are able to become self-supporting once they no longer have young children. About eighty percent of all women on welfare are in their teens, twenties, and thirties; only twenty percent are over forty.

It is perhaps easier to understand the plight of the mothers of the Project Teen-Aid girls than that of the girls themselves. At the time their mothers first became pregnant, it wasn't easy for the poor to acquire knowledge about various contraceptive devices, since hospitals were forbidden to give out such information. Moreover, the birth control pill had not come into widespread use. Abortions were illegal, and unless a girl was willing to risk her life and health in an illegal operation performed by a possibly disreputable doctor or someone who wasn't licensed, she had no choice but to go ahead and have her baby.

But the situation today is totally different. Easy, effective contraceptive devices are easily available to everyone who is sixteen or over, and the poor can get them free with their Medicaid cards. Moreover, abortions are now legal, and Medicaid will pay for these too.

The liberalization of the laws has had a striking impact throughout New York State and in the urban ghetto areas as well. Cumberland Hospital, where most of the women of Fort Greene go to have their children, has reported a steady decline in the number of live births since the abortion law went into effect. In 1970 the hospital recorded 2,502 live births; in 1971 the figure was 2,341; and by 1972 it had declined to 2,006. On the other hand, the hospital performed 1,134 abortions of all types in 1972. This means that almost one-third of all the pregnant women who entered Cumberland Hospital in 1972 had abortions.

The hospital is located on the grounds of the Fort Greene housing projects and draws eighty-seven percent of its patients from the immediate neighborhood. Most of the patients are on welfare, and Medicaid pays their hospital costs, which average between $126 and $132 per day. When their pregnancy is confirmed, women can get an abortion at Cumberland within ten days of their first clinic appointment.

According to a study by the Health Services Administration, there would have been twenty-four thousand additional children on the city's welfare rolls by now without New York's liberalized abortion law. Gordon Chase, the Health Services Administrator, said the study showed that abortion reform had allowed welfare mothers "greater freedom of choice in planning their families."

So why is it that the adolescents of Project Teen-Aid decided to go ahead and have their babies when they could easily have gotten an abortion?

"When you ask that, you're getting down to why they get pregnant in the first place," said Marie Swearer. "A lot of the kids come out of deprived homes, with very poor home structure and very poor love relationships with their parents. So the kids have their babies either to have a love object of their own or to demonstrate to their parents how a child should be raised—which of course they don't do, because they get hung up in the same emotional patterns as their parents. Or they use their child to sustain a brief relationship with the man, the putative father. They also may use the baby as a means of getting out of the home, setting up their own household. Sometimes their parents' household is just so bad they feel they can do better if they have their own kids and set up their own households. This way they think they can do better than their parents have done.

"So they don't want to abort. They definitely want their children. We've had only five adoptions in eight years, and just seven abortions. These kids are not into abortions at all. Your older black woman might be, but your younger one isn't. You see, the older woman might already have children, and she knows what it's really like to try to raise children on your own when you're poor."

There is a danger in the fact that these young girls depend so heavily on their babies to satisfy their own needs. A study undertaken by Dr. Arthur Green, child psychiatrist at Down-state Medical Center in Brooklyn, of mothers who abused their children showed that most abusive mothers tended to have just such a neurotic dependence on their child, expecting the child to fulfill their needs instead of the reverse. If such mothers feel they are rejected by the child, or that the child is not performing according to expectations, they tend to abuse him, Dr. Green says. Two-thirds of the mothers in the study said that as children they were abused by their own parents—just as many of the girls of Project Teen-Aid have been abused at home. It is a pernicious pattern.

Project Teen-Aid was begun ten years ago as an attempt to help pregnant teenagers get through a difficult period of their lives, to instruct them in health care, and to encourage them to continue working for their high school diplomas. Usually, once an adolescent in Fort Greene became pregnant she dropped out of school, virtually ending whatever chance she had of breaking out of the poverty cycle.

"It was not so much that pregnant girls were asked to leave the regular schools," Marie Swearer said, "but it was sort of suggested to them that maybe it would be better if they didn't stay through their pregnancy. So they just didn't feel welcome. Like, if you were the only pregnant kid running around school, you'd feel kind of out of place. And this type of thing—teenage pregnancy—wasn't so widespread then as it is now. This was back in 1963. I guess the schools have changed their attitude a lot since then, but in 1963 there was still a big stigma attached to a young girl getting pregnant, even in poor areas. So these girls would just drop out and then sit home with nothing to do.

"The idea for some sort of school to help pregnant girls

was first thought up by a visiting nurse. You know what visiting nurses do? They go into people's homes, make home visits. Well, this particular nurse used to come across quite a few of these pregnant adolescents while she'd be making her rounds, and when she looked into the problem she found there were no decent facilities for them anywhere. In the hospitals they were lumped in with the pregnant women, without having special facilities of their own.

"So she started out by getting some of these girls together and having group discussions with them on maternity and infant care, hygiene and other health matters. The groups got larger and larger, and soon they started having regular meetings at the Willoughby House Settlement. That's right here in the projects, too. For the first few years the meetings were run by visiting nurses and personnel from the Willoughby House Settlement. Then in 1966 or 1967 they hired two part-time teachers from the Board of Education to do remedial reading and math with the girls, and they found that this was very successful. The kids really did want to continue school.

"I think that about this time Georgia McMurray was working on a Board of Education committee for special children, and she proposed that the Board set up facilities for pregnant adolescents. The Board agreed, and six schools were officially started in New York City. We were one of them, and after we were officially approved we moved from the Willoughby Settlement to the place where the Senior Citizens Center is now. From there we moved here. But we're not funded by the Board of Education. We're part of the anti-poverty program, and our money comes from the Office of Economic Opportunity in Washington, channeled through the Fort Greene Community Corporation. For a time Georgia McMurray was the director of our school, but she moved on, and now she's the commissioner of the Agency for Child Development."

Project Teen-Aid bears little resemblance to a regular high

school. For one thing, it's located on the ground floor of a project apartment building and looks more like a crowded, cozy home than an institution. Tiny classrooms are squeezed side by side, right next to the reception desk and the offices of the director and the school principal. There are also a small examining room and places where the girls can lie down if they're not feeling well or if they're just tired. The atmosphere is strictly informal, cheerful and friendly.

Girls can start going to Project Teen-Aid whenever they feel that they want to leave their own school, say in their fifth or sixth month of pregnancy. "We pick up their education exactly where the kids leave off in their own high schools," said Marie Swearer. "If they come to us in the middle of the tenth grade, that's where we start with them. We're supposed to have a maximum enrollment of seventy-five girls, but right now we have ninety-one. We sort of count on the fact that not all the girls are going to be here on any one day, so we enroll as many as possible. Then, of course, you have kids who are out to deliver, so you have a few weeks where they don't come to school. Also, there's always some sort of illness around keeping girls out, so we can manage with an enrollment of ninety-one even though we're very cramped here. The attendance here is about eighty percent, which is a lot better than in the regular high schools around here. I guess the kids want to come. They're comfortable here. They're with other girls who are going through the same thing they are.

"Also, I think they feel they're being taken care of. We have at least two social workers here all the time, plus a full-time public health nurse. Also, we have people who go to the girls' homes to help them and help their parents, and to take them to the Department of Social Services and get them through all the red tape there. We have a ratio of about five kids to every adult here, and that's very good.

"One of the requirements of this school is that aside from

subjects like English, math, and history, the kids have to take a course in a saleable skill, which would be some sort of business subject. They also have to take home economics, which covers nutrition, money management, and all the things the kids need to know in setting up their own households. This is what we try to prepare these kids for.

"If they finish our program, they get diplomas from the high schools they went to before they came here. We don't have diplomas of our own, but we do have this arrangement with the regular schools. When Project Teen-Aid first started, our girls were mainly from the Fort Greene area, but now we're getting them from Brownsville, Bedford-Stuyvesant, and Jamaica. Some of them travel a long way to come here. Word gets around.

"Usually, when girls first come here they're not very highly motivated as far as schoolwork is concerned. Sometimes they've been referred to us by their guidance counselors in school or by Cumberland Hospital. These are the two main sources that we get our girls from. It's not usually that the girls have decided for themselves that they want to come here. They're just floundering around, and somebody says to them, 'Go to this place,' and they go.

"You see, they don't have very much to do anyhow. They're not as socially active when they're pregnant, so they feel they might as well come here. Also, they know we can help them with the Department of Social Services. But some of them do want to complete high school, or at least go on as far as they can before they have their babies.

"Another thing they get through us is much better health care than they would have on their own. A lot of poor people just don't like medicine and won't have anything to do with health care because of the clinic situation. After all, what can you say about the clinics at a place like Cumberland? The maternity clinic there might have 125 girls waiting to see three doctors from about eight to twelve o'clock—and this is *with* a separate prenatal clinic for adolescents. Cumberland is a municipal hospital with limited funds, so the kind of care pregnant girls get there is just minimal—not even that at times. The hospital just hasn't got the money or the staff, and the personnel attitudes are very poor. But the administration has been working very hard on that, and things are a little better now than they were before. Actually, our school has a pretty good relationship with the chief of obstetrics at Cumberland, and most of our girls from Fort Greene go there. We also made an arrangement with Brooklyn Jewish Hospital to treat our girls as a separate group. They have a prenatal adolescent clinic, an adolescent family planning clinic, and also an adolescent high-risk clinic.

"We make sure our kids are in some kind of prenatal clinic, because left to themselves they'd wait until the last minute to get prenatal care. Even though almost all our girls have Medicaid, their attitude toward medicine is very poor. Most of them don't want to go to a doctor unless they think they're dying.

"We have our own on-site prenatal examining room right here in the school, and we're getting some new medical equipment for it. The Chemical Bank is paying for it. They have what they call a 'street banker' who works out of their urban affairs department. His job is to go around the poor neighborhoods and see if there are any worthwhile programs that need money. Chemical is just giving money away—but only to programs or businesses that they feel are really valid. So this street banker came in here one day saying, 'Do you want anything?' And I said, 'Yeah. Do you want a list?' So he worked out this proposal to Chemical for us to get the medical equipment. This is the only program that Chemical has funded in Fort Greene that I know of, although they have funded quite a few businesses and social programs in Bedford-Stuyvesant.

"Anyhow, once we have this new equipment, we may be

able to get residents from Cumberland and Brooklyn Jewish Hospital coming over here to examine our girls. There's also a possibility of getting a doctor who's in private practice to come in here and set up a Medicaid clientele just for our girls. That way the kids would have their own private doctor who would take care of them right through pregnancy into delivery. That would be one of the best things we could do for our kids.

"I understand there are quite a few storefront health groups in the neighborhood now. I don't know how valuable they are, but at least they're doctors, so it means more doctors for the area. Before they came in I think the only doctor in private practice around here was Dr. Vitelli. The people use him because he makes home visits. He's an old fuddy-duddy G.P. who's been around since time immemorial, but he's got a lot of heart. And I guess that matters more than anything. There also used to be a private dentist down on Gold Street, but he's not there anymore.

"We really needed more doctors and dentists in Fort Greene, so maybe the storefront health centers are a good thing. They are an alternative to the hospital clinics, at any rate. But you have to remember that doctors can really make a killing in Medicaid, and they may not be really conscientious. Poor people don't usually know what questions to ask a doctor, and they almost never volunteer information, so you have to have a doctor who's really conscientious about his work. But somebody who's in a poor area making a killing on Medicaid is not likely to be so conscientious. He's interested in money.

"Our girls probably get better health care while they're in our school than they've ever had before. How long they stay in the program depends on them. If a kid is really having a hard time adjusting to the birth of the child, the girl may stay here a whole year or even a year and a half. It all depends on the individual, even after the child is born.

"We try to keep the kids moving out, because I can't see what purpose it serves to have them stay here indefinitely. This is a very sheltered kind of thing. It's not realistic to have them here too long. But they really seem to like it, at least socially. A lot of them say they like this better than the other schools they've been to.

"As far as I know, about seventy percent of our kids do go on to get their high school degrees, although not necessarily here. Some of them go back to their regular high schools after their babies are born. I think seventy percent is pretty good, considering that most of these kids are on welfare. And once they get their degrees, they usually do go to work. We don't have any real follow-up studies to prove this, but we have a lot of girls coming back here to visit two and three years after they've left here. They'll tell us, 'Well, I'm working now and I have another kid, and I'm going out with so-and-so.' So this is how we find out what's happening to them. It's not very scientific, but quite a few of the kids do return to visit, especially since so many of them live right around here.

"Most of our girls stay with their own families after they have their babies, and their mothers continue to get welfare money for their support as long as they're not working, plus money for the new grandchild. But if the girls don't want to stay with their mothers, or if they can't stay, they can sometimes be declared emancipated minors and get their own welfare budget from the Department of Social Services.

"This whole emancipated minor business is crazy, because it doesn't really depend on a girl's age. It all depends on which welfare center you're dealing with and which worker in the center. Like, we have a nineteen-year-old who couldn't be declared an emancipated minor, but we have sixteen-year-olds who could. Also, even if welfare says a girl can be an emancipated minor, the hospitals may not agree. For example, when a kid gives birth and wants to take her baby home to her own house, the hospital may not agree that she qualifies as an

emancipated minor—they have their own concept or definition of it. So nobody knows for sure what an emancipated
minor is. There are no guidelines. It's just arbitrary.

"If a girl can't live with her family and can't be declared an
emancipated minor, she has to be put into some sort of residence. We try to place them in what they call postpartum residences—places where girls live with their babies. The Louise
Wise Agency and the Foundling Home both have residences
like this, and even though they are mainly adoption agencies,
the residences have nothing to do with whether the babies
are going to be put up for adoption. A few other places have
residences like these, too, but there really aren't too many of
them. All placements have to go through the Bureau of Child
Welfare, which pays the costs unless the girls themselves can
pay. But most of our girls are very poor.

"We've had quite a lot of trouble placing some of our
girls in these residences. I think they have a kind of quota
system—like how many black women, how many white women, how many Puerto Rican women can stay in the residences at one time. Just a little while ago we tried to place
one of our Puerto Rican girls in the Louise Wise residence.
They did a whole psychosocial history on her. She went
through a psychiatric evaluation and a whole lot of things,
and afterwards she got a letter from them saying she was
accepted. But then they turned around completely and said
no. They didn't give any reason. They just refused to talk
about it. The only thing we could figure is that she's Puerto
Rican, and maybe they already had their full quota of Puerto
Ricans. Of course, it's illegal for them to set any kind of
quota where public funds are involved, but we never got
them to sit down with us and talk about it. There was no question about this girl being pathological or anything, no reason
to think she would do any harm to the other residents. She
was a very innocuous Puerto Rican girl.

"If we were a little more political, we probably could have

done something about this. But we just don't seem to carry the right kind of guns behind us. We were all very upset.

"After our girls leave here, if they get a job and start working, they usually rely on someone in their family to take care of their baby. Or else they rely on friends. It's family and friends, in that order.

"Then there are the little home day-care centers. There are hundreds of them in Bedford-Stuyvesant, for example. They're just little centers in people's apartments, with one woman taking care of, say, five kids, and all the mothers pay her. And of course there are the public day-care centers run by the city.

"But the public centers are in trouble right now, because the city is changing the eligibility standards and the fee scale. Working mothers aren't going to be able to use these day-care centers at all anymore unless they're earning so little that it's almost like they're on welfare. You see, the amount of federal funds available for these day-care centers has been cut back.

"It's not just the day-care centers, either. There have been federal cutbacks across the board. The maternal and infant care centers are being cut. A lot of clinics are going to be closed. Mental health clinics are going to be cut. The paraprofessionals in the schools are going to be cut. The people in the Agency for Child Development are absolutely terrified by these cutbacks, because of what it's going to do to their programs. Also, the Bureau of Special Services for Children, which handles handicapped, dumb, blind, and deaf, they're terrified about what's going to happen to their funds.

"I've never seen such a bad situation in my life. If I were paranoid, I'd say it was nothing but an attempt to screw the poor."

Until now, the public day-care centers in Fort Greene have been an outstanding example of the kind of high-quality service the city can perform for a poor community if it really makes an effort. The Willoughby House Day-Care Center—a multicolored rotunda located on the grounds of the Fort Greene projects—can probably match any private nursery school in the excellence of care it provides for children.

The Center accepts preschool children between the ages of three and six and has an enrollment of about 145. Working mothers can drop their children off at eight in the morning and pick them up at six in the evening, confident that their youngsters are being well cared for while they are away.

Not all the mothers work, however. Some are on welfare and going to school or to training programs. Others are supposed to be out looking for jobs while their children are being cared for, or home watching younger children. Still others are physically handicapped and unable to take care of their children the whole day. Thus, it is a flexible setup that helps both working and nonworking mothers.

Those who work pay a fee based on a sliding scale, with a maximum charge of twenty-five dollars a week. Although there is an income limit for working parents, this too is flexible—it takes into consideration the number of people in the family, the rent, and other set expenses. Generally, the children of parents who earn up to seventy-five hundred dollars per year are accepted.

Most of the children in the center come from one-parent homes where the mother simply cannot afford a full-time private baby sitter at anywhere from forty dollars a week on up—usually up. The day-care center, on the other hand, charges a relatively low fee and provides the children with breakfast, a full hot lunch, and three snacks at various intervals throughout the day, including juice, cookies, milk, sandwiches, and fruit.

The center itself is a sparkling-clean, spacious, cheery place, very airy and sunlit, with about seven or eight well-equipped playrooms lining the walls of the circular building.

To get to the playrooms, you have to pass through a large open area in the center of the rotunda which is used for group games, dancing, and singing. A piano, donated by a tenant in the projects, sits in the middle of the floor.

In addition to the games and activities that go on in the center, the children are regularly taken on trips to such places as the Coney Island Animal Nursery and the aquarium. In the summertime when the public school buses are available all day, the children go on long trips to state parks.

Because of the center's popularity, there is usually a waiting list of mothers who want to enroll their youngsters.

But all this is about to change. Under new federal regulations, only parents who earn fifty-four hundred dollars or less for a family of four will be eligible for public day-care services. It is estimated that this will render ineligible almost half of the thirty-four thousand children now enrolled in such programs throughout the city.

With so many children of the working poor eliminated, the centers would have more room for the children of welfare mothers, who would be required to look for jobs while their children were being cared for. If they could not find jobs after three months, their children would be dropped from the center. If they did find jobs, their children could remain in the day-care program—provided their jobs were so low paying as not to exceed the income limits. In short, if a welfare mother had the good fortune to find a job that paid more than a few hundred dollars a year above the poverty level, she would lose her day-care services. In many cases this would mean that she'd have to quit work to stay home with her children—and go back on welfare. So the cycle would begin all over again. Mothers who were already working at jobs that paid more than the day-care maximum were also afraid they would have to quit and go on welfare, since they would have no reliable place to leave their children.

Such insanity on the part of the Nixon administration—

which is supposedly encouraging people to get *off* welfare—
touched off a series of furious demonstrations by working
mothers, day-care teachers and administrators, and various
social service agencies. The result was a temporary victory—
the original day-care eligibility standards and fee scales were
allowed to remain in effect until at least July 1974. After that,
presumably, the battle will begin again.

To make matters worse, the city's Human Resources Administration announced that it was curtailing expansion of
its day-care program, and that it would open thirty fewer
centers than it had planned to open in the 1973–74 fiscal year.
The cause of the curtailment was the $2.5 billion ceiling that
was put on federal social services spending. The ceiling has
resulted in drastic cutbacks of all social service programs that
are funded in whole or in part by the federal government.

Jule M. Sugarman, the Human Resources Administrator,
noted that the cancellation of the thirty new centers would
mean that working mothers of approximately three thousand
children who would have been enrolled might have to go on
welfare because they could not afford private day-care
services.

The irony of all this is that public day-care services are being reduced just at the time when able-bodied welfare
mothers have been told that they *must* take jobs to work off
their welfare checks.

To determine how many welfare mothers are "able-bodied"
—that is, physically capable of working and supporting their
children—the city has begun a medical testing program. Those
who are medically unfit will be reclassified as disabled.

It is to the city's benefit to reclassify as many as possible,
because as of January 1, 1974, the federal government will
assume total public assistance responsibility for all welfare
recipients who are aged, disabled, and blind. At present, such
costs are shared by the federal, state, and city governments,
which also share the costs of the Aid to Dependent Children

program. It was estimated that if just 25,000 welfare mothers out of a total of about 250,000 are reclassified as disabled, the city and state will each save up to $12.5 million in 1974. Furthermore, the women themselves will receive more money if they are in the disabled category.

In the first week of medical screening almost ten thousand women were examined at twenty clinics throughout the city, and sixty-five percent of them were found to have severe disabilities. Although this was probably due to the fact that the most severely disabled women were the quickest to respond to the letters sent out by the welfare department, the city now estimates that about sixty thousand welfare mothers will legitimately meet the disabled standard.

The high number of women with disabilities was not startling, according to Charles Morris, deputy administrator of the Department of Social Services. "Poor people do not usually practice preventive medicine," he said. "Thus, during the course of a thorough medical examination it isn't unusual to find extensive disabilities."

But even if sixty thousand women are reclassified, it will still leave a very substantial number of welfare mothers who must be put to work, at least on a part-time basis, to earn their welfare checks. There aren't nearly enough part-time city jobs for them under the Work Relief Employment Project, which was supposed to become one of the major means of helping welfare recipients go on payrolls and was originally intended mainly for home relief clients, not mothers. Nor is private industry likely to help very much, since its need for unskilled labor is rapidly shrinking. No matter what the law says, it is impossible to imagine that jobs will be found for all the welfare mothers who are now required to work.

Even if jobs were available, there are simply not enough day-care facilities to accommodate all the children. In past years, before the law went into effect, many welfare mothers who wanted to work had to wait as long as a year before their children could be placed in a day-care center. To require thousands and thousands of welfare mothers to go out to work now without providing many additional day-care centers for them is just absurd.

In Fort Greene west of the park, there are just two public day-care centers for preschool children—one in the Fort Greene projects, the other in the Farragut projects—which accommodate a total of about three hundred children. When you consider that most of the 18,300 people living in the projects are children, you can see how ridiculously inadequate this is. The great majority of working mothers in the neighborhood don't even try to get their children into these centers, but make whatever private arrangements they can. Often they have to shift their children from one baby sitter to another. Or, if they rely on someone in their family and that person gets sick or can't help out anymore, they have to quit and go on welfare. But most of the women you talk to in the neighborhood say they would much rather be out working than sitting home and trying to get by on a welfare check. Although they don't seem to feel ashamed about being on welfare, at least not as far as their friends and neighbors are concerned (almost everyone they know has been on it at one time or another), they don't like the feeling of having to depend on the city, and they don't like the way they're treated by the welfare authorities. Few of them envision welfare as a permanent way of life, although some of them have been on the welfare rolls much longer than they ever expected.

Clara, a woman in her early forties with two children, has been on welfare for the last six years and knows just about all there is to know about the system. She is better off than most welfare mothers, because her youngest child is in school now and she is working part-time under the Work Incentive Program. In some ways she is typical of many welfare mothers in Fort Greene, but in other ways she is not—primarily because she's white and Jewish in a neighborhood where almost all other welfare recipients are black or Puerto Rican.

CLARA

"I had a lot of trouble when I first tried to get on welfare. My husband and I had split up, and he was supposed to be paying me a certain amount every week. I had just given birth to Jennifer, and I also had David, who was three and one-half at the time. Well, for a little while my ex-husband was able to give me money because he was working at the Dime Savings Bank on Flatbush Avenue. But then he had this accident, and afterward he lost his job. It was really his own fault. He had been messing around too much. He was always out—taking days off—and he was leading a very irresponsible life. Because of the accident he wound up in the hospital and then he didn't have money to send me anymore.

"So here I was, home with a one-month-old infant plus another young child, and I wasn't ready to go back to work and become self-supporting again. Before the kids were born I had been a secretary for a long time. I didn't get married until I was thirty, so I had quite a few years of work behind me, including the years I worked after I was married but before David was born. If not for the kids I would have gone right back to work and I wouldn't have even needed alimony, let alone welfare. I'm very antialimony. I don't think men should have to pay it. Child support, yes, unquestionably. But not alimony. When women are perfectly capable of going out and working, they shouldn't get any alimony.

"Anyhow, since I couldn't work now, I went to Social Services. At that time I lived in Flatbush, and I think I had to go to the Greenwood Center. I don't remember exactly what the procedures were, but they asked me a lot of questions, and I told them the facts. Then they said, 'Well, we'll have to go through our investigative procedure.' They got hold of my ex-husband and spoke to him. By this time he was out of the hospital, but he was on crutches. I don't know exactly what he told them, but certainly he had no reason to tell them anything that would keep me from getting welfare, because it was to his advantage if welfare helped me out. At this point I didn't have any money coming in at all, and neither did he, except what he might have put aside on his own. Whatever we used to have in savings together he had conveniently drained.

"While all this investigating was going on, I tried to get welfare to give me an emergency check, but all they kept saying was, 'Isn't there someone you can borrow from?' The worker who was taking care of my case, a guy named Newman, his attitude was, 'Look, I couldn't care less. You'll just have to wait. Somehow or other you'll manage.'

"My mother isn't well off financially, so I couldn't possibly borrow from her. I had to turn to my brother and sister, even though I didn't really want to do that. But they helped me get by and I did manage without an emergency check. After all, my brother and sister wouldn't let me and the children starve to death. It wasn't like with some people who don't have anyone at all to turn to.

"The real trouble was that this caseworker, Newman, was reluctant to put me on the rolls altogether. He kept telling me, 'There's more investigation that has to take place, and we're not sure. . . .' I remember saying, 'What's not to be sure? My ex-husband is not working, I have a month-old infant and a three-and-a-half-year-old son, and I'm not able to go back to work this second. I need money to live.'

"My sister went down to Social Services for me, and we called the top people, and somewhere along the line I did start getting assistance. But I was so enraged over the whole thing that afterward when it was all over and I was getting assistance, I sat down and wrote a letter to the commissioner of welfare—I don't remember who it was at the time—giving him an account of what I had gone through and the disgraceful way I was treated. I told him that Newman shouldn't be a caseworker because he didn't know how to handle people.

"Maybe as a result of that letter, Newman was subsequently taken off my case. From then on I had a succession of caseworkers, mostly because they all tended to leave the Department of Social Services with great frequency. They didn't stay on those jobs too long. In a way, the old system where you had an individual caseworker was a little better, because if you got someone who was sympathetic you could get a lot from them. But now we're on this group system where none of them know you personally, so I don't even bother to call them up.

"In a way it broke my heart to have to go on welfare, because when I was a child during the Depression my family was on relief. It was like I was right back where I started from.

"I remember how we all used to go to the clothing centers to get free clothes. They weren't used or anything. They were brand new, but everything was the same, like a uniform. I still remember the nightgowns they had there. They were all alike—every one of them was white with pink stripes—so me, my sister, and my mother were all walking around in identical nightgowns. It was the same way with the other clothes, like blouses and skirts. The other kids in school could tell if your clothes came from a center. They didn't fit right and they just didn't look right. So the kids would tease us, and it hurt.

"Now I was on welfare again, and I was getting $52 a week for the three of us. This was supposed to cover my rent, which at that time was $95 a month, food, gas, electric, and telephone. Actually, welfare didn't budget me for a telephone because they didn't consider it necessary, so in order to pay for it I had to cut down on other things, like food. There was a time years ago when they wouldn't let you have a telephone at all unless you had special permission. If a worker came to your house and found a telephone, he could have it taken out. But by the time I was on welfare they didn't really care if you had a phone or not, so long as they didn't have to give you anything extra for it.

"In this day and age I really think phones are a necessity, especially when you have young children. In order to try to get welfare to pay for my phone I got a letter from David's pediatrician saying I needed one because David had respiratory problems and I might have to call an ambulance or a doctor in an emergency. But welfare wouldn't go along with this. So I managed to pay for it out of the other money they gave me. I had no intention of doing without my phone.

"To this day I'll never know how I got along on that $52 a week, but somehow I managed. I mean, we didn't starve. Still, I wasn't accustomed to living like that, and I really used to feel bad when David would ask for some little thing—like a 19¢ coloring book—and I didn't have the money to get it for him. I had to pinch pennies very tightly. It's lucky that I happen to be very economically inclined. I'm very good with money. It doesn't flow through my fingers easily.

"That first year I was on welfare I had to go to my brother and sister only once or twice for a little extra money to hold me over until the next check. It's my nature that I never liked having to ask, even though they're my family and they would give it to me if I needed it. But I was never more than five or ten dollars short.

"After I was on welfare for about a year, I just got fed up with the way we had to live. As I said, we weren't hungry or anything, but it was rough and I didn't like it. I kept saying to myself, 'I've got to go back to work.' This was the summertime and the children and I were going to Brighton Beach every day. My sister financed the price of a locker for myself and the kids at this place in Brighton where they have a pool and baths. She kind of felt bad for us and she wanted us to have something to do during the summer.

"Anyhow, I met a lot of people there, and I used to talk to them every day. Not too many of them knew anything about my private life, but I got really friendly with a few people, and one day one of them said something to me about a work incentive program that the Department of Social Services had started.

"Well, I didn't have to hear another word. The next day I made a couple of calls and went down to my center, where I spoke to some caseworkers. With a lot of them it's amazing how little they know. They just don't know what the hell they're talking about half the time. This is so unfortunate. After all, people come down and they need advice, and who else can you go to? If the people who work for the welfare department can't answer your questions, who can? They must have publicized this work incentive program somewhere, but I hadn't heard about it before, and the workers didn't seem to know anything about it either.

"But finally I found someone who knew what he was talking about. You see, I wanted to know what I would be entitled to from welfare if I worked; how much of my salary I would lose or not lose. I said that I had two very young children who needed looking after, and would welfare pay for that? Jennifer was still too young for a day-care center.

"This man confirmed that there was a work incentive program but said that welfare would only pay up to a certain amount to have my kids taken care of. And I asked him, 'Do I have to find a baby sitter myself, or does Social Services recommend some place for me to go to have my children looked after?' So he suggested things like using the department's homemaker services, or else using people who are on welfare themselves so they can earn something, too.

"I remember arguing around this point. I said, "Look, there's a woman in my building who may be interested in looking after the children. She's a young married woman whose husband works, and she just sits home with no children of her own. She's very fond of my children, and she may be interested for a fee.' So the worker told me, 'Find out what she wants.'

"Well, I spoke to her and she was interested, and we arrived at a figure of something like twenty-five or thirty-five dollars a week for part-time work. I told the welfare center about this, and they said, 'All right. Have her send us a letter saying she's going to be watching your children for you.'

"All this was just preliminary because I didn't even have a job yet. But I had to settle these things first before I could go out and look, and this was taking a lot of time. You know, it's really dumb. The Department of Social Services offers this work incentive, and then they proceed to make things as difficult as possible for the woman. If I hadn't been so determined to work, or if I were less of a fighter and didn't have such a big mouth, I just would have dropped the whole idea. They don't encourage you to take advantage of the work incentive, in that they make everything so hard and complicated. A lot of people would just turn around and say, 'Oh, up yours!' and forget about the whole damn thing. But of course I wanted this for myself too. I happened not to mind going back to work. To me it wasn't a hardship. I had a skill and I knew I was able to earn.

"When all the baby-sitting arrangements were worked out, I went to the New York State Employment Agency. This was the first place I went to, because I had had experience with State Employment in past years, and I had gotten a number of good jobs out of them. You see, I was never a job-keeper in the past. I was a drifter. I went from one job to another. I hated staying in one place.

"This time they got me a part-time job at Long Island University. I worked four hours a day, from nine to one. I think I started at $2.25 an hour, so I was earning about forty-five dollars a week before taxes, and because of the work incentive program I was able to keep most of it in addition to my welfare grant. Plus they were paying my baby-sitting expenses.

"Do you know that when I started working, welfare sent me an extra check—an *unsolicited* check—because they figured I would need extra clothing that would be appropriate for an office? They thought I might only have had house dresses. So they gave me about one hundred dollars for additional clothes. This was something I hadn't even asked for, but I wasn't about to turn it down.

"Usually you don't get *anything* from welfare, even things you're entitled to, without nagging them for it. Like in the beginning when I first started getting welfare they had a policy of giving special grants for clothing and furniture when it was necessary. But no one in the Department of Social Services had ever told me this. I didn't know that you could call up and say, 'Look, winter's coming and my kids have outgrown their clothes and they need some new things,' and welfare would send you a check. Once I found out, I started calling up and getting what I was supposed to get.

"I'm a very persistent person. I manage to get my way. When I feel something is due me, I don't give up. I'll push for it. But a lot of welfare recipients have little or no education, and it wouldn't occur to them to fight for some of the things I've fought for. Social Services just sends them their checks every two weeks, and they assume that nothing else is coming to them because they really don't know better.

"I think this is very sad. You see, Social Services doesn't publicize clients' rights any more than absolutely necessary, because they figure if people don't know, it saves the department money. When the welfare rights groups came along a few years ago they publicized everything, and they started pushing clients to apply for whatever they were entitled to. But that wasn't good either, because people started demanding everything and anything, and it was such a drain on the welfare system that they cut out the special grants altogether. Now they put into your budget what the grants were supposed to cover before. This is really no good either. I mean, if they add $1.50 to the check they send you every two weeks to make up for what they used to send you in a lump sum for kids' clothes, well, what the hell is this going to buy? You don't save it up. It just sort of disappears into your food bill or some other bill.

"Even after I started working I still had to budget myself very carefully. I always knew how much to put aside for food, and how much for rent, and how much for gas and electric. You know, when you're feeding one adult and one infant and one small child, food can go a long way. Even now, with all this inflation, I find that food goes a long way. And David really eats now; he eats almost like an adult. But I try to buy economy-type meats, like beef liver. I sort of hate it, but by the time I get through preparing it, it really doesn't taste like liver anymore. You just wouldn't recognize it. And I buy chicken a lot, which I enjoy and the kids enjoy.

"After I was working steady for a while under the work incentive program, I was able to get some charge accounts. I'm very, very careful about them. I always know what I'm going to be billed at the end of the month, and I never pay two cents in interest charges, because I always have the money to pay off a bill in full. I never buy more than what I feel I can afford to pay. I mean I never receive a monthly bill from a department store anywhere near two or three hundred dollars like some people do, except when I buy furniture, say at Abraham and Straus. And even then I buy on a special charge account where I have ninety days to pay without being charged interest. Yes, there is a charge account like that. I make it my business to find out such things.

"After I was on this part-time job for a few months, I had a chance to move into a two-bedroom apartment right across the street from Long Island University. This was in University Towers, which is owned by L.I.U., and if you work at the school you can live there at a pretty low rent. The three of us had been living in a one-bedroom apartment for $95 a month, and now I had a chance to move into a two-bedroom apartment for $128. So I wrote a letter to the welfare department explaining how I could save on carfare and even on lunch money if I lived across the street from where I worked, and how I could spend more time with my children and cut down on baby-sitting costs. Welfare approved my application, and they gave me a maximum of $125 for my moving expenses. But the bill was more than that—it was about $150— and I had to pay the rest of it myself. If I hadn't already been working at the time I wouldn't have been able to manage that extra $25. But all in all, welfare was pretty good about my moving.

"The problem was, once I moved into the Fort Greene area I had to find a new baby sitter. This was very difficult because I couldn't get anyone steady. I kept worrying that I was going to have to stop working, and I kept having to take days off because sitters didn't show up. I thought I might even be fired if this kept up. Also, Jennifer was really a nervous wreck —always clinging and whining—because she had been shunted around to so many different sitters. David had started in a nine-to-three prekindergarten class in P.S. 307 when he was four, so he wasn't affected by the baby-sitter problem.

"Finally, when Jennifer was three, I went over to the Willoughby House Day-Care Center in the Fort Greene projects and pleaded with them to take her in, saying that I was desperate to find a permanent place for her while I worked. Well, the intake worker was sympathetic, and I got Jennifer in after not too long. You see, even though there's a waiting list, there's a big turnover every year when kids go into kindergarten or the first grade.

"I was very happy with that place. They had a good teaching staff and lots of really nice equipment, like sanded wood rocking horses. Jennifer had her breakfast there, plus a hot lunch. In the summertime the kids played in the sprinkler out in the back yard, and they went on lots of trips. Because I was getting supplementary welfare assistance I paid very little. I think it was something like two dollars a week. I started working longer hours now and earning a little more money, although it was still basically a part-time job.

"But welfare never gets off your back. They're always doing something to upset you. One day I came home from work and found a note under my door from my caseworker. She said she had an appointment to see me that day (apparently she had sent some notice that I never received), and that when she came I wasn't home. It was a little bit of a threatening note, and it said something like unless I contacted the center immediately my assistance would be discontinued. This wasn't a form. It was a handwritten note, and I was just livid. I thought, 'Goddammit, I'm out working, trying to help myself, and she's leaving me notes like this.' So I immediately got on the phone and screamed and hollered a lot. And she says to me, 'Well, how am I supposed to know you're working?' I said, 'Don't you have records? The Department of Social Services has known about my job from the day I started working.' It was never any secret to them that I worked. It was all done within the bounds. And I said, 'If you'd bothered to look at your folder, you would have known I worked.'

"Another time, after I had already been working for five years, they sent me this form asking if I could start working. So I wrote all over the form, 'I've been under employment incentive since 1968!' Really, one hand doesn't know what the other hand is doing.

"Take this employment incentive program. They start it one year and it's really a good thing. But they hardly publicize it at all, and then a year or two later they try to cut back on it. Like, when I first started working they reduced my welfare allotment by only about fifteen percent which was a pretty good deal. It made it worthwhile to work, even with the baby-sitting headaches. But only about a year and a half later I started reading stories in the newspapers about how they were going to cut welfare mothers' allotments by thirty percent or more if they had jobs. Well, I wasn't going to stand for that without a fight.

"I had sent away for a booklet from some sort of welfare organization at Columbia University that outlined people's rights. It told how much they were entitled to, the clothing, and all that. So when I was notified about cutbacks in the work incentive program, I got out this booklet and called a couple of people from Columbia who were listed in it. They suggested I go to South Brooklyn Legal Services for free legal help.

"So I went up there, and I saw a young woman attorney who I became involved with. I told her I felt the drastic cuts were not legal because they were taking the whole incentive away from the incentive program. She took this all down and said she would make a couple of calls to assemblymen and people who had some power to get things done. Within three or four weeks from the time she had said she was going to do something, she had done it. She had contacted somebody, and this somebody had written a letter to somebody else, and I was *not* cut. Maybe other working welfare mothers were cut, but I wasn't.

"People who are not really aggressive with welfare can wind up just banging their heads against the wall. They may be destitute, yet they can't seem to get through to people in Social Services at all. This is the saddest part of welfare, especially since you have the opposite situation, too—people who are riding around in Cadillacs getting checks, or people who own houses and go off to Florida who get checks.

"During the years that I've been working I've managed to

save a little between what I earn and what I get from welfare. So I do have a little something to fall back on if welfare cuts me off completely. There used to be a time when, if you worked at all, you could just forget about getting any help from welfare. And I think we're going to revert right back to that in the very near future—especially under our darling President Nixon. And then old Clara here is going to be living with her children on what she earns—and the thought of that scares me.

"It's not so much the welfare money itself. I'm earning a hundred dollars a week now at L.I.U., and I could probably get by without the thirty-five dollars a week I get from welfare, although it would be pretty hard.

"My basic fear is losing Medicaid. Last year David became diabetic. He was in Brooklyn Jewish Hospital for nine days, in a room with four kids, and I guess it was a pretty decent hospital. This happened to be the hospital of the doctor whose care he's under, but if I hadn't had Medicaid to pay for it, I would have had to send him to a city hospital like Cumberland or Kings County. I would be terrified to think that my child would have to go to a hospital like Kings County. I wouldn't put my child there for anything, unless there was absolutely nothing else I could do. It's a pretty sad state of affairs there.

"David almost did land up in Kings County because that's where he went for his initial testing. They confirmed that he was diabetic, and they were all ready to put him in. But I said, 'Oh, no, you're not,' and I got in touch with my regular doctor right away. You see, David wasn't comatose or anything. He was still walking and moving around, although they said his sugar was so high he was on the verge of coma.

"That same evening we got him into Brooklyn Jewish Hospital, and Medicaid covered it. I didn't have any other coverage at the time. L.I.U. pays only a little bit toward Blue Cross and Blue Shield, and employees have to pay all the rest themselves. That's much too expensive for me. I just can't afford it. L.I.U. does have major medical, though, and the school pays for that in full. But at the time David went into the hospital, part-time workers at L.I.U. weren't included in the major medical program. We are now, but there is a five-hundred-dollar deductible. This is a very big deductible. Where would I get that kind of money?

"Medicaid is such an invaluable thing. It pays for the insulin shots that David needs every day plus the disposable needles. If I weren't on supplemental welfare now, under work incentive, I wouldn't be getting Medicaid because I'm earning a hundred dollars a week. That's too high for me to qualify. Can you imagine? As if a hundred dollars a week for three people makes you well off. Their standards for getting Medicaid if you're not on welfare are so ridiculously low.

"With Medicaid, the kids and I were able to get into H.I.P. [Health Insurance Plan]. This means we don't have to go to the hospital clinics or those storefront medical centers on Myrtle Avenue. With H.I.P. it's almost like having a private doctor. Most people don't know you can join a H.I.P. center when you're on Medicaid, but it's perfectly legitimate. All I had to do was find a center that still had room for Medicaid patients. I was able to get into the Schermerhorn Center, which is in the downtown Brooklyn area. The children's pediatrician there is a delight. He's shown a lot of concern for David, and I think he's really given him the best care. The regular G.P. that I use at the center is not bad either. He treats everybody the same, whether they're on Medicaid or not.

"Last summer, because of David's illness, I guess I pushed for a little too much with the welfare department and I almost screwed myself up. I wanted to get David into Camp NYDA for a month—that's the New York Diabetic Association camp. They teach kids how to deal with their illness and how to give themselves insulin shots. It's a philanthropic place, and they charge people what they can afford. So I figured if I could get something from welfare toward David's camp expenses, well, what the hell, why not? I contacted Social Services and got some real creep of a dame on the phone who asked me all sorts of questions. They wouldn't pay anything for David's camp, but sure enough, two weeks later, I got a letter from them saying they were investigating my case to see if I was still eligible for public assistance. I had to come down to the center with my pay stubs and everything.

"At this point I was earning perhaps a little more than they had on their records because I've gradually increased my hours. I mean, they know I'm working more than four hours a day and for more than $2.25 an hour. They had down that I was working nine to three, but actually by then I was working nine to four.

"So when I came in with my pay stubs, this caseworker sat there looking at them for a long time. Then he says to me, 'A hundred dollars a week? That's a lot of money!' I swear to God, he said this. So I just looked at him and said, 'Really? Where have you been living lately?' He really scared me because he said he was going to submit the new figures, and Social Services might have to cut down on the money they were sending me, or drop me altogether.

"But then nothing happened. I never heard from them again. Maybe this worker got soft in the heart or something, I don't know. Or maybe to somebody else higher up it didn't seem like I was earning so much money. But I didn't hear a word about it, and now I just don't ask them for anything extra anymore. I put aside whatever I can for David's camp, plus I have to scrape up money for Jennifer's day camp for the whole summer. I never had to pay for her while she was young enough for the Willoughby Day-Care Center, which has an excellent summer program. But now if I don't send her to camp, what is she going to do all day while I'm working? Run around the streets? So I have all these extra expenses for the children just at the time when Social Services is thinking of cutting me off.

"They already reduced my check two years ago. I had gotten a rent increase here, so I went in to see if welfare would cover it. Well, when they saw what I was earning they not only wouldn't pay the rent raise, but they cut some of what they had been giving me. So between the rent raise and the welfare cut, I had about thirty dollars less every two weeks.

"I just got another rent increase, but I won't go anywhere near welfare at this time. I'm afraid to rock the boat. I know I'm on very shaky ground with them, and I just don't dare turn to them for anything for fear they'll cut me off completely. As long as they don't bother me, I don't bother them.

"The way I see it, what I get from welfare is just support for my children. Nothing I get is for me, really. Recently, Social Services has been very hot on the trail of my ex-husband, which is fine with me. They called me, and I've been more than willing to help if I could, except I don't have the remotest idea of where he is. Welfare seems to know more about where he is than I do. But frankly, even if they find him, I don't think it's going to do much good. He's a man who just picks up and moves on. He doesn't want to be found. He hasn't seen his children in a long time and obviously he has no desire to, for whatever his sick reasons.

"But if welfare wants to pursue him, fine. Let them try to get the money out of him. They could say to him, 'Look, you're working now and you're going to provide support for your children to the tune of thirty-five dollars a week,' which is approximately what I receive in welfare money. If he supported the kids, I wouldn't have to be on public assistance anymore. But then I wouldn't have Medicaid either, so in a way I hope he never starts paying up.

"It's unfortunate that people like myself or anyone else has to feel ashamed of being on welfare. It's not that I myself am ashamed of it, but it's the way people treat you. It's like a stigma. Sometimes I say to myself, 'I can't take this anymore.' I mean the whole idea of welfare. I have had things said to me over the last six years where I almost socked a couple of people.

"Once I had to go to the H.I.P. center in an emergency and I got a different doctor than the one I usually use. After he finished examining me he wrote out a prescription for some stuff, and I asked him to put it on a Medicaid prescription form. Well, he just stopped and looked at me—I guess because I'm fairly well dressed and because I'm white as well— and he says to me, 'What is someone like you doing on Medicaid?' I didn't answer him. I just let it pass over my head. But something like this leaves a very poor taste in one's mouth. It was such an uncalled-for remark. I mean, I'm on Medicaid and that's it. There must be a reason. Did he think this was supposed to be a compliment to me? That I didn't look the type? I mean, what's the *type?*

"Another time I was in the A&P on Myrtle Avenue. I was at the checkout counter with my food stamps, and there were some people in line behind me. I don't know what prompted it, but this creep of a checkout cashier—who obviously assumed that if you have food stamps you're just living off the city—turned to the people behind me and said, 'You know, it's unfortunate that *working* people have to wait.' I swear I almost hit her.

"I don't shop in the A&P anymore, but not because of that. First of all, I think it's a filthy store. It's poorly managed, it's unkempt, and the checkouts are impossible. Also, I don't find half of the things I want. So I shop Finast now, even though it's farther away from my house.

"But you do get remarks and looks from people when you're on welfare. They just assume you're sitting around all day waiting for your check to come. When you walk into a bank to cash a welfare check, or you're using your food stamps or your Medicaid card, you somehow get a feeling that you're a little less than the next person. You feel like you're being looked down upon, like they're thinking, 'Oh, a welfare check. Another one of those.'

"Maybe I'm overly sensitive about it because I don't think of myself as a typical welfare recipient. I don't like putting myself above anybody, but I do consider myself a more responsible person than a welfare recipient who doesn't sincerely want to make life better for himself, or at least try. It's true that I have a skill and I'm able to earn fairly nicely because of it. It's also true that a lot of people on welfare do not have any skills and perhaps can only clean house or do menial tasks. For that I blame the government, because they should have a lot more programs to teach people some sort of trade so they can go to work.

"But there are also people who can do things but would rather just sit on their hands. Even though I am someone who is involved with welfare, I must admit that I do look down on welfare recipients who can help themselves and don't— who don't care enough to do something about the way they live. I find it very hard to believe that anybody who lives only on welfare can be living any kind of a decent life. Or making any kind of a good life for their kids.

"I'm not against women who do a little conniving on the side, within reason. Like, let's say they're on welfare but they also get some money on the side from cleaning houses. There are a lot of women who do this. Maybe they earn thirty dollars a week and don't tell welfare about it. I say, more power to them. With what they earn, plus what they get from welfare, maybe they can live just a little bit better.

"I never did things illegally because, very frankly, I'm scared. It's a fact. I'm afraid of Social Services and I never really played games with them. I wouldn't say I've been *totally* on the up and up with them, but you can't be. You really can't be. I think that anybody like myself who kept them posted on everything right down to the dollar would just be asking for trouble. Like, I just got an increase at work of sixteen cents an hour. I'd have to be out of my mind to get on the phone with Social Services and say, 'Hey, I'm earning six dollars more a week.' I mean, that's a little ridiculous.

"I've worked very hard over the last few years. Not in terms of going to an office and slaving, because I happen to enjoy working. It's just the whole idea that I had to go to work when Jennifer was a year old, which I never would have done under normal circumstances. It broke my heart to leave my baby with a sitter every day when she was so young. I wanted to look after my child myself, and I probably would have waited until she was in school before I went back to work. But I wanted to live better. I wanted my children to be able to live better, and the only way to do it was to go to work. There was no other way. People shouldn't be under any illusions. You don't live good on what welfare sends you unless you're stealing from them or getting something from them that you're not entitled to.

"The work incentive program is really a good thing. It put me back to work and got me where I am now. My kids are not wanting for anything. If not for the incentive I might have tried to work without welfare knowing about it.

"Of course, there are poor people like myself who are so proud that they won't go anywhere near welfare. Sometimes it isn't even pride. It's the idea of going to these people at welfare and being treated the way you're treated. People just don't want to subject themselves to this. They're intimidated and harassed. But when I went to welfare six years ago, I just had no choice. I had no money coming in at all for my children or myself.

"In another two or three years maybe I'll feel confident

enough to let go of welfare completely, even the Medicaid. Because, you see, welfare is like an albatross around your neck. You're always worrying about it, always afraid they're going to find out that maybe you're earning a little more than they have on their records, or that they'll change the rules and cut you off all of a sudden."

7

Bilking the Poor

DIRECTLY across from the veterans' welfare center on Myrtle Avenue is a spacious store filled with the most elaborate furniture ever seen outside the Versailles palace. The spectacularly garish collection includes huge beds with crimson velvet spreads and massive, ornately carved headboards; lamps dripping with crystal and gilt; baroque dining room pieces; flamboyant sofas and elephantine chairs.

This dazzling showplace, called John Mullins and Sons, is unique on Myrtle Avenue. Most of the other stores on the street are small and unpretentious, and the household goods they carry have a practical, unadorned look about them. A number of small stores sell used furniture that is just too plain and modest to ever masquerade as antique. People who buy this merchandise don't get anything especially valuable or beautiful for their money, but then they don't pay very much either. It's a fair exchange, and everything is on a strictly cash basis. No credit.

A number of other stores sell inexpensive or used clothing; small appliances, usually at slightly under list prices; and an array of variety store items, also at somewhat cheaper cost

than places like Woolworth's or McCrory's on Fulton Street.
During the Christmas season one of the Myrtle Avenue variety
stores sells fancy name-brand toys for three or four dollars less
than Abraham & Straus or any of the other major department
stores. So it is not necessarily true that "the poor pay more"—
at least not in these small stores where the transactions are in
cash.

Nor are the supermarkets overpriced compared to food
stores in other areas. Yet many of the people who live in Fort
Greene seem to be under the impression that the supermarkets there do charge more, and that they are better off
shopping in middle-class neighborhoods where they will not
be cheated. It is not unusual to see groups of people from
Fort Greene driving over to nearby, upper-middle-class
Brooklyn Heights to do their weekly shopping, or even driving as far as Queens, where they are convinced they will get
more for their money.

But a price comparison of two supermarkets on Myrtle
Avenue and two in Brooklyn Heights—all done on the same
morning—showed that such assumptions are erroneous. An
assortment of twenty-one brand-name items cost $11.50 in
Bohack, the largest supermarket in Brooklyn Heights, and
$11.92 in Key Food, another Heights store. The same items
cost $10.70 in the Myrtle Avenue A&P and $11.08 in Finast.
So on Myrtle Avenue the poor pay less—sometimes.

However, this doesn't apply to *all* stores on Myrtle Avenue.
In any establishment where "easy credit terms" are bally-
hooed, the buyer had better beware. Some of these stores
seem to do most of their business by exploiting the poor, and
one of the worst offenders is that rococo palace, John Mullins
and Sons.

In June 1972 the Department of Consumer Affairs went to
court to stop Mullins from selling "decrepit merchandise to
low-income consumers." The department sued the furniture
company for "engaging in an unlawful scheme designed to

obtain payments from consumers for substandard, defective and unmerchantable furniture."

The State Supreme Court was asked to order Mullins to return all money collected from customers who were the victims of illegal billing and collection practices, and to issue a restraining order prohibiting Mullins from deceiving future customers.

Bess Myerson, then Consumer Affairs Commissioner, charged that "the furniture that customers see in the Mullins showroom appears to be sturdy and of reasonable durability. But what arrives in their homes are tables with cracked legs, wobbly chairs, soiled couches, unstable beds, and bureaus with drawers that don't work properly."

The formal complaint lodged against the store stated that Mullins asked customers to sign contracts containing blank spaces or incorrect totals. Once the contract was signed, the salesman would fill it in and would frequently make substantial errors in arithmetic, so that the customer had no way of knowing the true cost of his purchase.

One Brooklyn customer told the Department of Consumer Affairs that he had ordered a convertible sofa, two chairs, two end tables, and a coffee table from Mullins, and was told that the price was $299.95. When the furniture was delivered, the customer discovered that Mullins had sent him "flimsy junk . . . not the same quality as what we had seen and ordered at the store," and a regular sofa instead of a convertible one.

When the customer complained, Mullins told him it would cost an extra hundred dollars to exchange the sofa, even though the error had been made by the store's salesman.

"When consumers complain about the quality of the furniture delivered by Mullins, all they get are delays and phony promises that repairmen will be sent," the department charged. "And at the same time they are explaining why the repairman hasn't arrived yet, Mullins is demanding payment for their defective merchandise and incomplete orders."

Commissioner Myerson also charged that Mullins frequently failed to credit payments made by customers. She said that consumers were confused about the amount they owed because their bills were added incorrectly. In some cases, Mullins wound up suing customers for balances they had already paid.

"Customers who withhold payments on defective furniture are arbitrarily billed for late charges, sent repeated dunning notices, and/or telephoned by store collectors," explained Ann Farmer, an investigator for the department's Law Enforcement Division.

If the customer sticks to his guns and still refuses to pay, Mullins often takes him to court.

"Being sued by Mullins doesn't mean you are finally going to get a chance to tell a responsible person about all of the trouble you have had with the company," said Commissioner Myerson. "Mullins's customers are frequently the victims of 'sewer service,' [they are never given their subpoenas] and they don't know anything about the legal action until they have lost the case by default and their salary is garnisheed. Over ninety-five percent of these lawsuits result in default in favor of Mullins."

Aside from wanting Mullins to return all the money it had collected from customers in every default judgment it had obtained since 1970, the Department of Consumer Affairs insisted that the store stop advertising, selling, or delivering defective furniture. It also wanted the firm to provide Spanish-speaking customers with contracts and all other sale documents in Spanish as well as English.

Low-income people are particularly vulnerable to exploitation by places like Mullins. On their small salaries or welfare checks they usually can't manage to save anything, so when they need costly items like furniture they are often forced to buy on credit. The major department stores will not permit unemployed welfare recipients to open charge accounts of any kind, let alone the kind where the customer can pay off his bill in monthly installments. Nonwelfare, low-income shoppers also have a hard time qualifying for charge accounts in reputable stores. This means they must turn to other—possibly less reputable—establishments that will let them pay off their purchases in small sums over a long period of time.

The danger is that such stores may indulge in unethical and illegal sales practices, and then either repossess the merchandise or garnishee the customer's salary if he fails to pay. A garnishment can have a doubly disastrous effect, because often an employer will not want to be troubled by the extra paperwork involved in a garnisheed salary and will simply fire the hapless worker.

Ironically, low-income neighborhoods are apparently regarded as excellent locations by stores that habitually indulge in unethical practices. They make their profits by deceiving people who are poor and undereducated and who usually don't fight back—at least not in any effective way.

Another store of this type in Fort Greene is the J. Michael's furniture chain. Located on the outer fringe of the Fulton Street shopping hub, near the Manpower Employment Center, J. Michael's places ads such as these in its windows:

> Quick Friendly Credit!
> Deal Only With J. Michael's. No Banks or Finance Companies.
> We Give You the Credit Ourselves. We Never Give Your Account Over to a Bank or Finance Company.
> 90-Day Payment Plan Without Service Charge.

The furniture displayed by J. Michael's is not quite so ostentatious as that of Mullins, but apparently it is equally shoddy. The Department of Consumer Affairs has described the store as "the largest junkshop in Brooklyn"—a company that sells furniture that "self-destructs after it is delivered."

In September 1972, J. Michael's was also sued by the Consumer Affairs Department, which had received 130 complaints from irate customers. In a charge that sounded almost identical to the one lodged against Mullins, the department stated that J. Michael's sold defective, shoddy, cracked, and splintered furniture to its low-income customers and failed to make repairs when the goods fell apart. When disappointed consumers stopped paying, the company dunned and sued them by the hundreds. Most of these customers were also the victims of "sewer service" and never knew about the lawsuits against them until after they had lost by default and their salaries had been garnisheed.

One customer told the Department of Consumer Affairs that she purchased two thousand dollars worth of furniture from J. Michael's which began to fall apart after six months. The bed collapsed, a desk chair fell apart, the refrigerator door didn't work, the dining room table cracked in several places, and four straight chairs "are so wobbly I'm afraid to have people sit on them."

The woman said she had written letters to J. Michael's and had "done all of the pleading and begging possible to try and get them to replace or repair the furniture," but it was useless.

Another customer complained that J. Michael's had delivered floor samples in poor condition when she had specifically ordered and paid for new furniture. The woman told the store that the upholstery was coming loose and the color television set was cracked and didn't work properly, but her complaints were ignored.

Commissioner Myerson charged that "Customers are promised visits by servicemen but rarely are these visits made. When J. Michael's does agree to replace furniture, customers often find that the 'new' replacement items have the same defects as the original items."

Mullins and J. Michael's are probably the two biggest stores in Fort Greene that indulge in disreputable practices, but the

134 ☆ *Fort Greene, U.S.A.*

Department of Consumer Affairs has also launched active investigations against Busch's Jewelers on Fulton Street, and has received a number of complaints against several small furniture stores in the neighborhood.

The area's main antipoverty organization, the Fort Greene Community Corporation, has tried to alert low-income people to the dangers of buying on credit in such places, but it's a bitter lesson for them to learn when there's hardly any other way they can purchase the things they need—not luxury items, but necessities such as beds and chairs.

8

The Twin Terrors—
Crime and Drugs

O N E spring afternoon, two teenage boys were dawdling inside the Merit Farms food store on Flatbush and DeKalb Avenues. All of a sudden they snatched two cans of Coke from the cooler and dashed out into the street. While the store manager and two customers stood there, too startled to do anything, one of the fleeing youths unexpectedly turned around and ran back into the store.

"I forgot the straws," he said as he snatched two straws off the counter and raced out again.

After a moment of stunned silence, the manager said to the customers, "Did you see that? They're getting so goddamn brazen. They steal things right out from under your nose even while you're looking straight at them. And what can I do about it? I can't shoot a kid over a can of soda, and I can't go chasing after him and leave the cash register alone. I'm just disgusted. This kind of thing happens all the time, every day. Stealing is like nothing to these kids around here."

On the same day, a few blocks away, another minor episode occurred. Two very young boys, both of whom appeared to be under ten, were hanging around the corner of Myrtle Avenue and Ashland Place. They both seemed restless and fidgety, and they kept glancing up and down the streets. From time to time they would start heading up Ashland Place, then stop, look around, and fidget some more. Finally they spotted an elderly woman walking along the street and began following her. When she started to cross the street they made their move—they raced past her as fast as they could, shoving her and trying to snatch her bag as they ran. But they were still a little clumsy at the purse-snatching game, and the woman managed to fend them off. When the brief fracas was over, she began screaming at the children, who did not seem at all intimidated. While she admonished them they laughed at her, taunted her, and danced around her until she marched away in frustrated fury.

On another day in Fort Greene, several teenagers were walking along the streets with heavy sticks in their hands, casually bashing the windows of all the parked cars they passed. Their vandalism—which was carried out with an air of bored indifference—was observed by many people who were passing by at the time. But no one attempted to stop them.

Such incidents are commonplace in Fort Greene. They happen all the time, day after day, so that an air of lawlessness prevails on the street. These incidents are rarely reported to the police. After all, can a woman report an unsuccessful purse-snatching attempt? Can a store manager report two stolen cans of Coke? These are trifles that are too petty for the police to bother about, yet they have a very strong, adverse effect on the overall quality of life in the neighborhood. Every time someone leaves his house, he knows he is likely to see, or perhaps be the victim of, some petty crime that is carried out openly and with impunity. It is the abundance of such small offenses rather than major crimes that gives people the feeling they are living in anarchy.

Teenagers and children, who are the major perpetrators of these petty crimes, scarcely seem to recognize that laws exist. They are proud of their ability to steal—they brag about it at the slightest opportunity—and it is their total lack of fear, their indifference to any consequences that might result from their actions, that is most alarming to the residents of Fort Greene. In 1972 the neighborhood ranked second in juvenile delinquency in New York City.

Fear of crime is probably the dominant factor of life in Fort Greene, as it is in so many parts of New York City. Although the fear is highly disproportionate to the number of serious crimes that are actually committed, the fear itself alters the habits and life-styles of people. In Fort Greene, few people leave their houses after dark if they can help it, and stores close up early. By seven or eight o'clock the streets are practically empty. Evening social activities in the neighborhood have declined sharply, because the fear of going out at night overshadows the enjoyment of socializing.

In addition, residents of Fort Greene complain that their friends in the suburbs or in other parts of the city will not visit them, by night or by day, because they have heard such dire things about the area that they half expect to see blood flowing in the streets. Without firsthand knowledge of the neighborhood, the outsider's notion of it becomes grossly distorted—twisted by hearsay, rumor, and newspaper headlines that make it appear as if crime is the only activity that exists in low-income city neighborhoods. As a result, people living in the suburbs tend to have an even greater fear of these urban neighborhoods than the inhabitants themselves, enlarging the gulf between city and suburb still more.

Even the people who live in Fort Greene say that when they go away on long vacations their own fear of their neighborhood tends to increase; from a distance they picture the area as being even more crime-ridden than it actually is. Once they return, it takes a while for their heightened fears to subside a little. So it would seem that the farther away a person is from the urban scene, the more inflated his fears become about the actual amount of serious crime that exists.

The institutions located in Fort Greene are also adversely affected by crime and the fear of crime. L.I.U. has had great difficulty attracting students to its Brooklyn campus in recent years, and undoubtedly one of the factors in its declining enrollment is the fact that the school is located in the heart of a high-crime, low-income black neighborhood. A school like City College can flourish in the middle of Harlem because it is free, but students at L.I.U. have to pay sixty-six dollars a credit in tuition and twelve hundred dollars per year to live in the dormitory—and they just aren't willing to risk living in Fort Greene at those prices. The school has also been having trouble finding teachers for its evening courses, because most professors prefer to be safely out of the area before dark. Muggings and purse-snatchings have been occurring right on campus as well as on the streets.

According to the police, the most common crime by far in Fort Greene is purse-snatching. Next are robberies and burglaries. (Purse-snatchings are not defined as robberies by the police unless the assailant uses a weapon or assaults the victim in some way; if he just grabs her purse and runs away it is officially listed as a larceny. Thus, the official robbery figures are much lower than they would be if they included all purse-snatchings.)

Fort Greene is covered by two police precincts. The Eighty-eighth Precinct is responsible for the Fort Greene housing projects, the Kingsview cooperative, and all the small buildings and brownstones between Fort Greene Park and Pratt University. The ancient, decrepit station house is located near Pratt, and there have been persistent rumors that the Eighty-eighth would eventually merge with other precincts that are housed in more modern buildings. Residents of Fort Greene are bitterly opposed to this, fearing it would inevitably mean a reduction in the number of men assigned to their neighborhood.

The other Fort Greene precinct—the Eighty-fourth—is located in a sleek new building just across the street from the Fort Greene projects. Ironically, the projects are outside the Eighty-fourth's jurisdiction, so that if someone is robbed right across the street from the Eighty-fourth station house, he has to call the Eighty-eighth Precinct. The Eighty-fourth covers only the Farragut housing projects and University Towers in Fort Greene, the downtown Brooklyn shopping center, and neighboring Brooklyn Heights. The crime patterns in these three areas differ sharply. Shoplifting and pickpocketing account for much of the crime in the downtown area; purse-snatchings and robberies are most prevalent in Fort Greene, particularly in the hallways, stairwells, and elevators of the housing projects; and apartment burglaries are the number one crime in affluent Brooklyn Heights. Thieves who work in the Heights tend to be more professional, planning their jobs in advance and sometimes using sophisticated house-breaking tools, whereas crime in Fort Greene is the more spontaneous street variety. The Heights also has a large homosexual population, and in the past year there has been a rash of homosexual murders in the normally quiet neighborhood. In this type of violent crime, Brooklyn Heights ranks far ahead of Fort Greene.

According to the precinct-by-precinct breakdown of crime figures for 1972, there were six homicides in the Eighty-fourth Precinct out of a total population of 39,505, so that the precinct ranked thirty-eighth in homicides throughout the city. (There are seventy-one precincts altogether.) The Eighty-eighth Precinct had twenty-six homicides out of a population of 58,703, and it ranked sixteenth on a citywide basis. The highest homicide rate anywhere in New York was recorded by the Twenty-eighth Precinct in Manhattan, which covers part of Harlem. With a population of 57,472, the area had 117 homicides.

Partly because the Eighty-fourth Precinct includes the downtown Brooklyn area which attracts about two hundred thousand shoppers daily, there were more robberies recorded by that precinct than by the Eighty-eighth. The Eighty-fourth Precinct ranked eighth in robberies throughout the city, and eleventh in burglaries, whereas the Eighty-eighth Precinct was eleventh in robberies and twenty-sixth in burglaries.

According to a spokesman for the Eighty-fourth Precinct who has been on the force for more than twenty years, "over ninety percent of the street crime in the area is committed by guys under twenty-five. They're mainly kids who commit stupid crimes. Mainly junkies. But a lot of them start stealing very young, before they ever go near drugs. You have eight-year-old purse-snatchers around here, and you'd be amazed at how good some of them are at that game. After all, what do these kids have to lose? A lot of them have no name, no family structure. They've got nothing. One time we locked up a nine-year-old for pickpocketing, and it turned out that he had been arrested nine times before for the same kind of thing. And he was just a pint-sized little kid.

"With the older guys—the ones about eighteen or twenty—you find that a lot of them are unemployed or they have part-time jobs as dishwashers or porters or something like that. A few may be on welfare, or if they aren't on it themselves, in a lot of cases their families are.

"On the whole, the Farragut housing projects are safer than the Fort Greene projects. There's more crime, more militants stirring things up, in the Fort Greene houses. Those projects are so spread out, so vast, that anyone can just go in and out of there without being noticed. But Farragut is kind of isolated. It's surrounded by factories, expressways, and bridges, and the people who live there are sort of cut off from the rest of Brooklyn. When outsiders come in, the residents know it.

"You get a lot of robberies in Farragut, but hardly any homicides. Take this year, 1973. In the first six months there haven't been any homicides in Farragut, but we've already had four in Brooklyn Heights, and that's supposed to be a 'good' neighborhood. The homicide problem in the Heights is mainly a homosexual problem. Now, I got nothing against these degenerates, but they lend themselves to violence because of their life-style. If they would stay with the crowd they know it would be all right. But some don't hang out with a crowd. They go out into the streets and parks to pick up men, and a lot of times the ones they pick up are only looking to rob them."

Some of the youngsters from the Farragut and Fort Greene projects have discovered that they can make a lot of money by hustling the Heights homosexuals. Marie Swearer, the director of Project Teen-Aid, who grew up in the Farragut projects, noted that "quite a few of the kids in the neighborhood have become male prostitutes. This is particularly true among young Puerto Rican kids. They'll walk over to the Heights at night or on the weekends, and when they come back they'll tell you all about their experiences. They're not ashamed of what they're doing, and what can you tell them? They seem to think it's a better alternative than stealing, and they make quite a lot of money."

In general, the police from the Eighty-fourth Precinct say that Farragut gives them relatively little trouble, and they're grateful they don't cover the more violent, less stable Fort Greene projects. But Farragut too has its potential trouble spots. For example, about five years ago a yeshiva moved into one of the old Brooklyn Navy Yard buildings near the Farragut projects. About six hundred Hassidic Jews go to school there daily, and some three hundred are in residence. When the school first opened, there was continual friction, until the people in the neighborhood became accustomed to the presence of the Hassidim. But there are still occasional eruptions. One time a Puerto Rican youngster was struck on the head, receiving a wound that required six stitches. A rumor started to circulate that "the Jews did it," and soon a mob surrounded the yeshiva and began stoning it. But the police called on some key people they work with in Farragut—some of the community leaders—who learned that it was actually the boy's brother who had inflicted the wound. The Farragut leaders themselves were then able to disperse the mob before the police got there.

The great majority of police in both the Eighty-fourth and the Eighty-eighth Precincts are white, as are ninety-one percent of police throughout New York City. Of the city's 29,500 police officers, just seven percent are black and two percent are Puerto Rican. But the Housing Authority police who patrol the low-income projects are primarily black, and this gives them a decided advantage in establishing a good relationship with the residents. In the Fort Greene projects, the familiar "cop on the beat"—really a Housing Authority patrolman—works out of a station house located in one of the project's buildings. Kids from the area are always playing in and around the station house, seemingly fascinated by it, and they know many of the housing police by name, just as the housing police know them.

Yet these police are not so effective in preventing crime as they might be because there are so few of them. Just thirty-six housing police are assigned to cover the Fort Greene and Farragut houses on a twenty-four-hour basis. The projects cover an area of 57.9 acres, and the housing police are supposed to conduct an hourly patrol of all the walkways, all the staircases, every floor of every building, the basements, and the roofs. But with only twelve men for each eight-hour shift —not counting days off and time spent in court—such coverage is impossible.

In 1972 the housing police responded to 735 incidents of all types at the Farragut projects (which house 5,990 people), and to 2,298 incidents at the Fort Greene projects (where 12,200 people live).

Such figures included 24 robberies, 23 burglaries, and 2 homicides at Farragut; and 131 robberies, 72 burglaries, 2 homicides, and 4 rapes at Fort Greene.

Other types of incidents included family fights, assaults, auto thefts, health code violations such as urinating in the elevators (a very common offense in the projects, according to the housing police), possession of narcotics, and parking violations. Vandalism by children is a serious problem. More than half the children in the projects come from one-parent homes, and if that parent is out working most of the day, the children may be largely unsupervised.

Another critical problem is the large-scale theft of welfare checks. When a new system for check cashing was instituted in which the recipient had to show an identification card with his or her picture on it, the amount of check stealing declined. Now the thieves wait until *after* people have cashed their checks before robbing them, but the net result is still very much the same—the number of robberies in the projects on check days still runs very high.

The Housing Authority reported that serious crimes in the city's low-income projects declined twenty-nine percent in 1972, compared with a crime drop of eighteen percent throughout the city as a whole. The Housing Authority tries to publicize such figures to prove that public housing is much safer than critics believe, and that a housing project is not a detriment to a neighborhood, but such reasoning is an exercise in futility. People who live anywhere near public housing projects simply don't care how much crime goes on within the projects themselves; as long as the crime is confined to the projects they can safely ignore it. What worries them is how much crime is committed in the surrounding neighborhood by those who live in the projects. The Housing Authority doesn't offer any statistics on this despite the fact that it may be the crucial point in determining whether middle-class communities would be willing to accept the construction of low-income projects in their midst, as was planned under the city's scatter-site housing program.

In Fort Greene, the people in the middle-income apartment buildings and brownstones tend to blame the inhabitants of the projects for almost all the crimes committed in the neigh-borhood. Whether or not this is actually so, they *think* it is, so that prejudice against the projects runs very high among both white and black middle-class residents of Fort Greene. Far from being a united community, Fort Greene is actually comprised of two separate groups of people—those who live in the projects and those who don't.

Crime throughout the neighborhood seems to follow specific patterns. For example, several years ago there was one homicide after another in or around the middle-income com-plex, University Towers. None of the homicides appeared to be connected in any way, but residents began to get the feel-ing that their chances for survival were growing slimmer, and quite a few moved away. Later on, the danger shifted to the Pratt area, where there was such a rash of muggings and rapes that women started escorting their children to and from the local schools.

Sometimes a crime wave may be the work of just one culprit. Throughout the summer of 1972, a man who became known as the "elevator mugger" terrorized residents in Uni-versity Towers, the Kingsview cooperative, and Concord Village, a large housing development located between Fort Greene and Brooklyn Heights. The mugger always used the same modus operandi. He would sneak into a building, go up to the third or fourth floor, and push the "up" button for the elevator. If there was a lone passenger in the car when it stopped, the assailant would partially enter it and continue to hold the door open while he whipped out his knife and demanded the passenger's money. When he got what he wanted, he would step out of the elevator and let the door close, leaving his victim to helplessly continue the upward journey while he escaped down the stairs. This act was re-peated at least ten times in one week in University Towers, and many times thereafter in Kingsview and Concord Village as well as the Towers. Although undercover police were assigned to all of the mugger's favorite haunts, it was almost two months before he was finally captured in Concord Village.

The people in Fort Greene do not rely solely on the police for their protection. Tenant patrols have become increasingly popular in recent years. Some of the buildings in the Fort Greene projects have formed their own tenant patrols, and the housing police say this has had a decided effect in making the buildings more secure. The Kingsview cooperative, which is a favorite target for muggers because of the large number of elderly people in the development, has also formed a highly successful tenants' patrol. Just the sight of people sitting in a lobby keeping a wary eye on all strangers who try to enter the building seems to be a very strong deterrent to those with larceny in mind. One thirty-two-story building in Brooklyn Heights that was victimized many times has had no robberies at all since the residents organized a tenants' patrol.

In order to mobilize neighborhoods throughout New York to help the police fight crime, the Lindsay administration set up a block security program in which community groups that raised funds for security purposes could get matching funds from the city. The program was calculated to give a larger share of city funds to poor neighborhoods. Thus, a community group that could raise no more than fifty dollars would get matching city funds at a ratio of nine to one, or $450, whereas a group that raised as much as five thousand dollars would be matched at a ratio of just two to one. No group could receive more than ten thousand dollars. The funds could be used only for specific security devices that were approved by the city, such as bell-buzzer intercom systems, fences, a variety of locks, roof door bolts, window gates, floodlights, wire screens, police whistles, radio equipment, home alarms, walkie-talkies, and closed-circuit television sets. The program was financed by five million dollars in capital budget funds and two million dollars in expense budget funds.

Each police precinct was allocated a certain amount of money based on population in the area, and this money was to be divided among the various groups in accordance with how much money they themselves could raise. The Eighty-fourth Precinct, for example, was given a total of twenty thousand dollars for its neighborhood security program. About fourteen community groups wound up battling with each other over the division of this bounty—and all of the groups were from Brooklyn Heights. The Farragut projects, representing over five thousand people, did not submit any security proposals whatsoever. The police officer in charge of the program at the Eighty-fourth Precinct observed that "the people at Farragut just couldn't raise a nickel." So despite the fact that the security program was specifically designed to favor the poorer, most heavily crime-ridden areas, it was the middle-class block associations that walked off with all the money in the Eighty-fourth Precinct.

Much of the crime in the Eighty-fourth Precinct centers on the downtown Brooklyn shopping area. The police claim that they have blanketed Fulton Street so thoroughly and made so many arrests there that purse-snatchers and pickpockets have been driven off the street into the stores, where they ply their trades alongside the shoplifters. For the Fulton Street store owner, the crime situation has become a nightmare. Losses from shoplifting and employee thefts at Abraham & Straus run as high as eleven percent, according to police estimates, and there are persistent rumors that this Brooklyn landmark is eventually going to shut its doors. There are also complaints that the Brooklyn branch of A&S charges higher prices than other A&S branches for the same merchandise in order to offset its heavy theft losses.

Aside from the professional thieves who account for the bulk of the losses, a lot of shoplifting is done by teenagers and younger kids who come into the store in groups of four and five and try to swipe merchandise from every department they pass through. Almost every day the security guards are kept busy evicting kids from the store.

One of the housing policemen at the Fort Greene and Farragut projects recalled the time when he had to go over to A&S to look through their photo files of shoplifters, pickpockets, and assorted crooks. "I was surprised at how many of the photographs I recognized," he said, "because a lot of the kids from the projects turned up in the files. I didn't even know that some of them had ever been in trouble."

As in other parts of the city, youth gangs have begun to form in Fort Greene, although they are not nearly so large or so menacing as the gangs in the South Bronx—yet. In an attempt to provide a deterrent to the growth of these gangs, the Willoughby House Settlement, which operates out of offices in the Fort Greene projects, has restructured its youth program. With the aid of two foundation grants totaling thirty-one thousand dollars, the settlement has assigned five full-time and three part-time workers to provide group work and group counseling to neighborhood teenagers. In addition, the settlement house is intensifying its efforts to help teenagers train for and find jobs and to take advantage of educational opportunities. Over forty percent of the young men in Fort Greene between the ages of sixteen and twenty-one who are not in school are unemployed. The settlement hopes to recruit additional staff members to reach out directly to youth gangs in the neighborhood such as the Dukes and the Avenue Kings.

The Willoughby House Settlement is much more independent than other social service agencies in Fort Greene because it does not have to rely on the city, state, or federal government for its funding. Most of its money comes from foundations and private contributions, so it has not been directly affected by the Nixon administration's decision to abandon the antipoverty program and shut down the Office of Economic Opportunity.

But almost every other social welfare agency in Fort Greene has had to curtail its activities drastically or halt them altogether for lack of funds. The police fear that such cutbacks are eventually going to send the crime rate soaring and set off a new wave of militancy in the neighborhood. Although the police have no fondness for radicals and militants, they were delighted when the city hired many of them to work in the antipoverty programs. "It was like paying them to keep them off the streets and to draw them into the establishment," said one police spokesman, "and that was all right with us. It got them out of the way. But now that these programs are ending, the militants are going to be out of work and out of power, and they'll start stirring up the community again. People will follow them. Sure they will. When you get groups of people together they're just like sheep, and a strong leader can push them into practically anything. I don't want to see what's going to happen if we don't get some money in here to keep programs going and keep the militants employed."

For the past year or so, things have been somewhat calmer in Fort Greene as far as street crime is concerned, probably reflecting the eighteen percent drop in serious crimes recorded throughout the city. (The decline stemmed mainly from a sharp drop in crimes against property. Homicides and rapes actually rose somewhat.) In Fort Greene now you hear fewer stories of people being mugged, and while the fear of crime has not subsided in the least, people have some reason to hope that the worst may be over.

This drop in street crime is generally attributed to the methadone maintenance programs that have sprung up all over the city, as well as to the shrinking supply of heroin. With the price of heroin way up and the quality so poor that the drug is barely effective, large numbers of addicts have been virtually forced to turn to methadone. Even if they are not enrolled in one of the many legitimate methadone maintenance programs, they can easily buy a day's supply of methadone on the street for about five dollars. This means that addicts who may have previously needed to steal anywhere from forty to seventy-five dollars a day to support a heroin habit now only need about five dollars a day to keep themselves going on methadone—and unlike the problem with heroin, addicts do not need steadily increasing doses of methadone to satisfy their need.

This is not to imply that methadone is solving the drug problem. Methadone, taken orally, blocks the effect of heroin; it does not work at all on barbiturates, cocaine, LSD, speed, or other drugs, and it does nothing to curb the effects of alcohol. Also, when injected, methadone itself can produce a "high."

Far too many addicts on methadone are simply getting their kicks from these other drugs, and are still as spaced out and as incapable of leading productive lives as if they were on heroin. All methadone is doing for them is reducing their need to steal. In that respect, methadone is benefiting society as a whole. But its effectiveness in helping the addicts become fully functioning human beings is still debatable.

Long Island College Hospital, located not far from Fort Greene, has been operating three methadone maintenance centers in South Brooklyn for the past two years and has reported good results with its program—a majority of the patients in all three centers were either working, going to school, functioning well at home, or "able to control antisocial activities without dependence on heroin," the hospital stated.

One of the hospital centers reported that of the first 118 patients accepted in the program two years ago, only three were employed at the time. Less than three months later, thirty-seven of these patients were working and eight were in school or in job training. Another of the centers reported that "over one hundred of our three hundred patients are employed full-time, working in white-collar jobs, professional positions, as construction workers, service station employees, and in other jobs. Five are in college full time, thirteen in school part-time, four in trade schools, and four completing high school."

Walter Bryant, Jr., administrative director of the hospital's methadone centers, pointed out that "almost every addict, ninety-nine percent of them, who joined the program were in trouble before, and most of those who remain in the program are free of such trouble while in the program. They are no longer arrested for stealing, prostitution, abandonment, and similar difficulties. The process of changing a person's life-style is difficult. . . . Because of lack of education, severe socio-economic conditions and long years of waste, many are not employable, but while on the program they do not lead destructive lives."

Altogether, more than 620 addicts who continued as patients in the Long Island College Hospital methadone centers were helped to overcome dependence on heroin. However, the figures are somewhat misleading because they include only addicts who *continued* as patients in the program for two years; they do not include all those who dropped out and reverted to heroin usage or became addicted to other drugs. The number of these dropouts may be substantial, but the hospital report neglected to mention them.

One reason for the increasing enrollment in the methadone maintenance programs over the past year or two was the city's insistence that all addicts on welfare be registered in some sort of drug treatment program if they wanted to maintain their welfare eligibility. To keep closer watch on the Brooklyn addicts, the Department of Social Services assigned all of them to a single welfare center on Myrtle Avenue and Jay Street, where Fort Greene converges with downtown Brooklyn. The addicts have to come to the center twice a month to pick up their checks, and periodically must show proof that they are continuing treatment for their addiction. In addition, a computerized listing of all addicts on welfare was set up to prevent fraud and duplication. Between April 1972 and April 1973, after these systems were in effect, the number of addicts on welfare dropped from 34,000 to 19,615—a forty percent decline.

The great majority of addicts who are undergoing treatment are enrolled in government-funded methadone programs supervised by the city's Addiction Services Agency. Approximately thirty-three thousand addicts are registered in these clinics, and it is estimated that about forty percent of them are holding jobs, while the remainder are on welfare. Another eighty-five hundred addicts participate in the drug-free, psychologically oriented therapeutic communities such as Phoenix House and Odyssey House.

One clear sign that drug-related crimes are down is the fact that in 1973 the proportion of addicts among all suspects admitted to city prisons was about twenty-five percent, compared to forty-five percent in 1972 and about sixty percent in 1971. If the crime rate as a whole has not dropped proportionately it is because greater numbers of nonheroin addicts are now committing crimes.

The methadone program has had its adverse effects as well. At last count, some eighteen methadone centers had sprung up in Fort Greene alone. As a result, the neighborhood has been inundated with addicts, including those who come into the area to pick up their welfare checks plus those who come in to receive their daily dose of methadone.

Many people in the neighborhood are furious at what they consider the "dumping" of addicts into Fort Greene—especially since so many of the addicts come from other parts of Brooklyn, such as Bedford-Stuyvesant. The feeling is that Fort Greene has enough addicts of its own without having to import more, and that the proliferation of methadone centers is destroying certain parts of Fort Greene that were just beginning to be rejuvenated.

The outrage has focused on one particular methadone center at Waverly Avenue and Fulton Street. Estimates of the number of addicts receiving treatment here range from about 750 to as high as 1,200, with the bulk of the addicts coming from neighboring Bedford-Stuyvesant. The existence of this center has spawned the rise of the Fort Greene Crisis Committee, a group representing fifty Fort Greene community and block associations, which is battling to reduce the concentration of addicts in the area.

Many members of the crisis committee live in brownstones that line the quiet, tree-shaded side streets off Fulton Street. They are new homeowners—mainly black—and they have been renovating their three- and four-story houses over the last few years, converting them from dilapidated dwellings and rooming houses into well-kept charming townhouses. But the profusion of methadone centers in their area, and the Waverly center in particular, has made them fear that their efforts at urban renewal are doomed.

Anyone who walks along Fulton Street in the vicinity of the Waverly methadone center can understand the residents' fears. Addicts are everywhere—they are clustered in groups on the sidewalk, seated on parked cars, lounging in doorways or dawdling in the middle of the street, oblivious to passing cars. Many of them hang around the center for hours every day, drinking from bottles inside brown paper bags and yelling across the street to one another. Some of them appear to be as freaked out as if they were still on heroin. The large number of boarded-up and abandoned stores along this part of Fulton Street adds to the chilling, surrealistic scene. It is as if the addicts have taken over and everyone else has evacuated.

Although the loiterers—mainly the hard-core unemployed—may account for only a small percentage of the total number of addicts enrolled at the Waverly methadone center, their numbers are sufficient to scare people away from the immediate area. Whether the loiterers actually commit many crimes and assaults is a debatable point, but there is no doubt that their psychological effect is frightening. Residents are afraid to stand on a corner and wait for a bus on Fulton Street, or to go down into the subway. They are afraid to shop in the local stores, and they are afraid of being followed back to their homes.

The Waverly center is operated by the Addiction Research Treatment Corporation (ARTC), which receives funds from the city and recently announced plans to erect a $1.4 million skills training center for addicts to supplement its methadone-dispensing operation at Waverly and Fulton. The skills center would also be located in Fort Greene, at Waverly and Atlantic Avenues.

ARTC was created in 1969 as a nonprofit agency dedicated to rehabilitating hard-core addicts in Brooklyn. While basically autonomous, it has been supervised by a board of directors headed by former U.S. Attorney-General Nicholas deB. Katzenbach. The program itself is run by Dr. Beny J. Primm.

The Fort Greene Crisis Committee has accused ARTC of being "a substantial contributor to the destruction of the community's business and residential fabric," and with being a major factor in the sharp increase in addict loitering and crime in the Fulton Street area.

In response to such attacks, Dr. Primm said, "There has been constant harassment, and I and my whole staff are just about ready to hand the community the methadone, hand the community the patients, and say, 'You treat them.' Our program has constant evaluation and constant monitoring (from government agencies), and if this kind of program has to suffer these kinds of attacks, then my god, what will happen to all the little programs?"

The Fort Greene Crisis Committee also objects to another

large methadone center—run by the Narcotics Addiction Control Commission—located only about eight blocks away from the Waverly center. These two clinics, as well as the sixteen other methadone centers in Fort Greene, draw about sixty-two hundred addicts into Fort Greene daily, according to the Crisis Committee. "If the facilities develop and expand as currently planned, more than ten thousand addicts will be concentrated in and around the Fort Greene area by 1976," the committee charged, adding that most of the addicts will not be residents of the community.

"We welcome the opportunity to treat those in Fort Greene afflicted with drug addiction," the committee stated. "What we're objecting to is the dumping into Fort Greene of those addicts who live in other areas of Brooklyn and New York City. We accuse the city of refusing to meet its responsibilities toward its own addicted population."

No middle-class neighborhood would tolerate the presence of so many methadone centers in its midst for fear of being overrun by addicts, but because Fort Greene is predominantly a low-income black neighborhood without strong community leadership, it has been powerless to avoid being used as a dumping ground. The people in the public housing projects were just as opposed to the proliferation of methadone centers in Fort Greene as their middle-class neighbors, but they were not unified enough or strong enough to do anything about it. People who are living at the poverty level or on welfare have virtually no control over their own neighborhoods; the city does pretty much as it wishes with them.

In contrast, a solidly white middle-class neighborhood like Flatbush was able to force the ouster of a five-hundred-patient methadone clinic from its vicinity. (The clinic subsequently tried to relocate at Flatbush Avenue and Pacific Street—on the border of Fort Greene.)

It was not until larger numbers of middle-class homeowners began moving into Fort Greene—attracted by the availability of cheap brownstones—that strong, effective pressure was put on city officials and political leaders to reduce the concentration of addicts in the neighborhood. The mainly middle class Fort Greene Crisis Committee publicized the problem in newspapers and on television, and enlisted the aid of councilmen William Thompson and Fred Richmond and Brooklyn borough president Sebastian Leone. The pressure and publicity eventually got results, and by September 1973 controller Abraham D. Beame announced that he was going to stop payments to the ARTC methadone center at Waverly and Fulton unless the city's Addiction Services Agency took steps to end an "overconcentration of addicts in the Fort Greene area." At last report, the city was planning to reduce by more than half the number of addicts treated in Fort Greene. New clinics were being set up in the Brownsville and Bushwick areas of Brooklyn to handle the overflow from Fort Greene and reduce the loitering there.

Dr. Primm pointed out that ARTC would like to decentralize "down to a minimum of three hundred patients at any one site" if possible. The big difficulty in decentralizing is that there are so few neighborhoods in the city that will accept a methadone center—even a small one—without a fight. This is why it is so tempting to dump a lot of centers into the more passive poor neighborhoods, and to let these centers swell to monstrous sizes. It is simply the path of least resistance.

Despite the fact that methadone has become the most popular treatment for drug addiction throughout the city and that it is generally credited with helping reduce the crime rate, many people in Fort Greene are staunchly opposed to its use —particularly people who work closely with youths. Clifford Watterson, a parole officer in charge of the halfway house program for young ex-convicts at Long Island University, never recommends methadone to any of his parolees who start slipping back into drug usage. Instead, he tries to get them into a drug-free community such as Phoenix House, because he believes that this is far more beneficial to the addict in the long run.

"We want our people to stop relying on drugs altogether, and to face problems without a crutch," he said. "If they're on methadone they never really escape the drug habit—methadone is a highly addictive drug itself—and they're much more likely to pop pills or become heavy drinkers. It's all part of the same dependency bag.

"I would not be so opposed to methadone if it were used as part of a program that aimed at getting the addict off *all* drugs eventually, and included counseling, therapy, and all the other supportive services you need if you're going to effect any real change in people and enable them to stand on their own. I think a move is being made toward this type of treatment now, and I'm very glad to see it. But I think it's wrong to just maintain people on a drug like methadone indefinitely."

Marie Swearer of Project Teen-Aid shares Mr. Watterson's antipathy toward methadone. "I'm not for methadone at all," she said. "It's like taking poison. Also, some of these private doctors are really going to town with methadone. They just keep on giving out prescriptions to addicts for a good fee, and there's none of the therapeutic follow-up that should go with methadone treatment. It's just a kind of sick situation.

"We don't have much of a drug problem with our girls here. Most of the kids do smoke reefer, and we've had a couple of kids on barbiturates, which are really terrible— worse than heroin. Hardly any of our girls are heroin addicts, although many of their boyfriends are on it. The girls tend to avoid it. Why that should be, I just don't know.

"Even with methadone, the heroin problem in this neighborhood is still very bad. I don't think the methadone has been as effective as people say. I don't know about how things are in the Fort Greene projects, but I live over on the other side of Farragut, and I would say that more than fifty percent of the kids in Farragut are addicts right now. It's that high.

Every building has a shooting parlor, so to speak. You can find a contact in any building you want to, in the corridors, the staircases. If you hang out the windows you can watch the kids make contacts.

"The factories around Farragut are constantly ripped off by the drug addicts. They don't just hit them for small things. They walk off with television sets and IBM typewriters. I live in a private house, and the addicts hit us two summers ago and took about two thousand dollars worth of things. This was in midday when everybody was out on the street, and they just walked out the front door with everything. So there's constant ripping off, selling the stuff to people in the neighborhood, then ripping off again. If methadone is doing any good, I haven't noticed it."

The Federation of Addiction Agencies—a Brooklyn-based coalition of antidrug groups—has also come out against methadone maintenance, favoring instead methadone-to-abstinence programs. The federation stated, "Though methadone maintenance may be acceptable to some older addicts, many leaders in the community question the wisdom of addicting our youth to any narcotic as a so-called cure for heroin addiction. We continue to believe that the healthiest state of physical and mental well-being is a human body free of all drug support. Having witnessed methadone maintenance and the unsuccessful attempts by some insensitive researchers to saddle our communities with heroin maintenance, we rejoice at the now proposed development of methadone-to-abstinence programs."

However, the federation's optimism is apparently premature, for methadone maintenance programs continue to proliferate throughout the city. As long as they appear to be effective in reducing the crime rate, government officials are willing to give them priority in funding—regardless of whether or not methadone maintenance is the best long-term solution for the addicts themselves. As long as methadone keeps them relatively quiet, such programs will continue to be popular with city, state, and federal officials.

9

Housing

"IT'S BECAUSE of the public housing that this is not a more violent or more militant neighborhood," said Marie Swearer. "With all the cutbacks we've had in the poverty programs, day care and all other social services, we should have had a really good size riot by now. It would at least be an indication there's still some life in this community. But everything has been very quiet. Even the street gangs that started up a couple of months ago seem to have faded away.

"I think this is due at least partly to the housing. Everybody here in the projects has hot and cold running water, heat in the wintertime, and enough food. Those are your basics, and when people have those things they're not so dissatisfied that they're willing to put their heads on the block to riot. You go to someplace like the South Bronx where you don't have hot water and heat in the wintertime, and you have a lot of physical frustration and gangs that are active and violent.

"The housing here is at least adequate. A lot of people who move into the Farragut and Fort Greene projects have come from Brownsville and places like that, where their housing has been so bad that this place is like a panacea to them. So why should they fight? Why should they get up and do more than anyone else? They have everything they want now. There's enough food. The kids have money to buy candy. I see them buying hot dogs all the time from the stand on the corner, so there's enough money. If they don't have it, they steal it, so the kids aren't really dissatisfied. The parents aren't dissatisfied either.

"What has to be done in this community is to educate people to show them that they don't have what they should have. This housing here really is substandard in many ways, and the schools are substandard. But how do you tell somebody who comes out of a rat-infested tenement that this is substandard? To him it's not."

Regardless of what urban planners may think of most low-income housing projects—dismissing them as "vertical slums" —to the poor people of this city they are extremely desirable places to live; they are the best that is currently available. Waiting lists of families who want to get into the projects are very long, and once a family is accepted in a project, they tend to stay for many years. In this respect, a poor neighborhood that has a great deal of public housing tends to be a more stable community than an equally poor neighborhood where most of the housing is made up of tenements. It is also true that such a neighborhood will remain poor as long as the projects exist, and that in New York City it is likely to be a perpetual black and Puerto Rican ghetto, with little chance for any significant integration. Even in areas where interracial middle-income developments are located right across the street from the low-income projects, there is such a dichotomy between the two economic groups that the people in the projects remain essentially segregated.

In Fort Greene, at least, there is very little intermingling between the project residents and their middle-income neighbors, particularly since their children are zoned into different schools. Exceptions are found among people who grew up in the projects and subsequently moved to one of the nearby middle-income buildings. These people may have parents, other relatives, and old friends still living in the projects, and they form the main links between the middle-income groups and the poor. Marie Swearer is one of those who grew up in the Farragut projects and now owns her own brownstone just a few blocks away. Bob Wittich, a political reformer who also grew up in Farragut and ran for City Council in 1973, now owns an apartment in the Kingsview cooperative, directly across Myrtle Avenue from the Fort Greene projects. Elderly people in the projects talk of daughters who work as nurses in Brooklyn and Cumberland hospitals and have moved to apartments in University Towers, which is owned by Long Island University and is also across the street from the projects. Thus, the links develop as upward mobility takes place.

The Fort Greene projects were completed in 1944 and consist of thirty-five buildings, most of which are six stories high. The remaining buildings are either eleven or thirteen stories. Sprawling over many acres, with a maze of intertwining walkways, sitting areas, and play areas, the buildings contain 3,501 apartments and approximately 12,500 people. They were built primarily to house the war workers in the Brooklyn Navy Yard, according to standards that are now unacceptable for public housing. For example, the rooms are too small and the closets lack doors. Also, there is not enough recreation space in proportion to the number of people who live there. Because of the project's unwieldy size, it was eventually divided into two administratively independent sections—Walt Whitman houses and Raymond V. Ingersoll houses—both run by the New York City Housing Authority. However, the buildings continue to be known as "the Fort Greene houses" to people in the community.

The projects are like a small village in themselves. They contain an elementary school (P.S. 67), Cumberland Hospital, a library, a church, a day-care center, a housing police station, a senior citizens center, a high school for pregnant adolescents, and the Willoughby House Settlement. Shopping is located on Myrtle Avenue, which borders the projects.

Residents have complained of a marked deterioration of the projects in recent years, particularly in regard to faulty elevators and to the rampant crime and vandalism, both within the buildings and on the grounds outside. At the same time there have been numerous rent increases over the years. In response to these conditions a movement has arisen (although still a very weak one) to convert the projects into a cooperative owned and managed by people now living in the buildings.

The inspiration for this idea came from the conversion of nearby Wallabout houses—which had been built by the U.S. Navy in 1941 solely for navy personnel—into cooperative housing for low-income families. Wallabout was a federal undertaking in which the government, after closing the Navy Yard, rehabilitated the houses to provide one hundred and sixty-nine spacious apartments in the low-income range. Monthly costs per unit are a little higher in Wallabout than in the Fort Greene or Farragut projects, but families whose income has risen above the public housing limits can move in there. Most of the original residents of Wallabout came from the other two projects. Wallabout was intended mainly for large families, since forty-seven percent of its apartments have three or more bedrooms.

The Farragut projects, which were finished in 1952, consist of ten buildings that are thirteen and fourteen stories high. Approximately 5,500 people live there in 1,390 apartments. According to the New York City Planning Commission, Farragut "seems isolated from the life and opportunities of the city" because it lies on a slice of land that has been cut off from the rest of Brooklyn by the Brooklyn-Queens Expressway. Yet it is this very isolation that has made the Farragut projects a more unified and safer community than the vast Fort Greene projects on the other side of the expressway. People tend to know one another better in Farragut, and to know who lives in the immediate neighborhood and who is an outsider. It is harder for someone to commit a crime anonymously in Farragut than in Fort Greene, and the crime rate here is somewhat lower. This would tend to offset the theory by some urban planners that the height of a public housing project has the most direct bearing on the amount of crime within it—that is, the taller the buildings, the higher the crime rate. The Farragut projects are more than twice as tall as the Fort Greene buildings, yet there is less crime in that isolated enclave.

Well over twenty-five percent of the people in the Fort Greene and Farragut projects are on welfare. In earlier years the New York City Housing Authority did not accept welfare families in its low-income projects, nor did it accept families headed solely by a mother. Only the intact, two-parent working family was considered "worthy" of public housing. However, intact families did not necessarily *remain* intact. Before long there were many project families who had been split by separation, desertion, or divorce, and the mother had to apply for welfare to support her children. In these cases the families were generally not evicted, and eventually the Housing Authority dropped its nonwelfare, intact-family policy entirely.

Today, most people get into public housing after being on a waiting list for quite a while. But families who have been left homeless as a result of a disaster, such as a fire or the condemnation of their homes, may be given priority in public housing even if they are on welfare.

"Public housing is taking many more welfare families now than it used to," says Ann Rosenhaft, director of the Fort Greene Welfare Center, "although it's still hard to get anyone in because there are so few vacancies. Also, the welfare family in urgent need of housing tends to be a large family, and there are very few large units in the city projects, especially the older projects. In private housing you can maneuver a family of eight into five rooms or even four rooms if there's no alternative, but in public housing you can't. This is taboo under city housing regulations, and the city is very strict on overoccupancy. We don't have the option of saying, 'Give this family whatever is available.'

"Even when an appropriate apartment does open up, we run into problems because people don't want to leave their own neighborhoods. They would like to live in public housing, but they want a project that's near where they used to live, close to their old friends and neighbors. If they've been brought up in Brooklyn they don't want to go to the Bronx.

"Some of these objections I think are reasonable. If it's a family with children, moving to a far-off location means changing their schools and leaving the medical care that the family is used to and trusts, whether it be the local hospital clinic or whatever. Relocating means learning their way around a strange new neighborhood and finding out where all the agencies and facilities are. The welfare population is a lot more dependent on that kind of thing than a middle-income family. If a middle-income person has moved but wants to keep his old doctor, he'll just take a cab to the other side of town. But people on welfare don't have extra money for cab fares or even bus or subway fares, so they feel limited to facilities near their homes.

"We put far more welfare families into private housing than public housing. There are enough apartments in our area so that we don't usually have to put welfare families in hotels. However, in cases of fire or where there's a vacate order by the Department of Health, the city's Department of Relocation has to arrange for emergency housing—and that's hotel housing. Relocation pays their hotel bill for up to thirty days, and then we take over. But usually we get the family into an apartment before thirty days, so we rarely wind up paying hotel bills for our welfare families.

"Of course, it's always difficult to rehouse welfare families. On top of the race prejudice where black and Puerto Rican families are concerned, there's also a specific prejudice against welfare recipients. Landlords can reject people just because they're on welfare, and it's legal. It's still legal."

The supply of private housing in Fort Greene for low-income and welfare families has shrunk rapidly in the last few years with the influx of young middle-class people who have been buying up the old brownstones and rooming houses and renovating them for their own use. Rental apartments in these renovated houses are far too expensive for the poor. Each floor of a renovated brownstone in Fort Greene brings in about two hundred dollars a month, and many of the apartments are set up as duplexes. The owners usually live in one of the apartments and rent out the others.

"Renovation fever" has taken hold particularly in the areas around Fort Greene Park and Pratt University. The new homeowners tend to be a youngish, racially mixed group of middle-income people who are determined to stay in the city but want a lot of living space for a moderate price. When they first discovered Fort Greene about seven years ago, the dilapidated brownstones and rooming houses bordering the park were selling for about twelve thousand dollars. Today, they are in the thirty-thousand-dollar range, with another ten or fifteen thousand dollars needed for renovation. Still, they are a bargain compared to brownstones in Brooklyn Heights, Cobble Hill, Boerum Hill, and Park Slope—other areas in Brooklyn that are being restored through the private efforts of middle-class families, reversing decades of urban decay. In Brooklyn Heights the renewal process that began in the mid-1950s is just about complete, and it is almost impossible to find a brownstone there for under one hundred thousand dollars. In Cobble Hill and Park Slope, prices are up over fifty thousand dollars.

Fort Greene is a relative newcomer to the renovation scramble, and at present its brownstone area is totally mixed, both racially and economically. Welfare and low-income families live on the same block as middle-income families, and there is much more intermingling between them than between the residents of the public housing projects and their middle-income neighbors. Perhaps this is because the people in the brownstones are not so clearly branded as "low-income" or "middle-income," and since they share the same streets, their children play together and go to school together. It is almost an ideal urban mix, but it is not destined to last very long if the renovation process continues in the same way. As the prices of brownstones soar, the owners of rooming houses and other decayed brownstones where the poor live are very likely to sell their properties for large profits to renovation-minded middle-income families. The poor will then be forced out of Fort Greene into other neighborhoods. This means that the upgrading of Fort Greene will not have benefited them at all, because in the long run they will not be sharing in it.

Already many of the poor are disappearing, and the area is displaying some solidly middle class characteristics, such as the formation of block associations that are strong enough to have some political clout. These groups have been able to do things for the neighborhood that the poor were never able to do despite years of trying. For example, over the years many residents of Fort Greene had complained about the deterioration of Fort Greene Park, but nothing was ever done. However, when the middle-class block associations united in protest, the city took notice. In the fall of 1973 a nine-hundred-thousand-dollar renovation of the park was begun.

The process of converting the brownstone area of Fort Greene from a poor community into a middle-class one is being speeded up by the activities of real estate agents who bought up a lot of brownstones in Fort Greene a few years ago when they realized that this was a "coming" neighborhood. Some of the brownstones were sold a year or two later for a quick profit, while others were held on to and renovated in the hopes of snaring even bigger profits. The result of all this buying, selling, and renovating on the part of the real estate agents was to push up the prices very quickly.

Even in relatively undesirable brownstone sections of Fort Greene, such as a small area near the Farragut projects, housing prices have jumped tremendously in the last few years. Marie Swearer, who bought a brownstone around there in 1968, described what is happening in her neighborhood.

"When we bought our house it cost us only seven thousand dollars," she said. "The renovations are costing us about ten thousand, so we're getting a home for seventeen thousand dollars. There are only a few houses on our block, and the first one that was sold, just before we got ours, went for five thousand dollars. But the next house that was sold after ours went for ten thousand, then another house was sold for fifteen thousand. The last fellow who bought a house there, about six months ago, paid twenty-five thousand dollars. Some of the brownstone apartments on our block rent for as high as four hundred dollars—and this is just one block away from the Farragut projects.

"Only a few streets in our area have brownstones, like Water Street, Front Street, and Gold Street. It's a strange little area, with picturesque little homes and coach houses. An architect owns one of the houses, and an airline pilot owns another. A lot of the young people who rent go to Polytech and Pace College. Soon I think it's going to be an essentially middle class enclave."

The value of the housing in Fort Greene is highest in the area around Pratt University, where the people also have the highest incomes. The prices of brownstones at the outer edge of Fort Greene, near the Atlantic Terminal Urban Renewal area, are also fairly high. This is partly a reflection of the fact that people expect property values to rise sharply once the urban renewal complex is completed. This development will include two thousand housing units, a shopping center, and day-care facilities. About four hundred of the apartments will be low-income housing managed by the New York City Housing Authority, and the rest will be cooperative and low- and moderate-income apartments renting for about thirty-nine dollars a room. It is also possible that Baruch College of the City University will move to new quarters on a nearby site.

The Atlantic Terminal project may be the last to be built in an urban renewal area, because President Nixon's budget cutbacks slashed urban renewal out of existence. In addition, he imposed an eighteen-month moratorium on any new federally aided construction of this type.

The completion of the Atlantic Terminal project may very well hasten the conversion of the adjacent brownstone area in Fort Greene into a solidly middle class community. Such a development is not looked upon favorably by those who want the area to retain its economic mix. The Pratt Institute Center for Community and Environmental Development is currently doing a study to see if it is possible for the poor to share in the rejuvenation of their neighborhood by buying their own brownstones via some sort of mortgage pool or revolving fund arrangement. According to the Pratt Center, it may be possible for families with incomes as low as six thousand dollars a year to purchase their own homes, provided they can rent out two or three apartments to help pay mortgage and maintenance costs.

The study noted: "Applying this rental income [of about two hundred dollars per floor] to the building's carrying charges, and assuming that a substantial percentage of the labor costs of maintenance and upkeep would be absorbed by the owner as a form of 'sweat equity,' only $100 to $150 per month would be required to complete the building's carrying charges (mortgage, taxes and operating expenses). This $100 to $150 per month, which would provide a triplex apartment or a duplex apartment for the owner, . . . is well within the reach of a low- to moderate-income family earning approximately six thousand dollars per year."

However, such families would need considerable back-up assistance to insure against unforeseen disaster, the study said. In addition, there would have to be an expansion in the availability of mortgage and rehabilitation funds by the participation of mortgage pools and institutional investment capital. The study also suggested the possibility of establishing a community-based nonprofit Community Development Corporation that would try to obtain grants for a revolving fund of at least five hundred thousand dollars. This fund would be used to help people buy and renovate houses, and then rent apartments. Such programs would increase the amount of low- and moderate-income housing in the brownstone area of Fort Greene, and "stabilize the racial and economic mix now subject to rapid upgrading through renovation."

At present there are 115 vacant or nearly vacant houses in Fort Greene which are owned by the federal or city government. These houses in particular could be bought by low- and moderate-income families if their prices were kept well below the current market value of privately owned homes in Fort Greene. Eighty-four of the houses were taken over by the city because of defaults in the payment of property taxes. Ten houses are in-rem property—that is, they are in the process of being taken over by the city—and twenty-one houses are federally owned as a result of mortgage foreclosures.

The government evicted the tenants from most of these buildings at the time of the take-over, which in some cases was many years ago. The buildings have been standing vacant ever since, impeding the redevelopment of the neighborhood. The Pratt Center is suing the city and the federal government over these buildings on two grounds: the arbitrary eviction of tenants, and the threat to the environment caused by the empty houses (they are both an eyesore and a fire hazard). If such buildings were priced low enough to be purchased by poor and moderate-income families, such purchases might be an ideal solution for maintaining the neighborhood's economic mix.

The Pratt Center's study of housing in Fort Greene revealed that most homes were generally sound, but there were pockets of blocks that were extremely dilapidated, particularly where there were a lot of rooming houses. Many of these rooming houses were bought several years ago by real estate agents who have been acting as absentee landlords ever since. Presumably the agents intend to sell these houses when the prices go high enough, but in the meantime the rooming houses are badly overcrowded and in poor condition. In general, they are among the worst housing in Fort Greene.

The majority of other houses in the community are about fifty years old and are mainly row houses, brownstones and some tenement structures. Not surprisingly, welfare recipients are the main occupants in many of the substandard buildings and rooming houses, where rats, lack of heat and hot water, and intense overcrowding are common. The Department of Social Services has been forced to pay higher and higher rents for such dismal housing for its clients ever since the vacancy decontrol law went into effect. About two-thirds of the city's relief recipients still live in rent-controlled units, but the proportion has been going down as people move and as more apartments in the city become decontrolled. Some apartments in Fort Greene that rented for $65 a month just a year ago have soared to $125. The average rent for a family of four on welfare is now over $121 per month (in private housing, not in low-income projects). This represents about a twenty percent increase since December 1971, when the average welfare rental was $100.70.

The increase in rents is primarily responsible for the fact that total welfare costs in the city have risen over the last year despite the large drop in the number of people on the welfare rolls. This has led to demands by public officials that the Department of Social Services pay only a "flat grant" for rent—such as $115 or $125 for a family of four, for example. If the family was able to find an apartment for less than that amount, they could keep the extra money for other expenses. But if their apartment cost more than the flat grant, they would have to make up the additional costs out of their food or clothing allowances. The theory is that the flat grant system would inspire welfare clients to look for the cheapest possible apartments, and landlords would no longer be able to get away with charging the welfare department inflated rents for broken-down housing. In many cases it was discovered that the Department of Social Services was paying more for some apartments than were private tenants in the same buildings. The landlords seemed to regard this as a well-deserved bonus for allowing welfare clients to live in their buildings, and the welfare department silently acquiesced because it cost less than keeping the people in hotels.

However, a flat grant system can only work effectively—without punishing the poor—if enough decent low-cost housing is available in the city so that the demand does not outstrip the supply and force prices up. But in New York City this is not the case. There is a severe shortage of housing here, particularly moderately priced housing, and welfare clients are afraid that the inflationary rent spiral may continue indefinitely while the flat grant for rent remains the same. Under these circumstances they would certainly be forced into the worst possible housing and might even have to go without some of their food or clothing money to pay for a decrepit apartment. For this reason a number of social welfare groups have been fighting the flat grant proposals.

What is really needed in New York City is an increased

supply of low-cost housing, but this is not likely to come about in the near future, because the Nixon administration abruptly suspended a program under which the federal government was supposed to help build six million new housing units per year for the poor and those slightly above the poverty level through an interest-subsidy arrangement. President Nixon imposed the suspension in January 1973, on the grounds of waste and fraud in the building and lending industries, which received the bulk of the subsidies.

Instead of building any more new housing for the poor, the president has now proposed that those in need be given direct cash assistance to enable them to find decent housing for themselves on the private market. But in New York and other cities that suffer from a housing shortage, the effect of such direct cash subsidies may be only to push rental costs up still further, thereby nullifying the effect of the subsidies.

In New York City most of the new, totally private housing that has been built in recent years has been luxury housing. More modest middle-income developments have usually been aided by some city, state, or federal program. In Fort Greene there has been no new, wholly private apartment construction since before World War II, so the area has been very dependent on the government for its housing needs. All the middle-income buildings in the neighborhood went up under various urban renewal and slum clearance programs, so that the residents of the middle-income buildings as well as the residents of the low-income projects are in their homes as a result of government aid. Only the brownstone renovations were strictly private ventures. If the Atlantic Terminal Urban Renewal development had not been approved just prior to the federal cutback, there might have been no new residential construction in Fort Greene for years to come. As it is, the Atlantic Terminal program will provide only four hundred low-income apartments—not nearly enough to house all the poor who are being forced out of their apartments as the

brownstones and rooming houses in Fort Greene are renovated for middle-class use.

Where are the poor going? Mainly they are relocating in
neighboring Bedford-Stuyvesant and Prospect Heights. But
apartments are scarce all over, and in many cases an evicted
welfare family has to spend several weeks or months in a hotel
before they can find a new place to live. The hotel problem
is not so critical as it was a few years ago when so many welfare families were dumped into hotels and just forgotten for
a year or more. Now, as a result of strong public pressure, the
Department of Social Services is much more efficient about
getting families with children out of the hotels quickly.
Nevertheless, you can still see many children playing in the
lobby and on the street outside the Granada Hotel in Fort
Greene and around the many small hotels in nearby Brooklyn
Heights.

Once a welfare family has to move into a hotel for even a
short period of time, whatever stability or unity the family
had is likely to deteriorate rapidly. The children's schooling
is disrupted, and either they don't attend school at all while
they're living in the hotel, or they're thrust into a strange new
school where they have little motivation to "fit in" because
they know it's only temporary. Many welfare hotels have a
regular clientele of drug addicts and pushers, prostitutes, ex-
convicts, and ex-mental patients, and the welfare families are
forced into close everyday contact with these people. In addition, the ordeal of living in a cramped hotel room with young
children—without adequate cooking or refrigeration facilities
—puts an intolerable strain on a family.

One mother of three children who now lives in the Fort
Greene projects recalled the weeks she spent in the St. George
Hotel in Brooklyn Heights a few years ago as "the worst time
I ever had." She and her children had been forced out of their
apartment because of a fire, and they were given emergency

shelter in the St. George. But the days turned into weeks, and the family was unable to find another place to live. "Social Services wanted to send us to this apartment up in the Bronx," she said, "but I told them I wouldn't go. I don't know nothing about the Bronx. I'd lived in Brooklyn all my life, and I wanted to stay here. Only it was very hard for me to look for a place myself, because my kids were young and I couldn't drag them all around Brooklyn while I went looking. My youngest was only a baby then, and trying to take care of her in that hotel room was just terrible. They didn't have no refrigerator there, and just a kind of small hot plate for cooking. But I needed to keep things cold, like milk, so I would put the containers on this ledge outside the window. It was winter, and things stayed pretty cold. But one time I was reaching out to get the milk and I knocked a big can of juice off the ledge by accident. We was on the fifth floor, and the street down there was always full of people. So right away I jumped back from the window so no one should see me, and I thought, 'Oh, my god! I hope it don't hit no one.' You know, I was afraid that the people down there would think I threw it at them, and they'd come up and get me. But nothing happened after all.

"The four of us were living in that place for about three months, I guess. My oldest child was six, and he had been in the first grade where we used to live. But I didn't think we'd be in that hotel so long, and I just didn't put him into school around there. He didn't want to go anyhow, because he was scared of everything then. He just hung onto me all the time. He didn't want to go out to play or nothing. Anyhow, he missed a lot of school, and by the time he went back he was very far behind with his reading. A friend of mine finally found an apartment for us a couple of blocks away from my old house. It was really too small, and it was pretty broken down, but I would have taken anything to get out of that hotel. Then last year we moved into the projects here. We're living in building seven, and it's pretty nice. I guess it's about the best place I ever lived."

As bad as the hotels are for family living, they have been the only housing available for welfare recipients on an emergency basis. However, the Henry Street Settlement, in conjunction with the Department of Social Services, has been experimenting with a new type of emergency housing that could serve as a prototype for similar projects throughout the city. Called the Urban Family Center, the emergency housing units are located in a group of buildings in lower Manhattan that are operated by the New York City Housing Authority. These buildings are intended to provide decent temporary housing for homeless families who would otherwise be sent to welfare hotels.

The buildings can accommodate between sixty-two and eighty-eight families, depending on family size. A staff of about ten social workers from the Henry Street Settlement also live in the buildings so that they are available to provide services around the clock. Another fifteen people are maintenance workers. When poor families from Fort Greene or elsewhere are burned out of their homes, evicted, or left homeless for some other reason, they may be referred to the Urban Family Center by the Department of Social Services or the Department of Relocation. Homeless families can arrive at the center any hour of the day or night because there is always someone on hand to welcome them and help them get settled in one of the center's fully furnished apartments. Emergency food is also available at all times. One of the purposes of the center is to help these families find permanent homes, preferably in public housing, so families are not expected to remain at the Urban Center for longer than six months.

The Urban Family Center occupies two six-story old-style apartment buildings at 128 Baruch Place in Manhattan. The

director, Danny Kronenfeld, lives at the center along with
the rest of his staff. The relationship between the staff and
the welfare residents appears to be very close. Wherever Mr.
Kronenfeld goes, tenants call out to him, "Hi, Danny," and
many stop to talk for a few minutes. There is an intimacy
about the Urban Center that is totally lacking in any other
facility owned by the New York City Housing Authority or
even remotely connected with the Department of Social
Services. Formality and red tape do not seem to exist here,
and welfare tenants wander in and out of the center's office
with ease. The atmosphere is more like that of a comfortable
neighborhood clubhouse than a city facility, reflecting the
strong influence of its sponsor, the Henry Street Settlement.

"When people first come here, a lot of them are very defensive," said Danny Kronenfeld. "They think they're coming
into something that's run by the Department of Social
Services, so they're generally uptight. All their lives they've
had to deal with agencies that are not open and receptive to
their needs, so why should they see us as any different? Then
when they get here, they see we *are* different, and the suspicion and hostility disappear pretty quickly with most of
them. You see, they're given a decent apartment right away,
and they find they're welcome here. I mean, they really do
get a welcome when they come—there's always somebody here
to meet them, and it's a kind of open place. So the defensive-
ness usually disappears pretty quickly.

"Although the Department of Social Services has no control
over our day-to-day operations, we get all our money from
them. Welfare pays us the going hotel rate, which is five dollars per person per day. We're no cheaper than a hotel, but
for the same money our welfare families get furnished apartments with cooking and refrigeration facilities, plus all the
social services and counseling and recreation that we provide.
In addition, welfare doesn't have to pay restaurant allowances here as they do in a hotel. The families just collect their

regular welfare checks, except that their rent gets taken off their budget.

"The emphasis here is to help welfare people to continue functioning as *families*. We get the kids into school right away, and we try to make everyone feel like they're a part of our community for as long as they stay here. It's such a close setup that by the time a family is here for a week, they're very much a part of what's going on. They know the social workers and the social workers know them because everybody lives here together. It's not like they're going to an agency for counseling for an hour a week. Our workers really reach out to them. We're very aggressive, and we don't wait for the families to come to us.

"I think a lot of what had been seen as 'problem families' in the welfare hotels was the result of what happened to a family *because* it had to stay in a hotel, not because of how the family was before it got there. I think many families have been held together here who probably would have done much worse in a hotel.

"The way we're set up here is that we have apartments of all sizes to fit every family's needs. We even have five-bedroom apartments that can sleep ten or eleven people. These large units are made up of two two-bedroom apartments which are connected by a door. Most of the time this door is bolted shut, so that it's two separate units. But when we get a big family with eight kids or so, we open up the door so the whole family can fit into one place. We planned for this kind of flexibility when the buildings were renovated.

"Every apartment is fully equipped with furniture, linens, kitchen appliances such as a refrigerator and stove, pots and pans, dishes and silverware. In the empty apartments the beds are always made up so the place is ready whenever a family comes to us. Our facility is always open, and we can take in a family any time, day or night. And if a family comes to us after being in a welfare center all day and not eating, we can always give them something to eat.

"Our buildings are divided into six stairwells, and each one is like a small building in itself, because you can't go up one stairwell and cross over to apartments on another stairwell. You'd have to go back down and then come up on the other stairwell. So the Urban Center functions as if it were in six separate small buildings.

"A social worker is assigned to each stairwell, and he is responsible for the fifteen or so families who live in the apartments along that stairwell. The worker lives there, too, so he is always in contact with the families. Part of his job is to pull them all together into a stairwell council where they can thrash out their common problems, like if the stairwell is not being kept up well. Or the council may do things like plan a party for a family that's leaving.

"The first week that a family is with us, the worker spends a lot of time with them, helping them to settle in and helping them deal with some of the problems they may be having. He helps them fill out an application for a public housing project, so that gets into motion very quickly. Also, we have a licensed teacher here who's our liaison with the local schools. He visits the family the first week to make sure all the kids get registered in school.

"It's easier with the elementary school kids than with the junior high kids. The older ones don't seem to get hooked up to the school here as quickly as the younger kids, and a lot of them were just staying away because they couldn't adjust. Actually, a lot of them hadn't been able to make an adjustment to *any* school. What we did here was start our own junior high school for about fifteen kids who didn't want to go to the regular school. We went to the district superintendent and the local school board and had a teacher assigned to us. Our little minischool is considered an annex of the local junior high, and our kids get credit for all the courses they take. The attendance has been pretty good most of the time.

"We also have a youth program here. The Housing Authority let us have a basement lounge that we cleaned up and painted. It's open four afternoons a week for young kids, two evenings a week for teenagers, and two evenings a week for adults. It's a typical kind of lounge with Ping-Pong and dancing and pool. We also run an arts and crafts program in there.

"Some of the kids here are real problem kids, and we work with them more intensely than with the others. Our workers may get together with them in groups two or three times a week.

"There are some special problems in the Urban Center because it's so transient. But families do tend to stay about two, three, or four months, and they get to know each other very well. Friendships happen quickly here because the people feel they're all in the same boat. They've all been through a crisis, and they know that everyone else here has been through the same kind of thing. In many instances there's been a breaking down of racial and ethnic barriers much more quickly than you would see in another place. We've had a lot of white southern families who have gotten very close to black families here.

"Out of the first hundred families that came through here, about sixty percent were black, twenty-five percent were Puerto Rican, and fifteen percent were white. I would say racial tensions have been minimal. With one or two white families there were some racial overtones in relation to black families, but that was the exception rather than the rule.

"On the whole, there's a lot of visiting among families, lots of informal baby-sitting. Recently one of our mothers had a psychotic breakdown and we had to hospitalize her. Right away her three kids were taken in by other families who kept them for a week, until we were able to line up permanent homemaker service for the family.

"There is a lot of openness among families in the stairwells, but sometimes that in itself can be a problem. For example, on one stairwell the families got to know each other so well that there was almost an open door policy among them. But one of the families had a real problem kid who ripped off three or four of the other families. He just walked into their apartments and stole some things. This was a direct result of doors being open all the time, and kids being in and out of one another's houses.

"Aside from the incident with this one kid, there's been hardly any crime or violence here. It's very rare that we have incidents. Sometimes we get a mother who was having conflicts with her man back at home. Maybe there's been severe violence in the family, so she's taken the kids and left, and she winds up here. In cases like this, the man may come looking for her, and sometimes he catches up with her here. With these incidents we've gotten the police, but there's been very little internal crime.

"As far as drug use here, that has never become a public problem. If any drugs are used, it's done behind closed doors. I couldn't even venture to say if anybody is using drugs. A bigger problem is alcohol. There's about half a dozen families here with severe alcohol problems.

"We haven't legally evicted any families from here, but in two cases we did ask people to leave. There was this one family—a mother and five kids—who used to handle situations by pulling knives on other families. After this happened three times, we told the family they had a month to find another place and leave. And they did. They moved into private housing.

"Another couple with six kids used to let neighborhood derelicts bunk out in their apartment all the time. We gave them a certain period of time to clean that up, but they made no progress, so we asked them to leave. They also found private housing.

"We try to get our families into the low-income projects, and so far we've been able to place between thirty and forty percent of our people in public housing. Most of our people want to get into the public projects very badly, but they're not all eligible. For example, public housing won't take a welfare family that's had a history of poor money management, recent drug use, recent criminal records, or what they call 'socially undesirable traits'—which might mean an inability to handle their kids or things like that. These ineligible families can enter our housing preparation program, which deals with their social problems and helps prepare them for eventual placement in public housing.

"So far our largest families have *not* been our biggest problem families. Usually the worst trouble we have with them is getting them rehoused. The older public housing projects weren't built to handle really large families—like ten-person families—but some of the newer ones do have big apartments. We've been able to place all our large families in public housing so far, but it hasn't been easy.

"We've had only one family that's overstayed its six-month time limit, and it isn't even a large family. There are just three people in it. The main problem is their inability to pull themselves together to find a new place and leave here.

"We've placed a couple of families in the Fort Greene housing projects. Just recently we placed a young mother, Sylvia, who had come here with her little girl. Sylvia had grown up in institutions and foster homes, and she was a very lonely person. She got friendly with some of the people in the neighborhood here, and she used to bring them into her apartment. They really ripped her off. When she left here to move into the Fort Greene projects, welfare wouldn't give her any money for furniture. She had nothing at all. But sometimes the Urban Center gets calls from people who want to donate furniture to us, and we were able to give her a few things to get her started.

"About eighty percent of our welfare families here are one-parent families. But a lot of our two-parent families are in serious difficulty in that their relationships are quite strained. There have been a good number of cases in the center where either the husband walked out on the wife or the wife walked out on the husband. A lot of them really seem to be hanging together by a string, and if there's one thing we have to do more of here, it's family counseling. We have to find more ways of helping these people during the time when they're here.

"We have a lot of different programs going on right now. We have speakers coming down to talk about things like tenants' rights. One week we had a lawyer who spoke on welfare rights, and a lot of the women got so excited about it that they formed a welfare rights group. They've been meeting every week or so, and they've been discussing some important issues such as the proposal for giving welfare people a flat grant for rent. For some welfare recipients this would be a disaster, and our group wants to fight it. They've joined a neighborhood coalition which is also involved in fighting the flat grant. So you see, our people are really getting active and learning how to fight.

"We also have a health program here. We're hooked up with Gouverneur Hospital, and they service our people. They come down and register them for clinics. A month ago we had a mobile unit set up in our courtyard to do blood testing for sickle cell anemia. They've also done cancer testing here.

"Another area we'd like to get into a little more is helping our people with job training. We don't do a lot of this right now, but we have gotten some people into Manpower training programs. A couple of men got Class I chauffeur's licenses and jobs when they left here, so they've been able to get off welfare. We've gotten a couple of people into community colleges, and now we're beginning to work with a number of people who are interested in getting their high school equivalency degrees.

"A lot of people who come here would like to get off welfare, especially our young mothers. They would like to work if they could get some job training and child care. But there are others who don't have any ambition to get off welfare. It's hard to say whether it's a matter of feeling defeated, or whether they're just being realistic about what getting off welfare means if they have five or six kids."

If the Urban Family Center proves successful—and it certainly seems to be so far—it could serve as a model in setting up other emergency housing centers around the city. Such centers could replace welfare hotels entirely as far as families are concerned. Human Resources Administrator Jule M. Sugarman has said that his agency is also looking into the possibility of establishing a similar emergency housing facility for single persons who are still housed in welfare hotels, but this presents a larger problem because there are far more singles in the hotels than families.

At the formal opening of the Urban Family Center in December 1972, Simeon Golar, chairman of the New York City Housing Authority, said the center was "the best possible evidence that urban problems do not defy solution. We have brought together all of the required human services into a single well-organized place. When families face the horror of homelessness they now have a place to turn to—a place where the children can be enrolled in school, the entire family examined and treated medically, and a place where society can bring all of its social experience to bear on problems such as unemployment and antisocial behavior."

10

The Church in the Projects

YEARS ago, when Fort Greene was a heavily Italian neighborhood, the Church of St. Michael and St. Edward served as the focal point of religious life for Catholics in the community. The church building, which had been completed in 1902, stood out amidst the decayed housing and crumbling tenements that characterized the neighborhood. By the late 1930s, these buildings were among the worst slum housing in the city, and finally they were razed to make way for the Fort Greene housing projects.

Thousands of residents were evicted from their homes during the slum clearance, and the old church lost most of its parishioners for a time. The project buildings went up all around the church, dwarfing it, until it was completely enveloped within the sprawling public housing complex. But once the construction was complete, quite a few of the church's old parishioners moved back into the area, and many newcomers also became regular churchgoers, so St. Michael's and St. Edward's experienced a regeneration.

But this too was brief, for by the late 1940s the Italian Catholics began moving out of Fort Greene to the emptier, greener stretches of Brooklyn, where they bought private homes, or to the suburbs. Large numbers of blacks and Puerto Ricans took their places in the projects, so that by the start of the 1960s the Church of St. Michael and St. Edward found itself in the middle of a mainly nonwhite Protestant population. In the space of about a decade the old Catholic church had become irrelevant to its neighborhood—a white anachronism in the black ghetto of the Fort Greene projects. As one of the parish priests pointed out, "In this neighborhood, particularly, we are faced with the sad truth that we have almost no black or Hispanic ministers in the Roman Catholic Church."

Despite such handicaps, and in accordance with the widespread movement for change that has had such a shattering impact on the ancient traditions of the Catholic Church, St. Michael's and St. Edward's set out to become an integral part of the black community that surrounded it.

Beginning in the 1960s, its priests and nuns went out into the neighborhood and became involved in local politics and in campaigns to improve the schools, the hospitals, housing, and sanitation. If there was a community meeting to protest cutbacks in day-care services, the priests and nuns from St. Michael's and St. Edward's were there. If there was a demonstration to fight the closing of the BMT subway entrance near the projects, the priests could be found marching along with everyone else. If a board was set up to encourage new industry and more employment on the old Brooklyn Navy Yard site, the priests were involved. It was a merger of the sacred and the secular, reflected in the local church's avowed philosophy:

As committed Christians and concerned citizens, the gospel of Jesus Christ compels us:
  • To deepen our prayer life through the reading of the Bible daily and attending Mass each Sunday . . . [and] to register every eligible voter within the next six months;

- To accept the sacred responsibility of instructing our own children in the life of the Church . . . [and] to develop the housing project so that tenants will own and manage it for the well-being of families and senior citizens;
- To search our hearts for a sign of a special call from God to serve Him and our neighbors as dedicated religious people . . . [and] to establish a bail fund from the voluntary donations of our parishioners.

The significance of such secular activism is that it stems from an institution that is indigenous to the community—the local church—and is not dependent on funding from the federal, state, or city government. Almost all other agencies for social change in Fort Greene depend for their very existence on government money, so their activities are circumscribed by government policy. Only the church and the Willoughby House Settlement are wholly independent forces.

On the outside, the Church of St. Michael and St. Edward is still an imposing structure that stands out in sharp contrast to the uniformity of all the red-brick project buildings that surround it. But inside, the church's shabbiness is immediately apparent. With its cracked walls and faded, peeling paint, there can be no doubt that this is a poor church serving a poor community.

Nevertheless, there are several decorating touches that compensate for the lack of finery and at the same time make the church look far less formal than most Catholic churches. For example, an assortment of colorful flags hangs from wires that are stretched across the walls, including the American flag, the black liberation flag, and the Puerto Rican flag. A very long wooden divider—its many shelves covered with potted plants and flowers—stands a little distance behind the altar and serves as a backdrop.

But the showpiece of the church is the altar itself. Actually, this is a very odd-looking piece that most people find strangely familiar yet unrecognizable. Its identity comes as quite a surprise—the altar is actually made from a pillar of the old Myrtle Avenue El. As the church stated, "Our altar . . . is a visible sign of what we hope to do in every aspect of parish life. In dedicating the altar, we transformed something which was rather offensive into a symbol of hope. We found the sacred in the secular."

For the handful of old-time white parishioners who still live in Fort Greene and still attend St. Michael's and St. Edward's along with their black and Puerto Rican neighbors, the transformation of the church has been a little hard to take, particularly since the religious services have also been revamped and modernized. As one traditional, devoutly Catholic woman remarked, "I can accept all those political flags and that ugly altar, and I suppose I'll get used to the new things they do in the Mass, but every so often they replace the choir with a group of kids who sing that awful, loud rock music and even play guitars—right in church! That's just too much for me."

The church's main thrust at present is in the political arena. In its "state of the parish" report for 1973, titled, "I Am the Vine . . . You Are the Branches," the church noted, "At the heart of all we get involved in, to really show that we have a purpose and are united, we must develop political power. We will embark on a voter registration drive. Up to now, all the politicians could afford to ignore us because enough of us do not vote. If more of us voted in Fort Greene, then they would have to do more things for us.

"We would then be able to establish meaningful contacts in agencies and offices which attempt to control our lives. The housing office, the schools, the hospitals, the police department are but a few agencies where we will be heard. The possibilities are limitless.

"This parish will soon sponsor a workshop for political and community activity. This will deal with the past injustices, the present controversies, and the future possibilities of creative, *radical* change.

"We will support that person for public office who lives and works in this community and who is sensitive to the needs of the black and Hispanic people. He must be aware of the horror of watching our young people systematically murdered by those drug traffickers who are known to us and to the authorities. He must be aware of the horror of watching our youngsters systematically destroyed by an oppressive educational system which lacks understanding of the culture and background of the individual. He must be aware of the horror of watching all our people systematically degraded by an overwhelming and overriding disregard of basic human services by the city government, including:

- Welfare offices that require the poor to betray their human dignity;
- City hospitals that give lip service in place of medical service to the health needs of all our people;
- A sanitation department that picks and chooses the time of cleaning our streets;
- A park that instills a sense of fear rather than a sense of beauty in all who pass along its glass-strewn walks;
- A library that often fails to open when many citizens would like to make use of it;
- A Housing Authority that oversees buildings where terror rules the halls, where elevators often don't work, where incinerators spout forth smoke into a community that has the highest rate of tuberculosis in the city;
- Police services that are ineffective among our people who are driven to bolt their doors though they wish to dwell in peace, who dread going outside though they desire to walk in security, who become suspicious of

their neighbors though they long to share in a thriving community life."

The church estimates that between fifteen and twenty percent of the people who regularly attend its Masses on Sundays are not Catholic, just as the majority of the people in Fort Greene are not Catholic. Nevertheless, many of them send their children to the church's Sunday school to get a religious education. The situation is very much the same in the Farragut projects, where the local church was also built to serve a white Catholic population that moved away shortly after the projects went up.

St. Michael's and St. Edward's prints all its publications in English and Spanish and conducts services in both languages. The pastor is Father Anthony Failla, who is assisted by two very young-looking priests, Father Brian Callahan and Father George Wilders. Three nuns are also assigned to the church, but they live in Wallabout Houses—the low-income cooperative near the old Brooklyn Navy Yard—rather than in the rectory.

All of them are involved in the affairs of the communi.y, as well as church affairs. Father Failla is chairman of Community Planning Board No. 2, which includes the downtown Brooklyn area, the Atlantic Terminal Urban Renewal area, all of Fort Greene, and the Navy Yard Industrial Park. (Each of the city's community planning boards is responsible for determining its area's long-range needs in terms of schools, housing, commerce, etc.)

Father Callahan was elected by people in the community to the mental health advisory board for Cumberland Hospital. This advisory board was practically forced upon the hospital by the people in the area because they felt Cumberland was so unresponsive to their needs and had so few services for the mentally and emotionally disturbed.

Father Wilders is involved in the Fort Greene Federal

Credit Union—a cooperative plan whereby the joint savings of all members are used to make low-interest loans to any member who requests one for a specific purpose.

One of the nuns, Sister Sheila, works on the board of Project Teen-Aid to help pregnant schoolgirls. She and Sister Georgianna also .work with senior citizens, holding monthly social functions in the church basement and visiting elderly people in their homes. Sister Sally teaches classes in English for Spanish-speaking people.

In talking with the dedicated young priests and nuns of St. Michael's and St. Edward's, you get the feeling that they are far more concerned with social and political causes than with religious ones. Father Wilders greets visitors to the rectory dressed in a pullover sweater and slacks, so unless they already know who he is, they start out asking dubiously, "Are you a priest?" His manner, too, seems very unpriestly, very earthy, as he sits back and discourses on all the problems facing the Fort Greene community.

FATHER WILDERS

"Most of the bad things you hear about Cumberland Hospital are true. There are also good things going on in there, but in general they offer very poor health service. I remember one time a guy was shot up at the corner, right by the church, and we took him over to the hospital. At first we thought we could carry him there on a stretcher because the hospital is so close, the housing police wouldn't give us one. They also wouldn't take him over in a police car because they said the city could be sued. So we called an ambulance. It was forty-five minutes before it came—even though the hospital is just a block away. But finally we got him in there.

"Now this guy had a bullet through his heart, and that kind of emergency is supposed to take precedence over everything else. But the hospital wanted his Blue Cross number first, or his Medicaid card, and they were filling out all these forms. Meanwhile the guy's lying on the table unconscious and nobody's doing anything. So we started cursing and screaming, and then they started doing things for him. But he died on the table.

"Another time an elderly lady in the projects here thought she had pneumonia, so one of the sisters took her to Cumberland for X rays. Well, three or four weeks went by and the lady couldn't find out the results of her X rays. Finally, the hospital told her they had lost them. If she actually had pneumonia she could have died from it because of the hospital's negligence.

"What we're doing now is trying to get people to come together at the grass-roots level to put pressure on the hospital to give good service. We've already gotten Cumberland to agree to having an advisory board elected by the people in the community for all policies and programs relating to mental health. Cumberland didn't want these elections, but it had to have them. This was the first time the people actually had a voice in what the hospital was doing.

"The church's involvement in all this puts pressure on the hospital. We know who to call, whereas most people don't. People feel helpless when they're dealing with a big institution like a hospital, but actually they're not helpless. People can make a difference here on housing, health, and schools if they would only get together, if they would register to vote. That way they would have an influence on politicians.

"I think people around here are getting a little more organized now. Of course, there are nowhere near enough people involved in these things. Most people keep to themselves; they don't get involved. They live as if they're in a prison. They lock their doors and they don't even know who lives next door or on the same floor.

"In these projects here, the people don't have any say at all about the housing conditions. They're at the mercy of the Housing Authority. There are a lot of maintenance problems, like, sometimes the elevators work and sometimes they don't work. The maintenance people are very nice and they try to be helpful, but they're understaffed. The city had a job freeze on, so anytime a maintenance worker left he wasn't replaced.

"I'll tell you something, though. There are three or four maintenance workers here who also live here, right in the projects. You can tell which buildings they live in, because those buildings are cleaner than any of the others and the landscaping is nicer. The workers take care of those buildings more because it's their own homes. Eventually all these buildings should be turned into a low-income co-op, where the people who live in them also own them. That way they'll have control over their housing conditions.

"But even the way the buildings are now, they're a step up from a horrible tenement. At least they look better. Of course, the apartments here are all pretty much the same. All the rooms are small, and everyone has a living room/dining room combination.

"The worst part is, the people live in fear. Crime may be down, but the fear is still there. Things were really bad around 1970. That was a bad year. We had several speak-outs against all the crime. People put pressure on the housing police, and for a while they were more visible. But don't forget, the police cover three projects with close to twenty thousand people living in them. I figured out once that the police have only enough men to average one and a half police-men per tour for each of the three projects—and this one and a half includes the guy who's in the office answering the phone. With so few men, they can't patrol these projects the way they're supposed to under the public housing law.

"We haven't had any problems in the church with van-dalism or anything like that, although there was this one kid who was a pyromaniac, and he lit a couple of fires in the church. On the whole, though, there isn't any destruction. Also, there's no graffiti in the church.

"Kids will come in here and run around sometimes, because a lot of them don't know what a church is. One time some of them saw the poor box where people drop in change, and it said on the boxes, 'For the Poor.' These kids were seven or eight years old, and they read the sign and figured, 'That's us.' So they took the money.

"Just a little while ago there was this one kid who didn't like the way all our plants were arranged on this big wooden structure that's set up behind the altar, like a breakfront. So he came in and rearranged them. He put them all over the church, on the furniture, on ledges, on the floor. This wasn't a sneaky thing, because he told us what he did, and he said, 'Isn't it a lot better this way?' It took us two full days to find all those plants afterward.

"The schools around here do a lot of damage to the kids. Kids with good intelligence are destroyed. A lot of our kids go to Sands Junior High School, and so many of them are just consumed by it. Oh, it's unbelievable. Sands opened about ten or twelve years ago and immediately it was like a zoo. Really bad. Then in 1967 a new principal came in. He had a very good reputation—he was very well respected and well liked, and the people here were happy because they thought he'd bring some order into the school. But it's still a zoo, and the kids aren't learning anything. The kids are looking for discipline, so they act out. The teachers are young and inexperienced. The turnover of teachers is enormous. As soon as they get a chance, off they go to some other place. There are very few people there from year to year.

"We've had mothers come to the church telling us they're afraid because their kids are about to graduate from P.S. 67 and they're going to be sent to Sands. The mothers tell us, 'At Sands my child is going to be hurt,' or 'My daughter is going to be raped.' They want to get their kids into St.

James, which is a parochial school not too far from here, but there just isn't enough room for everyone.

"The elementary schools around here aren't that bad, although they have a very high turnover of teachers, too. In P.S. 67, across the street from the church, I would guess that the turnover is about eighty percent every year. But it's not really so bad, because there are a lot of paraprofessionals who work in the school—they're mothers from the neighborhood —and they stay with a class all the way through, from the first grade through the sixth grade. They break in the new teachers. The kids listen to them more than to the teachers, and a lot of the time they're effective in teaching the kids. So the discipline is a little better than it would be otherwise, if the mothers weren't there.

"Then there's P.S. 307 over in the Farragut projects. That was a More Effective School with a lot of innovative programs —until its funds were cut. You know, you don't mind when funds are cut from a program that isn't doing anything, but here kids were really learning to read and write, and all of a sudden—*whoosh*—out went the funds. You see, 307 had special grants from some kind of new reading program, and from what I heard the thing was working. The kids were at the level they were supposed to be in reading. But no more. It's all over now because of the cutbacks.

"We've been trying to get some of the older kids in our parish into the New Catholic High School, which is in Bedford-Stuyvesant. This school was set up three years ago, and it's the kind of place that's designed for the student. Everything is geared to individualized work. Kids go at their own pace under the guidance of teachers. So far we've gotten about thirty-five students into this school, and almost every one of them has really produced.

"The school has an internship program where kids can work on a specific project in the community for a week at a time—say, in a day-care center or a hospital—then go back to

school the next week and report on their project. They alter-
nate between school work and community work.

"One of the kids who we got into this high school graduated from Sands Junior High with a second grade level of
reading. He had above-average intelligence, but he was very
tight, very repressed—the kind of kid who would wind up in
jail in another year. Or else he might have killed somebody
or killed himself. That's how much tension was in him. And
a big part of his problem was caused by the schools he'd been
to. He just couldn't read. He's been in New Catholic High
School for about seven months now, and already he's up to a
fifth-grade reading level.

"This same kid also couldn't do any arithmetic in school.
He couldn't add, divide, or anything. Yet he had a newspaper
route where he did all kinds of bookkeeping. He knew who
owed him how much, or who was paid up ahead on their bills
—all kinds of fantastic bookkeeping. Yet in school he couldn't
do simple arithmetic. So the teacher has been using money to
teach him arithmetic, showing him how it's all the same thing.
Now he's doing pretty good in arithmetic, too. He's succeed-
ing in a lot of ways. He's on the swimming team and he's won
some medals. He's very proud of himself.

"I've seen changes like this in almost all of the thirty-five or
so kids from this parish who have gone to that high school.
Oh, of course a couple of them are just biding their time and
not doing much, but most are getting a lot out of it.

"Another good high school is Project Teen-Aid. Sister
Sheila works with that, and I think it is probably the best
poverty program in the city. That is, its money comes from
poverty funds. Now, on the whole, most of the criticism that
you hear about the poverty program is true. There's a lot of
money being wasted in it. But this Project Teen-aid has been
spending everything it gets for good, productive programs,
and if the funds are cut off, that'll probably be the end of it.

"Most of the pregnant girls in the school come from Fort

Greene, and others from Bed-Stuy and elsewhere. The school is really their salvation and makes it a very happy occasion for them to have a baby. When the girls first go there, they're very depressed, very down. They're pregnant and down. But the school gives them the tools to enable them to become strong people. There's an awful lot of girls who are saved each year by that school and turned into productive people. Comes graduation time, they don't want to leave. They're all tears. Listen, they found a school where they could be happy.

"Another good thing that came out of the poverty program was the Neighborhood Youth Corps. They would pay kids about thirty dollars a week to do some kind of work in the community during the summertime. The whole thing was meant to be a good working experience, so that after a year or two a kid would really know what's involved in working at a job. But each year fewer and fewer kids have been hired. It's all part of the cutbacks.

"Two years ago they hired kids in the Youth Corps to run a voter registration drive. The kids went around to all the apartments in the projects, and many times they knew somebody was in, but the person just wouldn't open the door or talk to them. They'd just look out the peephole. It was a very frustrating experience for the kids.

"They also set up a table downstairs in the street to try to get people to register, but this wasn't much good either. I think the twenty fellows and girls in the program each got only three or four people to register. But the kids learned something from this experience, because afterward they kept talking about 'How can we do it better?' You see, the registration around here is very low, and the voting is even lower.

"Probably the saddest situation here involves the senior citizens. There must be about two thousand elderly people living here in the projects, and nobody knows who most of them are. An awful lot of them live by themselves.

"There is a Senior Citizens Center in the projects right

around the corner from the church, and it's a very good thing for those who are healthy enough to walk over to it. They can get a free hot lunch there, which is very good and nutritious. But a lot of elderly people are too feeble or too frightened to leave their apartments very often. They don't have any communication with anyone, and many of them have been totally abandoned by their relatives. Sometimes they can go for days being sick, and nobody knows about it.

"To help these people we started 'Telecare'—a phone service for senior citizens in Fort Greene. We're asking volunteers to put in an hour or two every day just making phone calls to the elderly, to find out if they're alive and how they're feeling and whether they need anything. Some of our volunteers are senior citizens themselves, and they're fantastic as far as knowing who the other old people are. They're our prime source in getting up a list of elderly people in the projects.

"Our goal is to have every senior citizen get a call every day. They all have phones, even if they're on welfare, because with old people that's considered a necessity. Volunteers can come here to make calls to the elderly, or they can do it from their own homes. But if they use their own phones they don't have to make more than one call a day. We don't want this to be a financial burden on them. They can just pick one elderly person who they'll call every day—sort of like an 'adopt a senior citizen' program.

"Also, we have an extra telephone line here at the rectory just for senior citizens, so if there's an emergency they always have a number to call. We've mailed out this number to every elderly person on our list.

"Once a month we have a bingo game for the elderly down in the church basement. We get a crowd of about a hundred or so each time, and the noise is unbelievable. They like to play bingo and they really have a good time. It's a social thing. The first time, we put out a lot of different prizes, all nicely wrapped up. But we saw that the only things the old people were really interested in were the food prizes, like chicken, canned ham, coffee, and eggs. So this is what we give out now, and we hold the bingo game about three or four days before the Social Security checks come.

"All of us here at the church are involved in some sort of community program. I handle 'Telecare,' and I also work with the credit union. We started that about three years ago in conjunction with the Federal Credit Union System. There are about thirty people in it now who have pooled their money and amassed a fund of about seven thousand dollars in communal savings. Members can get loans from the fund for things like medical bills or furniture. Anyone can join who works in the area. It's a very solid thing because all the deposits are insured federally. People on welfare can belong to it, too. In fact, they're the best payers when they take a loan. Most of the members are very low income people, and they all do their best to pay off a loan. The worst repayers are three people who work in the poverty program. One is making twelve or thirteen thousand dollars. I don't know what's the matter with her, but she just can't seem to put her money away.

"The credit union is good because it enables poor people to get a loan for a big purchase—they don't have to buy on some installment plan where they pay exorbitant interest rates. I think that on the whole people around here are getting smarter about shopping. Even in things like food. A lot of people don't just rely on the local stores anymore. They get together and form car pools, and they go out to Pathmark in Coney Island, or to supermarkets in Flatbush or Queens, and they'll shop for a week or two weeks. Those stores out there have a bigger variety of stuff, and it's better and cheaper, too.

"Not too many people go to the A&P on Myrtle Avenue anymore. I think when that store's lease is up they're going to pull out. A few years ago the people in the community had a big meeting with two vice-presidents from A&P, a representative from the city's Consumer Affairs Department, and people from Operation Breadbasket who were conducting a boycott of A&P. One of the complaints against the store was that the things the chain listed on sale in the newspapers were being sold at the regular price in the Myrtle Avenue store. If a customer showed the manager the newspaper ad, he'd mark the item down for that customer. But anyone who didn't know about the special from the ads would pay the regular price.

"Also there were complaints that the chain would take left-over vegetables and fruits that it couldn't sell in its other stores in middle-class neighborhoods and bring them to Myrtle Avenue. So we would get the stuff here two days later. We would also see frozen foods sitting in the aisles, dripping, defrosted, and then they'd throw them into the freezer.[1]

"At that meeting the people from A&P just couldn't say anything. They couldn't answer any of these complaints. And, of course, the biggest complaint was about the guard in the Myrtle Avenue store. He was carrying a gun, which was against the law, and he didn't have a permit for it. He had killed a guy in the store for taking five pounds of potatoes. After that incident, nobody was in that store for a couple of weeks. I said *nobody*. After a while business picked up a little, but still it's nowhere near Finast.

"Finast is a little better place, although they got problems there, too. But you see, everybody knows Joe, the manager. He hires all kinds of kids from around here, and after people have gone shopping there once or twice they know his name. He talks to everybody."

---

[1] Many of the charges against A&P were never actually proven. Nevertheless, people in the neighborhood tended to *believe* they were true, rightly or wrongly.

11

The Elderly

THE "regulars" start drifting into the Fort Greene Senior Citizens Center about 9:30 or 10:00 A.M. A few of them settle down in battered old easy chairs in the front room, talking to no one, while others cluster together in animated, noisy little groups. They all know each other, for they spend all their days in the center, talking and gossiping. Most of them have nowhere else to go in their old age.

The center occupies a few small rooms in the basement of one of the buildings in the Fort Greene projects. It serves as the central gathering place for the elderly, most of whom live just a short walk away in the surrounding buildings. For many of them, the center is much more of a home than their solitary apartments, and they dread weekends when their "club" is closed.

The conversation in the rooms ranges from chitchat about friends and relatives to arguments over politics. A squat, white-haired woman of about eighty is describing a trip to Jerusalem she took years ago. A man in the next room is shaking his head and muttering to someone over a news story he just read about a ten-year-old boy who was shot by the police. Another man is talking about how President Nixon "has spies everywhere." There are many more women than men in the center, and some of them work on their sewing or knitting while they talk. Here and there someone wanders around as if in a daze, not fully aware of what's going on.

As the morning wears on, the enticing aroma of hot food permeates the small rooms, and by 11:30 quite a few more elderly people begin drifting into the center. Unlike the earlier crowd of "regulars," most of the newcomers keep to themselves. They don't seem to know many people. They have come only for the hot lunch, and they quietly take seats at several long tables in the lunchroom. For some, this will be their only meal of the day. Although the lunch is free, almost all the old people drop a little change into the contribution box so they can help pay for the center's activities. By donating their nickel, dime, or quarter every day they feel they are not receiving charity when they eat at the center.

About twelve o'clock, lunch is ready. The people fill up their plates with soup, fish cakes, stewed tomatoes, corn, and bread and butter. A coffee urn stands in the middle of the room where everyone can help himself to as many cups as he wants. During the meal, the conversation tapers off to a low murmur as people fix their attention on the food.

Afterward, most of the newcomers leave immediately, while others stay on for the afternoon classes given at the center. The janitor, a young black man of about twenty-five, cleans up the lunchroom. While he works, he explains that he is a Vietnam veteran who "took this job because it was the only thing I could get when I came back from 'Nam." He is very bitter. "People think of us vets as animals," he says. "They're afraid of us and don't want to hire us. This work is just something I'm doing for now, but I'm looking around for other things. In school I got training as an electrician, but I hear you got to pay about fifteen hundred dollars if you want to get into the electricians' union. So you can't do that kind of work unless you got some money to start with."

The afternoon class is an English lesson on "How to Write a Letter." About sixteen elderly people sit around one of the long tables in the lunchroom listening to a very young, pretty teacher explain the fundamentals of letter-writing. The teacher comes from New York City Community College a few blocks away, which has an Institute for Older Adults. All but two of the people in the class are women, and all but one are black. The only person in the group who is not a "regular" is the lone white woman, an Armenian who speaks very broken English. She usually leaves right after lunch, but today she has stayed for the letter-writing class because she wants to write to her daughter in Detroit.

Most of the people participate freely in the class discussion, and the most outspoken of all is Sam, a lean, agile, gray-haired man who says he is in his seventies but looks barely sixty. He is the president of the center.

When the class is over, two or three people leave, but the others stay for the rest of the afternoon, reluctant to depart until they must at 5:00 P.M. They will be back the next day.

The Fort Greene Senior Citizens Center is sponsored by several different groups. The staff—including the director, the assistant director, the cooks, and the custodial workers—is hired by the Department of Social Services. The New York City Housing Authority supplies the space, and the Willoughby House Settlement helps out with activities. The free lunch program is paid for by funds from the federal government.

The center has an enrollment of 242 members, but the daily average attendance is 58. However, enough food is always on hand so that if an unusually large crowd shows up for lunch, everyone can be served. The only requirement for membership is that a person be at least sixty years old.

The center helps elderly people with such things as applying for Medicaid, or for special subway and bus passes which enable them to ride for half-fare. Among the regular activities are arts and crafts classes, a sewing group, a nutrition class, bingo, piano lessons, a newspaper committee, a drama group, a choral group, and outings to such places as the aquarium.

Things are very slow at the center on the first and the sixteenth of every month when most of the old people stay home waiting for their welfare checks to arrive. Then they venture out to the stores to cash their checks and stock up with food. This can be a hazardous journey, because many teenagers lurk around the projects on check days, stalking elderly victims who might have a little welfare money in their pockets. The same is true on the third of every month, when the Social Security checks arrive.

Most elderly people at the center are on Social Security, but since they worked at very low paying jobs all their lives, or jobs that weren't included under Social Security until the last ten or fifteen years, their monthly checks are very small—too small to live on. That's why the majority are also eligible for supplementary welfare checks from the city. However, a few are just too proud to apply for welfare, and they manage to subsist on minimal Social Security payments. For them the free lunch program at the center is vital. (Those who receive average or larger Social Security checks are not even eligible for supplementary welfare payments, even though they too are desperately poor.)

Beginning in January 1974, the federal government took full charge of welfare assistance for people over sixty-five as part of its Social Security program. A welfare supplement for those who qualify is included in the monthly Social Security checks, thus erasing the stigma of "charity" associated with welfare.

Ironically, for some elderly people the recent increments in their Social Security checks proved detrimental. The small amount of extra money they received pushed them over the income limits for Medicaid and, in some cases, even for food stamps. The combined value of Medicaid and food stamps is far greater than the amount of their Social Security raise, so those people are worse off than before. They still have Medicare coverage, of course, but this pays only about forty-two percent of all medical expenses, whereas Medicaid covers everything, even drug prescriptions.

Many of the elderly people in Fort Greene live alone, victims of a highly mobile society. Their sons and daughters, nieces and nephews have all moved away, and they have been left behind. It is very rare nowadays to find several generations of one family living in the same neighborhood, even in a community as poor as Fort Greene. The young may not necessarily be moving to the suburbs, but they are looking for better neighborhoods, better opportunities elsewhere. Upward mobility does exist in poverty areas, but for the elderly who can't share in it, it only means increasing isolation.

Many of the people in the Fort Greene Senior Citizens Center mention children they never see anymore because they've moved so far away. And even if the elderly have a chance to move with them, very often they don't want to go. They are afraid they won't be comfortable in strange new surroundings, totally dependent on their children. So they stay where they are, spending their days in the center with other elderly people and reflecting on their neighborhood as it used to be. All of them live in fear now, because they are the main victims of the thieves and muggers who roam the projects. In addition, many of them have gone through the experience sometime in their lives of being uprooted from their homes by the city in the interests of urban renewal. Although they were supposed to ultimately benefit from such renewal, they seem to feel their lives were better before the city stepped in to "upgrade" their old neighborhoods.

204 ☆ *Fort Greene, U.S.A.*

SAM

"When I first came to live here a long time ago, there wasn't no projects yet, just a lot of old houses and shacks. I used to deliver ice and coal to people. I'd haul it all around town. This was a very safe neighborhood then. Very safe. It was all mixed around here. There were black people, Jewish people, Irish people, Italian people. All kinds. We all lived together here, and it was all right. You didn't see any muggings or things like that. There might be kids fighting once in a while, but there wasn't no snatching pocketbooks, no dope. Now there's nothing but dope.

"In those days Fort Greene Park was beautiful. Today it's all run down. People are scared to go in there 'cause if they do they could get mugged or even killed. But years ago on hot nights in the summer we used to go up to that park to sleep. The grass grew nice and green, everything was so clean. We'd take our blankets up there, but we'd have to get there early to make sure we got a good spot. I mean, you could hardly find a place to lay your blanket down in that park, there was so many people who used to go there. The place would be packed. Then we'd all go to sleep. Sometimes we'd wake up and it'd be pouring rain.

"But then people started moving away. Some people went to New York, some started moving uptown. When they started tearing down all the old buildings so they could put up the projects, that split up the whole neighborhood. I moved away to another part of Brooklyn. Later on I moved in with one of my daughters, but after a while she sold her house and moved out to Long Island. I didn't want to go to Long Island, so I put in for the projects. You see, all my kids had got married and moved out, and they got babies of their own. That left me and my wife alone. So I put in for the projects, and finally I came back here, to the place where I was raised. This was in the early 1960s, and I had been away from here more than twenty years.

"When I first came back it wasn't so bad. There wasn't so much dope, and it was still a little bit of a mixed neighborhood. Nobody was sleeping out in Fort Greene Park anymore, but the park wasn't too bad in the daytime. People used to go there on weekends and holidays to play basketball and tennis. A band used to come up there sometimes, and there would be dancing in the park. It was real nice.

"But then the dope started coming in heavy, and that's what made the neighborhood bad. This was around 1968. I don't know how it became so bad so fast. Everywhere you go now it's bad. You can't run away from it."

ADA

"I've been in Fort Greene all my life. That's sixty-seven years. I was born in this neighborhood, on Fleet Place. It's called Fleet Walk now because it's inside the projects, but before the projects went up it was called Fleet Place. I lived in a building that had three floors and a basement and a front stoop. The toilet was in the yard.

"Around 1940 we all had to move from here 'cause they knocked all them old shacks down. There wasn't nothing around here but shacks, and you had them pushcarts all along Myrtle Avenue where you could buy onions and potatoes and everything. Those were the good old days. Oh, we had a few rats running around the houses, but I'd rather live in that time than this. Then you weren't afraid to walk the street any time of night you wanted. You weren't afraid someone would snatch your pocketbook. We were safer then. Certainly we were. If anyone came over to you and said something to you, all you'd have to do is start hollering and he'd be *gone*. But not nowadays.

"People got along a lot better, too. There wasn't what you call no racial trouble. I went to school with Italians, Jews,

Polacks, Spanish. It was all mixed. I played many a day in an Italian mother's house, and her children would come over to my mother's house. If any of us children did something wrong, and any of the mothers saw us, they'd hit us and send us home.

"For instance, if I was being bad out on the street and your mother saw me, she'd make me go home. Then when she seen my mother, especially on Saturdays when they'd all be shopping and getting their vittles for the whole week, your mother would say, 'I seen your daughter and she was doing this and that.' And then my mother would come home and say to me, 'Sadie says she seen you. What was you doing?' And if I tried to say I hadn't done nothing, my mother would say, 'Oh, so she's lying, is she? You got so big now you can call her a liar?' And I would get punished for whatever I did. That's the way it was with everybody then.

"But nowadays you can't put your finger on these kids, you can't punish them now. That's why they're so bad. And you can't talk to their parents, neither. No, indeed. I said to this one mother yesterday, 'Look what your child is doing. He's pulling the little trees and bushes down.' And she says, 'Well, my child ain't the only one out there doing that.' So I said, 'Don't you worry about the others. You talk to your child and maybe the others will take lessons from him.' But she couldn't see it.

"Anyhow, when they tore down all the shacks around here, I moved to a place very far down on Myrtle Avenue. I stayed there until I was able to move back into the projects. My new apartment was much more sanitary than what I had lived in before in Fort Greene. It was much more airy, and the rent was lower, too. Anyhow, it was at first. Gradually it kept going up.

"For the first twelve years or so I lived in Building Nine. Then this Spanish lady's apartment caught on fire, and our whole floor had to move out. You see, the fire came out into the hall, and the paint on the walls was all burned. If that lady hadn't left her door open the fire never would have spread. She also had her windows open, and the wind just carried the fire all over. The firemen said it was the old paint on the walls that helped spread it. I was really scared 'cause my door got sealed and I couldn't get out. They had to take crowbars and break the door to get me out. All the apartments on the floor got a lot of smoke and water, and then the beams buckled. That's why we all had to get out. So I moved over to Building Two.

"Oh, I been around here a long, long time. When I was a little girl I went to the Number Five school. That's been turned into Brooklyn Tech High School now, but then it was a grammar school. Sam went there, too. That's how long we've known each other. It was a nice school. My son grew up here and went to school here, too. He was my only son, but he got killed. When my sister's kids were growing up they got along pretty well in the schools. It was better then than now, with all the dope and stealing. Her kids are all grown and married now, and they don't live around here no more. But my aunt still got a home over on Ashland Place. It's a brownstone, and it's right next door to that casket company, between DeKalb and Fulton.

"The neighborhood is terrible now. I mean real terrible. You're not safe in your own house. You know, I'm scared to even go to my incinerator. I haven't been robbed yet, thank God, but I've had boys knocking on my door trying to get me to open it. Just the other night some boys knocked on my door and one of them says, 'Here's your paper, lady.' I said, 'I didn't order no paper,' and he says, 'Well, open the door and see.' I said, 'Uh, uh. I don't want no paper.' And they kept insisting I open the door, but I wouldn't do it. That's a common trick. They do it all the time.

"You're not even safe in the stores. Yesterday I was with this lady in the A&P. We was looking at the steaks and I was saying, 'Oh my god! It's cheaper to eat your money than to buy this meat.' Anyway, I got a little steak for a dollar or so, and she got something, and while we were talking this little boy got in between her and me. Then another little boy who was with him says to this lady, 'Excuse me, but you shouldn't buy that steak. You see that white lump in there? That's fat.' And she says, 'Well, I know it's fat,' and she went off to the check-out counter. But when she looked for her food stamps in her coat pocket, they wasn't there. The boy who got in between us must have been picking her pocket, and the other boy started talking to her so she wouldn't notice. So she didn't have no stamps, and she had to pay for the things with money she had otherwise. It cost her $20.50. The stamps that was stolen from her was worth eighteen dollars.

"They have a cop in that A&P, but I don't know what he does. If he sees kids in there not buying anything he should throw them out. What do they have a cop there for if he can't keep them kids out?

"The stores around here are no good. Like some of those furniture stores on Myrtle Avenue. You got to be very careful with them. When I buy anything there I always pay in cash. Once I bought a washing machine at one of those stores on Myrtle and I paid $165. Only a day or two later I saw the exact same washing machine at Friendly Frost for $113. It was the same make, same style, same everything. So I goes back to Myrtle Avenue and I tells the owner of the store what I saw, and he calls up Friendly Frost to find out if it's true. They tell him, 'Yes, we're selling that machine for $113.' But he wouldn't give me back the difference anyhow, and he wouldn't take the machine back.

"His store is bad enough, but Mullins is worse. That's the last store I would buy in. I don't think their furniture is quality stuff at all. Cardboard. J. Michael's is another bad place. I ordered a breakfast set there. It was a set I had seen in the store, but instead of sending me that set, they sent me a different one. I complained, but they told me, 'Oh, no. That's the set you bought.' And I said, 'No, it isn't. The set I bought had an edging on it. This set don't have no edging.' But they wouldn't do nothing about it. It wasn't a bad set. It lasted quite a while. Only it wasn't the model I ordered.

"I come to this center every day except Saturday and Sunday. There's a nice group of elderly people here. I'm one of the oldest members—not in age, but in attendance. I started coming when it was just a little place in the basement of the library in the projects. Then it moved to two other places in the projects. It wasn't run by Social Services then. It was private. I think Willoughby House started it.

"When I leave here, I go straight home. I don't open my door no more unless one of the neighbors comes over. And they better call me on the phone first, because if they knock on my door and I don't recognize their voices, I just don't open the door.

"We used to have a choral group down here that met in the evenings. We was all scared to go home afterwards, and one lady used to call the Youth Patrol on Myrtle Avenue to get someone to walk her home. But I say what's the sense of them walking you to your door downstairs when you still got to go in the halls? The halls are the worst yet. At least when you be outside you can holler. But when you're caught in the halls and they pull you into the staircases, no one hears you. In my building they even raped a woman upstairs in the hallway. Maybe the Youth Patrol would walk you right up to your own door if you asked them, but I never tried it because I don't stay out that late anymore.

"I don't even go to church in the evenings. We have our communion at night, and I won't go at night. My church is pretty far from here, in Bedford-Stuyvesant, and I have to take two buses to get there. Coming back I have to change buses on the corner of Marcy and Dekalb. It's very bad around there at night. There is a delicatessen on that corner and he used to stay open late, but he don't stay open much anymore. I don't even think he's open on Sundays now. So I just don't go to church at night, and I miss it. I been in that church a long time. I sung in that church for thirty-seven years."

SIRANOOSH

"I am the only Armenian in projects. I live here thirteen years, but I have no friends here. No one comes to visit me. Before I move here I live in New York, near Columbia University. Where I lived was very nice. In my building and all over there were lots of Armenians. Everybody Armenian. I got nice friends over there. I know everybody and I raise my children there. I used to play cards with my friends, talk. We would knock on ceilings and walls to each other.

"Then the city tore down our houses. They told us all to move out, but we got no place to go. Every day I go to the office and I tell them that people can't find places to live. I holler and I holler, but nobody listens to me. I say, 'Why you not build a new house for people in their own neighborhood before you throw them out of where they live? Don't send people to strange places all over.'

"But they keep breaking down the houses, and I lose all my friends and neighbors. My house was the last one left. It was condemned by the city, but I was still living there. Everything was broke. There was no more heat, no hot water, no janitor. I was afraid to go upstairs, so I used to ask policeman to bring me upstairs.

"Then the city said they were going to move me out, into the Fort Greene projects in Brooklyn. So I cry and cry. I always lived in Manhattan, raised kids in Manhattan. What I want with Brooklyn? The city gave me so much trouble I got sick. Then they sent me here and I lost all my friends, lost everything. I don't even know where most of my friends are now. They moved here, there, everywhere. Some, I know where they are but I don't want to go visit. I'm afraid. They're in bad neighborhoods just like here, and I'm afraid to go there.

"When I come here to Fort Greene, I don't know nobody. I keep my door closed. I just say hello to a few people, and I go inside my own apartment. I don't go in nobody's house. Nobody. I come to this center every day for lunch, then right away I go home. Here there are only Spanish and black. I am all alone.

"After lunch I go right in my house and take off my clothes because I know I don't go out again. When I was in New York, I don't take off my clothes until late at night when I put on my nightgown and go to bed. But here I take my clothes off right away after lunch because I don't get no visitors. I am inside my house before three o'clock every day. After three it's not safe. You can't go out. I don't like it, but what can you do?

"Before, I used to go all over city with my husband. We even go up to Bronx to play cards, and we come home at four o'clock in the morning. Nobody touch you then. Nobody bother you.

"I come to this country in 1920, after the war. I am an exile and I don't got nothing. I come here with nothing. I was engaged to an Armenian who was living in America. I never seen him before I come here—Armenian people arrange marriages like that—and my first day in this country we got married. It was just a legal ceremony so I could stay in America. If I not marry right away, he think maybe they put me out.

"I don't know what was happening that day. I don't know English. I don't know nothing. My fiancé take me to somebody's house, and a man with a book was there. He was talking. I sat around and didn't say nothing. Then my fiancé tells me, 'We're married.' I say, 'What kind of marriage is this?'

"But we don't live together yet because it was not a real Armenian wedding. I stayed at these people's houses, and every day my husband come over. He buy me clothes, shoes, gloves, everything he buy me because I don't got nothing. He take me to all his friends' houses and to his family. His family nice. They make me sit down, don't even let me wash a teaspoon. They tell me, 'You had a hard time in Europe. You take it easy now.' Then we had a real wedding, very nice wedding in Armenian church. Then we had very nice party, much people, much friends. Everybody there, they bring a lot of presents.

"At first we get a four-room apartment on West Side, on 133rd Street. My husband pinned a piece of paper with my name and where I live right here, under my skirt. That way if I lost, I show somebody the paper and they tell me how I get home. I can't ask because I don't know English. Nothing I know, nothing.

"When I have baby, my husband has to find Armenian doctor because I can't talk with no other doctor or with nurse. My baby was born in house—all my babies born in house—because I can't speak English and don't want to be in hospital. I have four babies. Three girls and one son. They all married now. My son live in Maryland near Washington. One of my daughters live in Detroit, another live upstate near Kingston, New York, and one of my daughters live in Long Island. After they marry and my husband die, I am all alone. Then the city started breaking down my house.

"So now I live here thirteen years and I got nothing, no friends. My children don't visit me because they're afraid to come here. I write to them. I want to write a letter in English but my spelling is no good. My children say, 'Mama, you send it. We'll know.' But I want it to be better so I go to this

English class here. They have this class once a week. Tomorrow they have singing lessons with another teacher. I like the singing and I like the English. I like going to them better than going home right away after lunch and closing my door.

"I was robbed four times here, twice inside my building in the elevator. They push me inside and rob me. Now when I come downstairs I don't go in elevator. I walk. But going upstairs to the sixth floor I have to ride even though I am afraid. Once I take elevator up to sixth floor and two boys were waiting. They knock me down and hurt me and take my pocketbook with my Kennedy half-dollar in it. I was saving that, I never spent it. Then the boys run away down the stairs, and I yell out the hall window. Everybody outside look up, but nobody call police.

"Another time the police did come. It was when I was walking home from the Carvel store on Myrtle Avenue, and a boy follows me into my building and takes my pocketbook. I yell and yell, and right away a neighbor comes running down the stairs and says, 'What happened, what happened?' I was scared, and he took me inside and called police. They come and ask me questions about what the boy looks like. I say, 'He was wearing red jacket. He was not too colored and not too white.' But they never find him.

"You got to be very careful because sometimes boys try to get into your apartment when you're going in. Once a boy followed me into the elevator and got out on the same floor with me. I never saw him before. I got my key in my hand, but he's standing near me and I'm afraid to open the door. The boy says, 'Why don't you go inside?' He tells me his father is a housing policeman and they live on the seventh floor of my building. But I'm thinking, 'You live on seventh floor, why you come down to sixth floor?' So I said to him, 'Yes, I want to go in. I'm very tired. But I lost my key. I'm waiting for the housing policeman who's coming to open my door.' So I wait there maybe a half-hour and I hope that one of my neighbors will come along in hallway. But I don't see nobody for half an hour. Other times doors are always opening and closing, children playing in hallways, but not now. I don't see no one. Finally, my neighbor comes out of elevator. As soon as I see him, I open my door fast and I go inside. Later my neighbor tells me they catch that boy robbing someone else in the building.

"I used to go to a singing group at night. It didn't finish until 10:30, so I went to the Youth Patrol on Myrtle Avenue and asked them to meet me at night when I'm coming back from singing. They met me two or three times, but the last time I wait and wait and they don't come. I have to go home alone. I was carrying a shopping bag, and suddenly two boys ran past me and cut off the handle of the shopping bag with a knife, very quick. Then they took the bag and ran away. So I don't go out at night now.

"I can't sleep good at night. Lots of people are yelling outside, making a lot of noise. Kids are roller-skating in hallways until very late and nobody says nothing to them. The children play very wild, like billy goats. They climb all over. One day outside a little girl threw a ball right in my face and I start to bleed. I yell at this little girl, and she says, 'I didn't do nothing.' Then two other girls with her say, 'That's right. We're her witnesses. She didn't do nothing.' So I go to housing police, but what can they do? I am disgusted.

"Things like that never happen when I was in New York. There was nobody breaking into your mailbox there, nobody leaking in the hallways. Here, they break everything. There's broken glass all over. I just want to stay in my own home and rest. I don't go visit nobody."

Despite their fears and loneliness, the elderly people who congregate in the Senior Citizens Center are far better off than others in Fort Greene who are totally isolated. Some are too feeble or too arthritic to venture out every day, and just leave their houses briefly once or twice a week to buy some food. Others barricade themselves in their homes, virtually paralyzed by fear of what might happen to them outside.

The priests and nuns of St. Michael's and St. Edward's have been trying to find out who these elderly people are, and the nuns visit as many of them as possible. In one apartment they found a frail old woman on welfare whose only recreation was looking out her window and watching TV in the apartment across the way. When her neighbor's shades were down, she was totally cut off from the outside world. The nuns were able to get a used television set for her, which helped ease her loneliness somewhat.

The nuns have also helped elderly people get free homemaker and housekeeper services through the Department of Social Services. Many old people on welfare are simply not aware that such help is available to them to enable them to keep on living independently in their own homes. The Fort Greene Senior Citizens Center and the social services departments at Brooklyn and Cumberland Hospitals also try to help guide the elderly through the welfare maze so that they can get whatever services they need. But the problem is enormous because of the large number of isolated elderly people and the reluctance of many of them to ask for help.

Under a new law passed several years ago, children are no longer legally responsible for the financial support of their parents, so the burden on the welfare department has become much greater. Welfare workers who deal with the elderly are very bitter about this law, feeling that it mainly protects the rich who are able to support their parents but don't want to. As one worker said, "The law certainly doesn't protect the poor man, because someone who is earning only ninety-five dollars a week and has five children could easily show in court that he isn't able to support his parents. I know there was a time when they were dragging all these people into Family Court to produce all their bills and earning statements, and most of the time it turned out that the children themselves were very poor. The legislators said the new law would put an end to this kind of harassment, and it did. But the people it really helped were the rich.

"For example, in my center many of the old people have children who are doctors and lawyers—children they put through school—and these children won't help support their parents at all, so the old people wind up on welfare. I also happen to know that a former director of this center had a mother who was on public assistance, and you know what a welfare center director earns—at least eighteen thousand dollars and up, depending on years of service."

One factor that discourages children from supporting their parents voluntarily is that the parents would not automatically be entitled to Medicaid that way, whereas they would if they received welfare. Children who might otherwise be willing to support their parents or at least supplement their income may decide not to out of fear that they will be overwhelmed by medical bills. They feel it is safer and smarter to put their parents on welfare.

Dolores Roberts, a social worker at Brooklyn Hospital, has found that one of the biggest problems with the elderly is that they just don't know they are entitled to such things as Medicaid, food stamps, and half-fare passes, or they don't know how to apply for them. In addition, many of them are too proud to accept welfare, or else they are discouraged by the requirement that they have no more than five hundred dollars in the bank. Many old people would rather hang on to savings of one or two thousand dollars than accept welfare money. Their savings give them a sense of dignity, a feeling that they are not totally impoverished and dependent. Also, the savings may be set aside for their funeral, to make sure they aren't buried by the city. Whatever the reason, they would rather struggle along without welfare than give up their small bank accounts. It is simply a matter of pride.

According to Ms. Roberts, some elderly people still suffer extreme deprivation just to keep their pride intact. "There was one elderly woman who used to attend our arthritis clinic from time to time," Ms. Roberts said. "After a while I found out that she had hardly any money at all and wasn't eating very well. She had never applied for Social Security, never applied for welfare, and never got a Medicaid card. A man she had raised from childhood used to bring her some money and some food every couple of weeks, and that's what she lived on. She really needed that Medicaid card because she couldn't ambulate very well. She was supposed to have special crutches that cost a lot because with her arthritis she couldn't hold regular crutches.

"This lady was very strong against charity, and she didn't want to accept anything from the government. I went to her house to talk to her and I finally persuaded her to apply for Social Security. I helped her get her birth certificate, and then I went with her by cab to the Social Security center. While she was waiting for that first check to come, I arranged for her to get an emergency welfare check—and do you know what she did? She sent that emergency check back. So the welfare department mailed it to her again, and again she sent it back, this time with a note, 'No charity.' What's more, it took me eight months to convince her to accept Medicaid.

"In another case, a mother and a daughter were both in the hospital at the same time. The mother was sixty-seven and she had been living with her daughter, who supported her. Last month the mother was admitted to the hospital because of a cardiac condition. While she was here her daughter also became very sick and was brought to the hospital unconscious. The daughter was still unconscious last week when it was time for her mother to leave the hospital, but the mother didn't even have a key to the daughter's apartment. She also didn't have any money.

"The first thing we had to do was go through a special legal procedure to open the daughter's pocketbook and get the key to her apartment. Then we tried to get welfare for the mother, but she didn't want it. She just refused. Now, what can you do in a situation like this? You feel responsible for the person, and you can't just let her leave the hospital with nothing. So we gave her some money out of our petty cash fund. I also gave her some money out of my own pocket because I just couldn't see this lady going home to an empty apartment without food. If the social services director at the hospital knew that I had done this, she would be furious. We're not supposed to get personally involved with the patients."

Ms. Roberts handles a caseload of 125 to 150 patients per month. Most of them are elderly people. About half are on welfare, and almost all of the others are poor enough to be eligible for Medicaid. Ms. Roberts helps them with their home and family problems, assists them in getting welfare, Medicaid, and food stamps if they don't already have them, and arranges for the purchase of any special equipment they might need—such as wheelchairs or crutches—with Medicaid paying the bill.

She has had quite a few bad experiences in trying to deal with the welfare centers and has found several of them very uncooperative and very rigid. "In one case there was a patient in the hospital who was living on very small disability benefits, and he really needed some welfare help," she said. "But the people at the welfare center investigated him and said his income was thirty-five cents more than the limit, so they turned him down. Isn't that incredible? I've seen a lot of cases where people who desperately need help from welfare don't get it.

"One center I like to deal with is the Wyckoff Center, which handles most of the cases from the Fort Greene projects. I've gotten to know people there and I have a good relationship with them. They're very helpful and cooperative.

In dealing with welfare centers, so much depends on which caseworkers you get. Some can look at the whole situation and be flexible, while others go strictly by the book. It's all so arbitrary that you're never really sure in advance whether you can get welfare help for someone or not."

New, stricter welfare regulations are also causing problems for Ms. Roberts and her patients. For example, the Department of Social Services used to give extra money to welfare recipients who needed more expensive foods for special diets. This practice has been curtailed, so that many welfare clients can no longer afford the special foods they need. This cutback particularly hurt the elderly, because so many of them require special diets. Funding has become tighter all around, and foundations have not been giving out much money for these purposes either. In cases where her clients are suffering because they can't afford the kinds of foods they're supposed to have, Ms. Roberts works with the hospital nutritionist to try to find inexpensive substitutes for necessary items, such as collard greens in place of escarole.

The red tape that is involved in dealing with welfare and Medicaid is almost ludicrous. For example, one day Ms. Roberts spent most of the morning trying to arrange for an ambulette and oxygen tank for an elderly Medicaid patient who was scheduled to enter the hospital that afternoon. Ms. Roberts had filled out a myriad of Medicaid forms and made about eight phone calls before the arrangements were completed. But then she learned that in order for the woman to get from her third floor apartment to the ambulette she needed to be equipped with a *portable* oxygen tank. Ambulettes do not carry this type of tank, so a more expensive ambulance had to be provided. Once again Ms. Roberts had to fill out a pile of Medicaid forms and place another six or seven phone calls. The ambulance could not be sent out until a Medicaid payment was guaranteed. Because of the confusion and the heavy paperwork involved, the sick woman did not arrive at the hospital until several hours after she was supposed to be admitted.

Ms. Roberts also handles the job of getting housekeeping services for her elderly Medicaid patients who can no longer take complete care of their homes by themselves. In cases where they are too feeble or too disabled to continue living at home, she arranges for placement in nursing homes. All nursing homes receive some government money, so they must accept a certain number of Medicaid patients regardless of whether they are voluntary (nonprofit) homes or proprietary homes. There is often a very long wait before beds are available for these patients, although private patients can usually get in right away. Approximately five-sixths of all the nursing home beds in the city—19,779 out of 24,000—are occupied by Medicaid patients.

The average nursing home in Brooklyn charges approximately $234 per week, far beyond the means of Ms. Roberts's clients. But she advises people who have a little savings to enter a home privately at first, even if they can only afford it for a month or so. When their money runs out they can continue to stay in the home under Medicaid—but meanwhile they will have had the chance to select one of the better facilities and to be admitted right away. If they enter as Medicaid patients from the start, they will be limited to whichever nursing home happens to have Medicaid openings at the moment.

There are two nursing homes in Fort Greene, and although, from a quick glance around the main floor, both appear to be fairly well kept, Ms. Roberts does not include them among the handful of homes she feels are particularly good. "When you're looking around for a nursing home, you've got to go above the first floor," she says. "The first floor is usually clean and beautiful. But if you go one flight up and you get the smell of urine and feces, you realize the patients are not being cared for.

"Just this week I visited two homes that were no good at all. I saw old people who were sitting and lying in feces and drenched in urine. Some patients were sitting there half-dressed with trays in front of them, just staring at their food. They needed someone to help feed them, but no one did. The help was just standing around in the hallways talking to each other and enjoying themselves. I was so upset that I couldn't even talk to the head nurse. I just walked out in tears.

"A lot of nursing homes are like this. The patients are treated miserably, but their families think they're being taken care of, and they forget about them. They just go visit them once in a while. But the families shouldn't trust the homes. They should come in themselves and help out a little because almost all these homes are short-staffed."

The total amount of money that Medicaid pays out to the 161 nursing homes in New York City has risen phenomenally in the last four years. In 1969 the nursing homes' claims amounted to $76,484,769; by 1972 they had reached $262.3 million. Recently, state officials began poking into the legitimacy of these claims and discovered a substantial amount of overbilling, particularly in relation to the quality of care the patients were getting.

A more sensible and humane solution to the problem of what to do with disabled elderly poor people would be to allow many more of them to remain in their own homes, watched over individually by housekeepers or practical nurses paid for by the Department of Social Services. At present, far too many elderly people are sent to nursing homes who really don't need total, twenty-four-hour care, but because of welfare or Medicaid restrictions it is easier to put them in an institution than to get home services for them. If the emphasis were reversed so that home care was relied on more heavily, the cost to the city, state, and federal governments would probably be less than it is now with the emphasis on nursing homes —particularly if the housekeepers and practical nurses were recruited from the city's pool of welfare recipients and given special training for this type of work. Such a policy would provide many more city jobs for welfare recipients, in addition to offering far more personal, individualized care for impoverished elderly people.

12

Health Care for the Poor

TEN years ago, if a poor person in Fort Greene got sick, practically the only place to which he could go for treatment was the clinic at Cumberland Hospital, a municipal institution. Needless to say, he couldn't afford a private doctor, and even if he could, there were hardly any private doctors practicing in Fort Greene. Brooklyn Hospital, the only other hospital in the community, was a voluntary institution that charged a hefty fee for its services. If the person had to be hospitalized for a serious illness or needed an operation, again the most likely place he would wind up was Cumberland, since Brooklyn Hospital accepted only a small number of indigent patients.

Thus, a poor person in Fort Greene had very few options regarding medical care. It was Cumberland or nothing, and the conditions at that hospital were so bad—with severe overcrowding and intolerably long waits at the clinics—that most poor people avoided going for medical treatment until they were desperate. Illnesses or conditions that might have been easily corrected in the early stages went untreated too long, frequently resulting in chronic ill health. The general health level among the poor has always been lower than that of the population as a whole, due at least partly to the lack of adequate medical care. This is why it is really not surprising that so many welfare mothers were found medically unfit to work during the recent screening by the Department of Social Services.

A major step toward correcting this situation was first taken in 1965 when the medical assistance program—commonly known as Medicaid—was created by the addition of Title XIX to the Social Security Act. This extended federal aid for medical care to medically needy families and individuals who were not necessarily on welfare, as well as to the medically needy aged. It was left to the states to set the income limits in determining who was "medically needy." Welfare recipients automatically fell into this category, but today under New York State law, only the poorest of the working poor are eligible for Medicaid coverage.

This was not the case when Medicaid first became operational in New York in 1966. At that time the earnings limit for a family of four was set at six thousand dollars net income (the equivalent of about seven thousand dollars gross). This original standard was one of the most liberal in the country, but it didn't remain that way for long. As soon as the New York state legislators realized that about forty-five percent of the state's population would be eligible for Medicaid this way, they hurriedly lowered the cutoff point to fifty-three hundred dollars. In 1969 they lowered it again, to five thousand dollars net income for a family of four. In 1971 they slashed it still further—forty-five hundred dollars—but they were not able to implement this low figure because of a court ruling that such cutbacks would cause irreparable injury to the medically needy. Thus, the cutoff point for Medicaid coverage in New York State remains at five thousand dollars net income for a family of four (approximately fifty-seven hundred dollars gross income). The cutoff for a family of three is four thousand dollars; for a couple it's thirty-one hundred dollars; and for a single person it's twenty-two hundred dollars.

However, families with these incomes do not get *total* Medicaid coverage in all situations; in many instances they have to pay a percentage of their medical bills themselves. Only welfare families and those earning under four thousand dollars net for a family of four are entitled to full coverage.

Full Medicaid coverage is a precious asset for the poor. It entitles them to inpatient care in hospitals or nursing homes; X-ray and laboratory services; physical therapy; outpatient care in clinics or by qualified physicians, dentists, nurses, optometrists, and podiatrists; routine dental care; drugs; eyeglasses; and transportation to obtain care. All of these benefits are absolutely free to anyone who has full Medicaid coverage, and the provider is reimbursed by the Medical Assistance Bureau. Typical expenditures for the four-person family receiving Medicaid amount to approximately thirteen hundred dollars a year.

In Fort Greene, Medicaid has had a profound effect. First of all, it opened up Brooklyn Hospital to welfare recipients and to the working poor who were on Medicaid, thereby relieving some of the overcrowding at Cumberland. Voluntary institutions such as Brooklyn Hospital don't care whether a person is covered by Blue Cross, a major medical insurance plan, Medicaid, or some other health insurance program—as long as he is covered by *something* and the hospital is guaranteed payment. In fact, it is better to have Medicaid than to have the Blue Cross–Blue Shield twenty-one-day plan. Once the twenty-one days have been used up and the patient has no more funds, Brooklyn Hospital will transfer him to Cumberland, if possible. But Medicaid patients can stay indefinitely; there is no limit.

Medicaid patients have much the same choice of hospitals as middle-class people. They can go to such places as Methodist Hospital, Brooklyn Jewish Hospital, or Long Island College Hospital, all of which are located in Brooklyn, relatively close to Fort Greene. But the working poor who earn a little too much to qualify for Medicaid do not have the same range of choices. Unless they are fortunate enough to work for a place that provides free or very low cost hospital coverage for its employees, they are still largely limited to municipal institutions like Cumberland.

Medicaid was also responsible for the growth of storefront medical centers in Fort Greene and other poor neighborhoods, bringing an influx of desperately needed doctors, including general practitioners and specialists such as dermatologists, cardiologists, and so on. Dentists also operate out of these centers, so that a great many services for the poor that were once offered only by hospital clinics are available through these small medical groups. Although there is still a great deal of suspicion among people in Fort Greene regarding these storefront medical centers, at least they are a possible alternative to the hospitals—another option for those on Medicaid. But here again, people without Medicaid cannot take advantage of this option unless they're willing to pay the ten or fifteen dollars that the storefront doctors charge for a non-Medicaid visit.

It is also possible for people on Medicaid to join an H.I.P. center—as Clara did—although they might have to do a bit of hunting around before they find one with openings for them. This is another option that the non-Medicaid working poor do not have, for it is unlikely that they can afford H.I.P. coverage on their own.

The possibilities that Medicaid opens up for getting first-rate health care for the poor are virtually unlimited. For example, almost all the pregnant girls in Project Teen-Aid are on welfare and covered by Medicaid. This makes it possible for the school to implement its plan to bring in a private obstetrician-gynecologist who will accept Medicaid reimbursements and will care for the adolescents throughout their pregnancy and delivery. Other groups, such as infant-care, day-care, or after-school centers might make similar Medicaid arrangements to guarantee that the children receive regular checkups and are tested for such things as sickle cell anemia. The children are particularly in need of better health supervision, because what they receive through the elementary schools is notoriously inadequate. In 1972 the school health coordinator for District 13 checked over the records and discovered that more than four thousand students in the district (which includes all of Fort Greene) had never been inoculated against *anything*. Some students were in junior high school and had no health records at all. Such facts are coming to light now that school decentralization is in effect.

The advent of Medicaid has at least made it a realistic possibility for people in poverty areas to receive decent health care. Those on welfare, in particular, no longer have to worry about whether they will be able to get the medical care they need. Medicaid pays for everything, so they are fully covered. In effect, an application for welfare constitutes an application for Medicaid, and the eligibility continues as long as the person is receiving public assistance—even if it is only supplementary assistance with a very small cash payment.

The big difficulty with Medicaid arises with the working poor. If their income rises above four thousand dollars net per year for a family of four they are still entitled to Medicaid coverage, but they have to pay varying percentages of their medical costs themselves. In some cases this is very little, but in other cases it can amount to several hundred or even thousands of dollars, thereby nullifying any improvement in their standard of living due to higher earnings. In such cases it may actually be more beneficial for the working poor to go on welfare than to work. As a 1973 study in public welfare by Blanche Bernstein showed, where the working poor and Medicaid are concerned, "It would be hard to imagine a

more confusing and complicated set of arrangements to determine who pays how much for what types of care under
varying economic circumstances." A Medicaid recipient who
gets a raise of five hundred dollars a year, for example, may
find himself in debt because he has to pay such a large percentage of his medical bills. Whereas if he hadn't gotten the
raise, his medical expenses would have been fully taken care
of by Medicaid and he would have been better off in the end,
according to the study. "The effect of this incomprehensible
and arbitrary system which may expose such families and individuals to heavy medical bills, often exceeding any additional income they might secure, can only be to encourage
many families to retain their welfare status at all costs. For, as
welfare recipients, they have certainty—certainty of access to
full medical benefits with no co-payments."

In Fort Greene it's very common to hear people say they
would like to go on welfare mainly so they can get Medicaid
coverage. If they have chronic health problems they are afraid
of being limited to Cumberland Hospital, which has a reputation of being bad in everything except "gunshot wounds, knife
wounds, or acids."

The hospital is certainly convenient for the people in Fort
Greene, since it is located in the center of the projects. Yet its
emergency ambulance service is notoriously slow, and people
who live just a few blocks away complain that they have had
to wait half an hour or longer before an ambulance from
Cumberland responded to their call.

As with many municipal hospitals, Cumberland's main
problems apparently stem from a shortage of nurses and aides.
This is what patients complain about most frequently, rather
than the type of treatment and attention they get from the
doctors. On the whole, people seem satisfied with the doctors
at Cumberland, and many prefer them to the doctors in the
storefront medical centers. One elderly woman who lives in
the projects and does not have Medicaid contrasted her ex-

periences at the Myrtle Avenue health center with her experiences at Cumberland:

"I went to the Myrtle Avenue doctors one time and they
were too expensive. They charged me ten dollars for the examination. Then they gave me a prescription and told me I
could go to the drug store next door to have it filled. The drug
store is part of the center, and that place wanted $9.50 for that
medicine. If I had known how much it would have cost, I
wouldn't have given the prescription in. I won't go back there
no more.

"It wasn't even any serious sickness. I just had this pain in
my chest, and the doctors didn't even hardly examine me.
They just felt my pulse and my heart, and they didn't tell me
what was wrong with me or nothing. They just told me to
come back. It was so fast. I went right in and came right out,
and that cost me ten dollars.

"I have a friend who goes to the Myrtle Avenue center. I
don't know if she's satisfied, but she goes there all the time.
Not me. I go to Cumberland when I'm sick. I guess Cumberland is just like any other hospital. You have to wait until
your turn comes. I was there three weeks ago for an emergency, and I didn't have to wait too long that day. I had this
bad pain in my side, and the doctor examined me very
thoroughly.

"The doctors at Cumberland have been pretty good with
me, but I don't think they were too good with my husband.
He has arthritis and gout, and the doctors at Cumberland told
me he wasn't ever going to walk no more. The doctors at
Brooklyn Hospital said the same thing. But at Brooklyn they
didn't get him out of bed. The nurses didn't even take him to
the therapy he was supposed to go to. So I said to them, 'You
don't know whether he can walk or not 'cause you don't take
him to therapy.' I used to go there in the evenings and get him
out of bed myself because the nurses wouldn't do it.

"Finally I put him in this nursing home that's farther out

in Brooklyn, and now he's walking just like he was before. I knew he was going to walk again because he had that ambition. He's doing good at the nursing home as far as walking, but it's really a bad place. I don't like it at all. I'm going to take him out of there in a few weeks. The nurses are all right, but those patients—they go around doing whatever they want to do, and nobody really tries to stop them. I just don't understand it."

Another woman—a welfare recipient who lives in the Fort Greene projects—went through six operations at Cumberland Hospital and had no complaints at all about the doctors. "The doctors there are very good," she said. "Them Indian doctors, them Korean doctors, and them Japanese doctors, you know, they're wonderful. They're excellent. And there's no problem about talking to them because if a doctor don't understand you there's always an interpreter for you. When I go to the clinic now I get the same doctor all the time. Oh, he's a doll. That's one blessing."

A great many foreign doctors are doing their residencies at both Cumberland and Brooklyn Hospitals. They rotate between the two institutions, working for a few months at Brooklyn, then for a few months at Cumberland. They mainly treat Medicaid patients who don't have any attending physicians of their own. According to some of the nurses at the two hospitals, the foreign residents are much better with the black and Puerto Rican Medicaid patients than the American attending doctors, many of whom are described as "very prejudiced." One nurse in the cardiology unit at Brooklyn Hospital said that some of the attending physicians "go into a rage if their own patients are put into a four-bed room together with a welfare patient. These doctors sometimes scream at us, 'Why is *he* here?' as if they think the welfare patient smells bad or something. It's the way a truck driver might act, but you don't expect that kind of thing from doctors. If the welfare patient happens to have a good location in the room, say, near a window, the doctor may even move him away and give his own patient that spot.

"The foreign residents aren't like that," she added. "They tend to treat all the patients the same, and they're just furious at some of the attending physicians. A lot of the nurses are really furious, too, and we would love to tell off some of these attending doctors. You know, nurses get very disillusioned about doctors after a while."

The shortage of nurses and aides, particularly at Cumberland Hospital, can lead to situations where disabled patients miss meals simply because no one has the time to feed them. The Fort Greene woman who underwent six operations at Cumberland said that many times her food was cold before someone got around to feeding her, or else she didn't get fed at all. "You see, sometimes when you're sick you can't reach the tray to feed yourself," she said. "If you're a patient who can help yourself, you're all right. Then Cumberland's not a bad place. But if you're so sick that you can't help yourself, you're out of luck. Your food just sits there on the tray, and after a while people come around with a wagon and take the trays away, and you wind up not eating.

"All the time I was in that hospital I said to myself that if I ever got well I was going to come back and help feed the patients as much as I could. And that's just what I did. At first I didn't know if I would be allowed to go up and feed people, so I used to sneak up there. But then one time a nurse caught me, and she said, 'Why do you sneak up? Why don't you sign up as a volunteer?' And I said, 'Well, how do I go about that?' So she told me to go downstairs, and what room to go in, and I did. I volunteered. I used to feed everybody. I would even go upstairs to the dining room and get coffee for them. I'd make sure the patients ate their breakfast and lunch and had all the water they wanted. I was only supposed to be there for breakfast, but I never went home until after lunch. I wanted to be sure everyone had at least two meals. I don't know how they got along at suppertime, but I bet a lot of times they didn't eat. This happens on the wards, even in the private rooms. It doesn't make no difference. Whether you pay or don't pay, it don't matter. 'Cause I seen 'em pay and get bad treatment."

The same type of neglect exists regarding the patients' cleanliness and comfort. An elderly woman at the Fort Greene Senior Citizens Center told of visiting a friend of hers who was in Cumberland with cancer of the spine. "She had got so that she couldn't move at all, it hurt her so bad. She was always messing her clothes and the bed, and they'd just let her lie that way for hours. Me and another neighbor used to go up there to visit her, and we saw the way her bed was. But I knew where they kept the sheets, so I told the other neighbor to keep watching out while I went to steal some fresh sheets and bring them back. Quite a few times I changed her whole bed.

"The people who work in Cumberland tell you they ain't got the time to keep changing sheets for one patient when they got so many patients to take care of. Sometimes they get very disagreeable and nasty to patients who soil their beds. I heard one nurse say to a patient, 'What do you think, I've got all day to spend changing you?' But when you're an invalid patient you can't help yourself. That's why they're supposed to put bottles and things on you, to protect your bed and keep you from getting bed sores. But some don't have these bottles and things on them, and they have no control, and they can't help themselves. The nurses can really be nasty to these patients. I seen 'em do it—especially them West Indian nurses. Oh, my god. They're terrible. They don't have no patience at all. They come here from somewhere else, some other country, and they tell you what to do. I wouldn't recommend none of them.

"I was in Kingsboro Hospital once where a West Indian

nurse knocked the medicine right out of my hand. You see, I couldn't swallow it down right away, and she said to me, 'You take it *now* or you don't take it at all.' She spoke in this West Indian accent. So I said, 'Well, I won't take it at all then, 'cause I can't scoop it right down.' Then she just reached over and knocked it right out of my hand."

(Antagonism between American blacks and West Indian blacks is fairly common in Fort Greene. American blacks, no matter what their economic or social status, often feel that the West Indian blacks look down on them and behave arrogantly.)

The hospitals in Fort Greene are microcosms of society as a whole, with the same types of conflicts, power struggles, and animosities that exist on the outside. Brooklyn Hospital recently was thrown into turmoil when its director of nursing was fired, allegedly as a result of a secret meeting between six attending physicians and the top hospital administrators. According to several nurses, the physicians were upset because the nursing director—who was white—had been hiring a lot of black nurses and promoting others into high positions. Both the assistant and associate directors of nursing, who had been appointed by the director, were black. In addition, the director had encouraged her nurses to be less subservient to the doctors and to speak up for what they thought was right. She disparaged the old formalities that required a nurse to stand up when a doctor walked into the room, and to give up her seat if there was no other available for him. According to Dorothy, a white nurse in the cardiology division, "Some attending doctors are really fanatical about these little traditions. They have very strong ideas about what a nurse should be and how she should behave—and if she doesn't stand up as soon as they walk into the nurses' station, they're outraged. These are usually the same doctors who hate welfare patients. It's all part of the same type of values."

Frances, a black nurse who works with children at Brooklyn Hospital, was very upset when the nursing director was fired. "She was a very dynamic person and I liked her very much," she said. "I found her very warm, very understanding. But the doctors were mad because she was hiring so many black coordinators that they had nobody white to go to anymore. Also, some of the white nurses didn't like her—particularly the nurses who had graduated from the Brooklyn Hospital nursing school. They had monopolized the supervisory positions until this director came in. But she opened new avenues, put new jobs into effect, and filled these new positions with black people. So the white nursing supervisors didn't have all the power anymore, and they didn't like this. I think they got together with some of the attending physicians who had pull with the board of trustees, and they helped get the nursing director kicked out. Actually, nobody really knows for sure why they fired her, but we feel we have a pretty good idea.

"The woman who is now the acting director of nurses is black, but I think she's a very weak person. I think she's being controlled by the administration."

Frances lives in Fort Greene, not far from Brooklyn Hospital. Not long ago she was promoted to a supervisory position on the hospital's nursing staff, replacing a white nurse who had left. The problems she is having in her new position are a reflection of the power struggle that is going on in the hospital as larger numbers of black nurses move into positions of authority. Given the fact that Brooklyn Hospital is located in a predominantly black community, and that its patients are mainly black, it was both natural and inevitable that such a struggle should arise on some level of the hierarchy. In the hospital—as well as in the schools in Fort Greene—the emerging prominence of blacks in supervisory and administrative roles has been met with stubborn resistance, and their climb has been slow.

FRANCES[1]

"This is not the first supervisory position I've had at the hospital. A while ago I was made head nurse in another section of the hospital. I followed a white head nurse there, too, and the staff really resented it. I don't think they ever accepted the fact that I was the head nurse. They wouldn't do anything I asked without an argument, and the whole thing turned into one big hassle. I was ready to leave. I had taken as much as I could take, and I was ready to become a public health nurse.

"But then I was offered the supervisor's job in this section, and I took it. I've been working at it only a short time now and I'm hoping things will get better, but right now I'm having some of the same problems I was having before. The majority of my staff is white and West Indian, and no matter what I say or what happens, they always tell me how my predecessor would have handled things. The West Indians at this hospital are mainly from Jamaica and Trinidad, and some are from British Guiana. I think most of them would rather have a white supervisor than a black supervisor, even though they're black themselves. You find this with a lot of American blacks, too. They'd rather be working for a white person. Maybe they're jealous when another black gets into a higher position, or maybe they've just been brainwashed by white society, I don't know.

"With the white nurses, particularly if they're Australian, a black supervisor will have a hard time. The Australians are a very prejudiced group of people. They do not like blacks at all. I don't know why the administration brings these girls from Australia into Brooklyn Hospital, into a black neighborhood. And if the girls move into any of the hospital apartments, like the ones they have in University Towers, then they're living in a black neighborhood.

1 Not her real name.

"When the hospital recruits foreign girls to be nurses—girls from the Philippines or from Australia—the brochure really misleads them. It shows a picture of Grand Army Plaza, which makes the girls think the hospital is located in a very nice environment. But Grand Army Plaza is nowhere near the hospital or Fort Greene. Also, the brochures show lots of pictures of Brooklyn Heights, so when these foreign girls see the brochure, they think they're coming into a totally different kind of neighborhood than what actually exists around the hospital. It's very misleading, and a lot of the foreign nurses who come here are very dissatisfied. Especially the Australians. I don't think we've had any of them stay longer than six months.

"The hospital wants foreign nurses because they get paid the lowest scale. They are not licensed in New York State, so they have to get a permit that allows them to work as R.N.s for a while until they take their licensing exams. As long as they only have permits they're on a totally different pay scale than we are.[2]

"There is a problem with the foreign nurses, especially the ones who work with children and who are in contact with the children's parents all the time. These girls are not used to dealing with black and Puerto Rican people and welfare mothers. They have a very difficult time relating, and the mothers resent them. It's partly a language problem, but it also has to do with different mannerisms and customs. It's funny, but this problem does not exist with the foreign doctors. For some reason, the parents seem to relate very well with the foreign doctors.

"But there is trouble between the foreign nurses and the Puerto Rican mothers, in particular. We have a large percentage of Puerto Rican kids, and their parents are very

[2] A spokesman in the nursing office reports that Brooklyn Hospital stopped sponsoring foreign nurses at the start of 1974, and now hires only nurses who already have their New York State licenses.

difficult to deal with. The Puerto Rican mother is a very protective mother, very suspicious of the hospital. They can't understand a nurse telling them that they mustn't pick up their child and hold him all the time and carry him all around the hospital when he has pneumonia. They think the nurse is just being nasty or is neglecting the child.

"Also, the foreign nurses tend to take things lightly—they don't show too much concern. I mean, if a parent tells you something about her child, no matter how insignificant it is to you, just make sure you're showing concern about what she's saying. But the foreign girls don't, particularly the ones from the Philippines. They're not warm with the children at all. They are strictly professional, a little cold, and the parents resent this.

"At Brooklyn Hospital, mothers can stay with their children from ten in the morning until seven at night. But when seven o'clock comes, the Puerto Rican mothers don't want to go home. And when you tell them visiting hours are over, that's when the trouble begins. The mothers become very hostile to the nurses, to the hospital, to the doctors, to every-body there because we won't let them stay until their child goes to sleep, or won't allow him to have an extra pack of sugar. Puerto Ricans feed their kids an awful lot of sweets. They feel that for a child to drink anything it must be syrupy sweet, and they have a powdery sugar kind of thing that they put into formulas. The children become used to this and they won't take a bottle of milk unless there's a lot of sugar in it. So the hospital has to put sugar in these babies' bottles.

"If we were to try to stop these mothers from being at the hospital all the time, they'd just as soon sign their child out. They'd much rather do that than be away from their child for a time. They are really a very concerned group of parents —more concerned than the black or the white mother. The Puerto Rican mothers really believe that they are essential to their children.

"With the black mothers, in some cases we have the opposite problem. They bring their children to the hospital, and then we don't see them at all. We have to send telegrams saying, 'Please come and take your child home. He has been discharged for two or three days.' Sometimes we have to track them down, contact Social Services or refer the matter to the police department. They eventually come in. I'm not saying this happens with a majority of black mothers, or even with a large number of them. But it happens with enough so that it's a problem. We hardly ever have this kind of problem with the Puerto Rican mothers.

"The American nurses at Brooklyn Hospital can kind of understand these mothers because we're used to dealing with them. We've gotten our education here in the city and we've worked in hospitals here, so we're familiar with these kinds of mothers. But for the foreign girls it's very hard.

"The hospital has even more foreign doctors than foreign nurses. Just about all our residents are foreign. I think we have only two residents in my section who are American. The foreign residents get along very well with the patients, but we ourselves have a communication problem with them. It's very bad sometimes, and that really creates a problem. They can't understand you and you can't understand them—at least not until you've worked with them for a while and gotten used to the way they talk so you can figure out what they mean.

"The residents switch off between Cumberland Hospital and here, and from what they tell us, Brooklyn Hospital is like heaven compared to Cumberland. The residents have a lot of trouble with the nurses over there. Like, if they want to do a spinal tap on a child at Cumberland and they ask a nurse to help them, the nurse might say, 'You go in and hold that child yourself or you get someone else to hold him because I don't have time.' They're very short on staff at Cumberland. But also, they have a very large percentage of West

Indian nurses, and they are very difficult to work with. West Indian people are extremely difficult to work with. Nurses, technicians, I don't care what. They don't consider themselves as being black like we are. They consider themselves West Indian. So they come here with this superior attitude that they're better than the American blacks. Whether they have an equal education to us, or whether they can come up to us economically, it doesn't matter. They still feel superior. This makes it hard for us to deal with them as far as work is concerned, and it's also hard on the black patients.

"Most of our patients here are covered by Medicaid. As soon as our private patient load drops a little, the hospital administration pushes for more Medicaid admissions because that's sure money. So we're dealing mainly with patients who are really poor, and we get a lot of the same problems that the municipal hospitals have.

"For example, when I was working with infants we always had some unwanted babies in the nursery whose mothers never took them home. We called them our 'boarders,' and they would stay with us for five or six months until the social service department of the hospital found some place for them, like a foster home. This is not the kind of thing that happens very often in a hospital where most of the patients are middle class.

"But things are changing here now because of the abortion law. Before the law was passed we always had at least four boarders at any given time, but since the law has been in effect we get maybe one boarder every few months. We have far fewer unwanted children now than before. Actually, we have fewer births here altogether. In the regular nursery we have a capacity for twenty-six babies, and before the abortion law we used to be full to capacity all the time. Now, we rarely have as many as twenty-three babies.

"The babies that are left with us now usually have something wrong with them, and that's why the mother doesn't want them. Some of them are mongoloids, and they usually have cardiac problems, too, so we keep them for a good length of time. Not long ago we had a mongoloid child who was born to an older couple. The man was about fifty, and the mother was in her mid-thirties. This was their first child, and they couldn't accept the fact that he was not normal. They just didn't want him at all, so they picked up and went to Florida and left the baby in the hospital. We finally placed that baby in a foster home with an Italian couple who seemed very pleased with the child.

"Another child we had for a long time was also born to older parents. The mother was about fifty-six and the father was about sixty. They were really old people to be having a baby. The mother evidently had had syphilis for years and didn't know it, so it was never treated. Well, that baby was just a mess. He was brain damaged, had just one eye, and had a cardiac problem. He had some of everything. We kept him here at the hospital for a year and a half, and he became our baby. We taught him to talk, to walk, to eat, everything. We gave him Christmas and birthday parties. His mother used to come to see him, but she couldn't take care of him. Finally the hospital placed him in a foster home, and I understand that the people have adopted him.

"There are also cases with newborns where there are such bad problems in the home that we don't know if we should let the mother take the infant out of the hospital. If we sense there is a problem, the social service department will get visiting nurses to go out and check the home and tell us if they feel the baby can go into that setting. This is done especially with drug addicts. We just had a case where the mother was an addict but she had been getting methadone treatments. Her baby was born addicted to methadone, and we had to give him tranquilizers until he passed through the withdrawal stage. Babies who are born addicted to methadone go through a much more severe withdrawal than those born addicted to heroin. The visiting nurses went into this mother's home and found that everything was adequate, so she was allowed to take her baby home.

"We have another case now where the mother really doesn't want the baby. She is white and the father is black, and she has a number of other children. I don't know why she didn't have an abortion. The father is putting pressure on her to take the baby, but I think it's a very bad situation to give the child to this mother when she doesn't want it. There's a real danger that this child will be abused.

"We get a number of cases of child neglect or child abuse, which we refer to the Bureau of Child Welfare. But usually the hospital loses out in these cases, and the child goes back to the parent. You see, the Bureau of Child Welfare just doesn't have any place to put all these kids, so they give the parent the benefit of the doubt.

"Sometimes a mother doesn't actually abuse her child, but she is really too incompetent to take care of him. We had one little boy who was brought in with pneumonia when he was nine months old. When the doctors did a work-up on him, they found out that he also had sickle cell anemia. The mother knew he was a sickle, but she had never taken him for treatment. It didn't mean anything to her. She didn't even tell the doctors that he was a sickle baby. This mother was a very hostile girl, and even after our doctors spoke to her, she rejected everything they told her. She threatened to sign the kid out of the hospital numerous times when he was still very sick. Finally, when he was better and the hospital said, 'Okay, take your child,' she didn't want to take him. Now she keeps bringing him back. She's a very mixed-up, unstable person, and she really shouldn't be caring for a baby.

"We get a lot of babies and children from the welfare families who are living in the Granada Hotel. The hotel is about two blocks from here. Gastroenteritis and intestinal viruses are very common among the hotel kids. So is diarrhea.

We hardly get any cases of malnutrition, though. Basically, I guess they get enough to eat, although a lot of times it's a matter of getting too much of the wrong kinds of foods and not enough of the right kinds. Some of the parents need to be educated on what they should feed their children.

"When we get older kids who have to stay in the hospital for long periods of time—like rheumatics or kids with kidney disorders or heart problems—the hospital gets a teacher to tutor them. We have a regular teacher from one of the local public schools who works for the hospital regularly. The only trouble is, this teacher is not a very strong person, and these kids frighten her. She's afraid of them—their language, their hostile attitude. They can really wrap her around their fingers.

"Last summer we had a seventeen-year-old girl who had been on drugs and had hepatitis. She was a senior in high school, but she really had no interest in school and wasn't even planning to go back to graduate. Most of the time in the hospital she would watch cartoons on TV or draw with crayons. Several times when I was in there with her, this teacher would come in and say, 'Okay, it's time to do some schoolwork.' And the girl would say, 'Oh, hell. I don't want to learn anything.' Then the teacher would tell her, 'You have to get an education to get a job.' And the girl would say, 'Oh, that's a lie. I can go into any one of these department stores and be a salesgirl if I wanted to. I don't need an education.' Well, the teacher didn't know how to deal with this, so she would just pick up her books and leave.

"You see, these kids can sense as soon as she walks in the room that she's petrified, and they give her the business. I mean, from age six to age sixteen, they give her the business, so while they're in the hospital they really don't learn anything. They fall very far behind.

"It's really a shame, because we used to have a very good

teacher here. She was a very big woman, over six feet tall, and she frightened the kids. They didn't bluff her too much, and she was able to get them to do some work. But then the board of education transferred her someplace else, even though she didn't want to leave the hospital. We wrote to the board and asked if we could keep her because she was so good, but it was no use.

"A lot of the children here are from problem families and families on welfare. I must admit that I resent some of the things that people on welfare get that I don't get. Like, if I got sick and had to be hospitalized, who would take care of my house for me and watch my child when he wasn't in nursery school? People who are on welfare can get a home-maker to come to their house every day. The Department of Social Services pays for this. But I couldn't get a homemaker from the city if I needed one. The middle-class person gets no help whatsoever.

"Sometimes we have cases here where we feel the mother needs someone in her home to help with a sickly child, or to be with her other children while she spends time in the hospital with her sick child. If she's on welfare she has no problem, because the city will provide a homemaker for her.

"There are cases where welfare mothers abuse this service. Like the time we had a little girl with leukemia in the hospital who really needed her mother. She was dying. A home-maker was taking care of everything in the house just so the mother could be at the hospital with the little girl, but the mother must have been out partying all the time because she never came here. There are other cases where mothers go shopping or visit friends or whatever, but they don't come to the hospital to sit with their kids even though that's what they've got the homemaker for. This annoys me. I argue with our social service department about this all the time. I say, 'We're telling you that this mother has not been coming to the hospital at all, yet you're going to continue paying for a homemaker for her?' The little girl with leukemia died without her mother ever coming to see her.

"If you're on welfare, our social service department will find better housing for you under certain circumstances. Like, when kids are hospitalized for lead poisoning we won't let them go home until the house is lead-free or until their family has moved to another apartment. Social service will investigate and help them find better places to live. Social service only helps welfare patients. We can request social service for a private patient if the doctor consents to it. But in these cases, social service can only advise; they can't really help.

"We have a very strong social service department at Brooklyn Hospital. Most of the workers are very dedicated people. There's no limit they won't go to to help people in the hospital who are on welfare."

The Board of Health is another agency that provides a number of medical services for the poor. A pediatrics clinic, located in the Fort Greene projects and run by the Board of Health, has an excellent reputation in the community. Mothers can bring their children to the clinic for regular checkups and can get free formula and free vitamins if they can't afford to pay for these things themselves. The nurses there instruct the mothers in how to care for their babies, and sometimes if a mother doesn't show up for an appointment, one of the nurses will phone her or go to her home to see what's wrong.

Diane, a white public health nurse who works in the Fort Greene area, felt that her two children received better care through the clinic than from their own pediatrician, so she brought them there regularly for several years. Diane herself has gone into many homes in Fort Greene to check on potential health problems. For example, when she was working with the schools in the community, she would be sent to the homes of children who were repeatedly absent to find out what the problem was. She went into the Fort Greene and Farragut projects, as well as brownstones and tenements "where welfare families were living in apartments that were in such bad shape they should have been condemned, even though the welfare department was paying very high rents for these miserable places," she said.

In one instance she was sent to the home of a family with five children, one of whom had simply stopped coming to school. "This was a really pathetic situation," she said. "It turned out that the mother was totally blind, diabetic, and obese, and all the kids were very badly cared for. There was no father. The oldest child had been staying home from school to help the mother, but conditions were just deplorable. Urine and feces were all over the place. The ceiling was about to fall down and rats were breeding on top of the ceiling. We had the Department of Sanitation come over to clear out the rats and to check and see if the building should be condemned. Also, since the family was on welfare, we arranged for a homemaker to come in every day and take care of things."

Living conditions in the projects are far better than in most of the brownstones and tenements, Diane said. "The project apartments are usually kept very nicely. But in the Fort Greene projects, going into the elevators is like going into a public urinal. There is a very strong odor in those elevators. This is not the case in Farragut. There's no smell at all there."

For a time, Diane was a nurse at Sands Junior High School, across the street from the Farragut projects. "Working there was a really frightening experience," she said. "The kids there are very rough, very tough. They would intimidate the teachers and the nurses. For example, a kid would come in and say, 'I'm sick. I can't go to classes today.' The kid's whole manner and attitude would be so threatening that the nurses would be afraid to call him a liar and say he's not sick. There was one black nurse who was very good, though. She was able to handle the kids better than most of the teachers."

The health supervision of schoolchildren in Fort Greene, which was not too good to begin with, has declined still further now that the schools have stopped giving immunization shots to children because of the cutback in federal funds. Parents are left with full responsibility for taking their children to the Board of Health for shots since nothing is being done inside the schools. In a neighborhood where it was discovered only recently that four thousand schoolchildren had never been inoculated against anything, this latest turn of events is more bad news.

The cutbacks in health funds grew out of the Nixon administration's refusal to spend nearly $1.1 billion in funds that Congress had intended for major health programs in 1973. Such miserly behavior has a far more calamitous effect on poor neighborhoods than middle-class ones, because the poor are almost totally dependent on government-financed health programs of one kind or another. If the squeeze is on federal funds, the poor are the first to feel the pinch.

The programs for which funds were withheld had been created by Congress to meet specific health needs, such as protection from disease, mental health care, health manpower (to enable more people to become medically fit to work), and improved health services of many kinds.

The administration's decision not to spend the large sums that had been appropriated by Congress for these programs was criticized sharply by representative Paul G. Rogers, chairman of the House Commerce Committee's Health and Environment Subcommittee. "Unless these health needs in fact do not exist, or have been met, or are being met by alternative superior programs, then these impoundments must be considered a sad failure of our government's commitment to serve its people," he said.

The Nixon administration has also proposed new regulations requiring that health programs for the poor become financially self-sufficient. As published in the *Federal Register,* the proposed regulations said health service delivery projects "must become basically self-sustaining community-based operations with diminishing need for direct or indirect" federal support. Congressional opponents of the proposal feared it would doom many programs that now serve the poor, such as programs for migrant workers, neighborhood health centers, and about half of the community mental health centers.

President Nixon also proposed a reduction in Medicaid and Medicare benefits. Certain "low priority" Medicaid benefits, such as dental care for adults, would be dropped altogether. In the case of Medicare, the elderly would have to pay a bigger percentage of hospital and doctor bills, so that a sixty-day stay in the hospital would cost a Medicare recipient a minimum of five hundred dollars, compared to seventy-two dollars under the present law.

If all of the president's proposals go through, the harm they will cause in poor neighborhoods like Fort Greene may be severe enough to minimize the health benefits that were so recently gained through the introduction of Medicaid.

13

In the Schools

U N T I L 1888, the school system in Brooklyn was officially segregated. Colored School #1, located on Willoughby Street where the Kingsview middle-income cooperative houses now stand, served the black children of Fort Greene. It was one of three "colored schools" in the city of Brooklyn, but the other two—in Williamsburg and Bedford-Stuyvesant—were built later on, mainly to serve blacks who had fled from New York City during the draft riots of July 1863.

Colored School #1 was a dilapidated old building where children were taught the three Rs, and not much else. It stood in rather dismal surroundings, for when the schoolchildren looked out the windows all they could see was the Raymond Street jail across the street and the city morgue. If they looked in the other direction they saw the city cemetery and the poorhouse.

In 1888 the entire faculty and student body from Colored School #1 were transferred to a new school, P.S. 67, a block away. Although this school was also entirely black at first and was still known as a "colored school," the racial composition gradually changed as the neighborhood changed. By the early

1940s there were many poor Italian, Irish, and Jewish children in it along with black children. Although many buildings in the area were torn down around this time to make way for the Fort Greene housing projects, P.S. 67 was left standing while the projects went up around it. Thus, it became the main elementary school serving the children from the projects. At first these projects were fairly well integrated, but over the years they became increasingly populated by blacks and Puerto Ricans as whites moved out. Today, P.S. 67 has come full circle—once again it is, in fact, a "colored school," with blacks and Puerto Ricans making up 97.6 percent of the student body.

Even at that, P.S. 67 is not the most totally segregated school in Fort Greene. That distinction belongs to P.S. 56, which has a black and Puerto Rican enrollment of 99.1 percent (blacks account for 93.6 percent and Puerto Ricans for 5.5 percent).

All of the schools in Fort Greene belong to Community School District 13, which also covers Brooklyn Heights and small portions of Bedford-Stuyvesant and Park Slope. On a districtwide basis, blacks and Puerto Ricans far outnumber white pupils, and the majority of them are extremely poor. In 1972, 13,000 children out of the district's school population of 24,166 were eligible for free lunches because their parents earned less than four thousand dollars per year (for a family of four).

If *all* the families in the district sent their children to the public schools, these facilities would not be so totally imbalanced either racially or economically. The area is far more mixed than the school statistics would indicate. But the middle-income families in District 13—both white and black—generally try to avoid sending their children to the public schools, preferring either parochial or private schools. For many of these middle-income families, paying private school tuition is a great hardship, yet they continue to do it. If tuition payments become intolerable they generally move to a different part of Brooklyn or to the suburbs rather than switch their children to the Fort Greene public schools. Low-income families, if they can possibly afford it, also try to keep their children out of the local public schools by sending them to parochial schools.

This means that the children in the public school system in Fort Greene come primarily from the poorest families in the community, with just a smattering of middle-income youngsters thrown in.

Judging by the reading scores in District 13 over the past several years, parents have every reason to dread sending their children to the local schools. On every grade level on which they've been tested recently, the children in District 13 have been well behind the nationwide norm. Even schools that were slightly above the norm five or six years ago have fallen behind. The chart on the following page shows the comparison between District 13 reading scores and the nation-wide median scores.

The scores reveal that children in the lower grades in Fort Greene schools were more likely to be reading on or near their proper grade level than the older children. But as they progressed through school they gradually fell further and further behind, so that by the time they reached the eighth grade in junior high school they were approximately three years behind the national norm. (The results were similar in low-income areas throughout New York City and in other urban areas across the nation.)

In 1973 the board of education conducted another citywide reading test and computed the results to show what percent-age of total students in each school were reading at or above grade level. In District 13 there was only one school—P.S. 7-8 —where as many as half the children were on grade level. (P.S. 7-8 is a paired school that links the mainly black children from the Farragut housing projects with the mainly white

School	Grade 2 (nationwide median is 2.7)					Grade 5 (nationwide median is 5.7)			
	1967	1968	1970	1971	1972	1967	1970	1971	1972
P.S. 3	2.8	2.3	2.5	2.6	2.4	4.3	4.1	4.2	4.2
P.S. 7-8	2.9	2.5	2.5	2.2	2.3	6.2	4.1	4.8	4.2
P.S. 9	2.6	2.9	3.4	3.0	2.7	5.3	4.6	3.9	4.5
P.S. 11	2.3	2.5	1.9	2.5	2.4	4.7	3.6	3.0	4.1
P.S. 20	2.6	2.6	2.2	2.2	2.3	4.9	3.7	3.6	4.2
P.S. 44	2.5	2.3	2.3	2.5	2.3	5.3	4.1	4.4	4.5
P.S. 46	2.3	2.2	2.0	2.3	2.2	4.7	4.1	5.7	3.7
P.S. 54	2.2	2.3	1.9	2.3	2.3	4.4	3.5	3.8	4.3
P.S. 56	2.3	2.1	1.9	2.4	2.0	4.1	3.7	4.5	4.2
P.S. 67	2.3	2.6	2.9	2.3	2.2	4.3	3.6	4.3	4.6
P.S. 93	2.4	2.8	2.1	2.5	2.3	4.4	4.1	4.1	4.6
P.S. 133	2.2	—	2.0	2.4	2.2	4.2	3.9	3.8	4.4
P.S. 256	2.4	2.3	2.1	2.3	2.3	4.4	4.6	4.4	4.4
P.S. 270	2.5	2.6	2.6	2.5	2.3	5.1	4.6	4.5	4.4
P.S. 282	2.4	2.3	2.0	2.3	2.1	4.6	4.1	4.1	4.4
P.S. 287	2.7	2.5	2.1	2.5	2.4	4.4	3.9	3.8	3.5
P.S. 305	2.6	2.5	2.5	2.4	2.1	4.9	4.1	4.3	3.8
P.S. 307	2.7	3.3	2.8	2.4	2.1	5.2	4.6	4.3	4.5

School	Grade 6 (nationwide median is 6.7)		Grade 8 (nationwide median is 8.7)			
	1967	1968	1967	1970	1971	1972
J.H.S. 117	4.7	5.0	6.7	5.7	5.6	5.8
J.H.S. 258	4.9	5.0	6.3	5.8	5.6	5.5

School	Grade 7 (nationwide median is 7.7)		Grade 8 (nationwide median is 8.7)			
	1967	1968	1967	1970	1971	1972
J.H.S. 265 (Sands)	5.7	5.6	—	5.4	5.0	5.5
J.H.S. 294 (Rothschild)	5.6	5.9	—	5.7	5.5	6.0

Comparison between District 13 reading scores and the nationwide median scores.

children from Brooklyn Heights.) In the majority of other schools in the district, just twenty-five percent *or less* of the children were reading as well as they should have been. In P.S. 67, the school in the Fort Greene projects, only 16.8 percent of the students were on their appropriate reading level.

The relative success of P.S. 7-8 comes after a long period of instability and decline that began immediately after the schools were paired ten years ago, in 1964. Prior to the pairing, P.S. 8 served the children from Brooklyn Heights, and P.S. 7 served the children from Farragut. The Heights school was considered excellent at the time, and there was a lot of pressure from liberal, idealistic Heights parents to have their school paired with the Farragut school. It was thought that both facilities would benefit from the arrangement, since they would become entitled to special funding and equipment, plus additional teachers who were specialists in various fields. Several other schools in New York City became paired at that time, and it seemed as if pairing might be the answer to the quest for high-quality, well-integrated education.

Under the pairing arrangement, all the children from the Heights and Farragut were to attend the Heights school, P.S. 8, from grades one to four. This meant that the Farragut children would be bused into the Heights for those four years. For the next two years, in grades five and six, all the children would be switched to P.S. 7, and the Heights children would have their turn at being bused to school. The number of grades in each school were not evenly divided, because P.S. 7 is a very small, very old, and only partially fireproof building, and it could accommodate only two grades of paired children. However, both schools kept their own individual kindergartens because it was felt that five-year-olds were too young for busing.

The pairing arrangement started off with a great deal of fanfare and high hopes, but within a very short time disenchantment set in among many Heights parents. They felt that the paired schools were not getting all the special services and extras that had been promised, and that the whole setup was not working out as well as they had expected. They vented their rage on the new principal who had taken over at the time the schools were paired, and within two years they went to court to try to have her removed. The action was not successful, and the principal is still there.

While the battle raged, more and more Brooklyn Heights parents began looking around for other schools. Although the Heights already had several private schools in the neighborhood, such as Packer and Friends, a new private school for intellectually gifted children—St. Ann's—was started partly in response to the demands of Heights parents who wanted to snatch their children out of P.S. 7-8. St. Ann's was an immediate success, and in the first few years of its existence it practically replaced P.S. 7-8 as the neighborhood school for Heights children. White enrollment in the paired public schools dropped sharply as many Heights parents—who had provided the impetus for the pairing in the first place—abandoned their support. Reading scores declined from averages that were above grade level until 1967 to averages that were substantially below grade level by 1972.

But as the tuition costs in private schools accelerated and apartment rents in Brooklyn Heights soared out of the stratosphere, fewer Heights residents were able to afford a private education for their children. Newer parents, who had not been involved in either the initial drive to have the public schools paired or in the disillusionment that followed, decided to give the paired schools a try—not out of idealism but out of necessity. Many of these parents found the schools far better than they had been led to expect, despite the falling reading scores, and they in turn began encouraging other Heights parents to send their children there.

In 1972 a vote was taken among the Farragut and Brooklyn Heights parents to determine whether P.S. 7-8 should continue as a paired school. By that time it was the last remaining paired school in the city, since all the other schools that had experimented with pairing had dropped it. A significant number of parents from both Farragut and the Heights wanted to end the experiment at P.S. 7-8, too, but the supporters of pairing won out and the school remains paired—the last survivor of a once highly touted plan for achieving good integrated schools in New York City.

(At the time of the voting, one cynical Heights parent remarked that the only reason she voted to continue the pairing was that "P.S. 8 is in District 13, which is a mainly black district, and it's pretty militant. I think they really hate the Heights school, and if we weren't paired with the Farragut school we wouldn't even get pencils from the district office. School decentralization doesn't seem so great when you're the only whites in a black district.")

In the last year or two, P.S. 7-8 had defied the pattern of other inner-city schools. White enrollment in grades one to four has gone up instead of down, so that by 1972 it reached forty-two percent—up from thirty-four percent in 1970 and 1971. In addition, the proportion of children who were reading at grade level or above jumped to 51.4 percent in 1973 (the highest percentage of all District 13 schools), compared to 30.0 percent for 1972 and 34.4 percent for 1971. According to national standards, the "average" school would have half its pupils at or above grade level and half below, so P.S. 7-8 is now an "average" school.

The paired school seems to have finally stabilized, ten years after its inception, and there no longer appears to be much danger that Brooklyn Heights parents will wreck the racial balance by refusing to send their children there.

However, the school still has a very serious flaw in that it is far less balanced in grades five and six than in grades one to four. Once the Heights children finish the fourth grade, their parents are generally not willing to have them bused into an all-black neighborhood for the last two grades. They much prefer to have the Farragut children bused into the Heights. As a result, only twenty percent of the children who attend the two upper grades at P.S. 7-8 are white, in contrast to forty-two percent in the lower grades. Part of this imbalance is due to the fact that P.S. 7-8 feeds into Rothschild Junior High School in Fort Greene, and hardly any Heights parents send their children there even though it is their district school. Since they intend to switch their children to private school at that point anyhow, most of them decide to do it two years earlier to avoid the busing altogether.

This situation has led to a strong movement among Heights and Farragut parents to build a new school that will go from kindergarten through the eighth grade and will serve both neighborhoods. Most parents agree that this would probably be better than the paired schools, both of which are very ancient structures anyhow. The source of friction is where this school should be located, since the Farragut parents want it closer to their community and the Heights parents want it closer to theirs. Since the Heights groups are more vocal and better organized and have better political connections, they will probably get their way if ever a new school is built.

In general, the Farragut parents tend to be less involved in school politics than the Heights parents. Fewer of them show up at PTA meetings, and last year the school had a difficult time finding a Farragut parent who was willing to serve as co-president of the PTA along with a Heights parent. It is a difficult, time-consuming job, and no one wanted it. Finally they found a divorced father who actually lives in Jamaica, Queens, but whose children go to P.S. 7-8, who was willing to take on the job.

Despite the vicissitudes of the past ten years, P.S. 7-8 appears to have become one of the better schools in District 13, at least as far as reading levels are concerned. Of course, to keep things in perspective, it should be remembered that almost half the children in P.S. 7-8 are *not* reading up to grade level. Nevertheless, the results at that school were still far better than the results in other District 13 schools in 1973. For example, in P.S. 9, which had the next highest reading scores, almost two-thirds of the children are not up to grade level.

Both the Farragut parents and the Heights parents speak highly of P.S. 7-8 now, although the two groups often have very different ideas as to how their children should be educated. For example, the low-income black and Puerto Rican parents from Farragut are generally much more conservative and traditional in their attitude toward school than the Heights parents. When the open classroom system was introduced in P.S. 7-8, with its nontextbook approach to learning, many black parents objected very strongly and did not want their children to participate. They preferred a much more structured, orderly school setup where children sat at desks, worked from textbooks, and got regular homework assignments. That way the parents could keep track of exactly what their children were doing in school and how well they were doing it. To these parents, a solid, traditional education meant a possible escape from poverty for their children, and they did not want to gamble with any learning experiments.

The Heights parents, on the other hand, had already "made it" in the world and were fairly confident that their children would too. They were more concerned about their children's creativity being stifled in a traditional setting and therefore were much more willing to experiment with the latest educational theories.

When the first open classrooms were instituted at P.S. 7-8, they were on a voluntary basis; parents had to request that their children be put into one of these classes. A great many Brooklyn Heights parents did so, and quite a few Farragut parents also agreed to give it a try, although reluctantly. But after the first year, many of the Farragut parents switched their children back into the traditional classrooms. "It seemed just like a kindergarten to me," said one Farragut mother. "My child would come home and I'd ask him what he did in school today, and he'd say, 'I made jello.' For math they used to give him these sticks to play with [Cuisenaire rods] instead of a book, so that child couldn't add three and three. He wasn't doing too good in reading, either, so I put him into a regular classroom and now he's doing much better. At least I can see that he's really learning something."

P.S. 7-8 tries to get an even mix of Heights children and Farragut children in the open classrooms, but each year there is a bit of a struggle to persuade Farragut parents to let their children participate.

The same type of objections to the open classroom experiment cropped up in many other schools in Dictrict 13, with the same pattern repeating itself everywhere—the white middle class parents generally favored the new, looser approach, and the low-income black and Puerto Rican parents generally opposed it. It was as if they were afraid to play experimental games with their children's education, even though the traditional teaching methods were not working very well.

Speaking about the opposition to open classrooms at P.S. 307, which is across the street from the Farragut projects, Marie Swearer said, "I think the teachers blew it more than anything. They didn't really explain to the parents what was going on, and when the parents walked into the classroom it looked like a zoo. You know, it was totally individualized study, with all the kids doing different things. The parents were upset about it because they didn't feel their kids were learning anything. Like, they didn't understand why a kid would be working with wood or playing with water or making peanut butter. I guess the teachers never told the parents that the kids were learning how to use measurements this way, learning about volume. I know the parents were very much against the new program."

Until a few years ago, P.S. 307 was a More Effective School

(MES). This meant that it had a larger staff and smaller classes than most public schools, more teacher's aides, and more individualized instruction, as well as a resident child psychologist and several guidance counselors. In addition, it had a prekindergarten for four-year-olds plus a full-day kindergarten for five-year-olds instead of the usual half-day session. P.S. 307 was also one of the first public schools to try the open classroom approach.

Because of its special nature, P.S. 307 was open to children from outside the district—that is, outside the immediate Farragut area—and bus service was provided for all who needed it. Quite a few children were bused in from all over Brooklyn, and some came from the middle-income pockets in Fort Greene, such as the University Towers buildings owned by L.I.U., the Willoughby Walk houses owned by Pratt, and the Kingsview cooperative houses. These children would ordinarily have gone to their own district school, P.S. 20, or to private and parochial schools. But because P.S. 307 was an MES school it sounded attractive enough so that parents were willing to try busing their children into the Farragut projects. Quite a number of those who were bused in were white, so that the school's white enrollment rose to about fourteen percent.

The creation of MES schools like P.S. 307 was another widely heralded attempt to improve the quality of education in poverty areas and prevent children from falling behind in reading. Yet MES too was eventually abandoned as a failure. Argie Johnson, science coordinator for District 13, explained that "MES just didn't prove anything. Those kids were not advancing any more than the schools that were not MES schools. The teachers' union had been pushing MES at first, but after a citywide survey was made on the impact of MES and nothing conclusive came out of it, they dropped the whole idea. All the MES schools were dropped."

At P.S. 307, the elimination of the MES program meant a

sudden jump in class size from about twenty-four to close to forty students. Parents were furious, and they protested loudly at the start of the fall 1972 term. After a lot of switching around, classes were eventually reduced in size to about twenty-eight students. But a lot of the extra services and personnel—such as the resident psychologist and the additional guidance counselors—were eliminated, so the school no longer had the same appeal for outsiders as it once had. Although children are still being bused in, they are a very small group now.

Another school in Fort Greene that once had this kind of reverse busing is P.S. 20. As late as ten years ago, this school had the reputation of being one of the best in Brooklyn. This was one of the main reasons why the tenants of University Towers and the Kingsview cooperative were so eager to have their buildings zoned into this school instead of into P.S. 67, which was just half a block away in the Fort Greene projects.

In the early 1960s, P.S. 20 was singled out by a group of white parents in Sheepshead Bay who were looking around for a good interracial public school for their children. This was the era when blacks and liberal whites had optimistically joined forces in the nationwide nonviolent civil rights movement, and in keeping with the idealistic spirit of the times, the Sheepshead Bay parents did not want their children to attend the virtually all-white schools in their own neighborhood. So they chose P.S. 20 and began busing their children in.

The reverse busing appeared to work well for a time, and school administrators were clearly very pleased that P.S. 20 had been selected for this busing program—so pleased, in fact, that after a while many black parents began to feel that favoritism was being shown to the children from outside the district. For one thing, just about all of these children were put into classes for the brightest children, even though some of them did not necessarily belong there. This left less room in the top classes for black children, and several who should have been in were excluded. (Although the top classes are no longer identified by number in the public schools, they still exist, and everyone in the schools knows which ones they are.) Furthermore, since the white children who were being bused in and the white children who lived in Fort Greene were all grouped together in just a few classes, they tended to form a separate clique.

In each grade, it was mainly the top class that got special books, such as the Bank Street readers. They also went on trips to places like Washington, D.C., while the other classes in the grade didn't go much farther than Fort Greene Park. As one angry mother put it, "If it was really important academically and socially for the children to go to Washington, then *all* the children in the grade should have gone."

By 1968, many of the black parents in P.S. 20 had begun to feel that their own children were not benefiting at all from the reverse busing arrangement. It was also becoming very clear that integration alone would not necessarily improve a school, since the reading scores of the children in P.S. 20 were declining year after year, just as in every other school in District 13. On a nationwide basis, a movement for black power was replacing the movement for integration, and this too had an effect on school politics. Resentment and anger on the part of many black parents toward the white principal resulted in his sudden resignation in the middle of the spring term in 1968. Following this, P.S. 20 became one of the first schools in New York City to choose its own principal. A fairly militant screening committee made up almost entirely of black and Puerto Rican parents interviewed a great many candidates for the principal's job, and to just about everyone's surprise they recommended a white man—Richard Alexander. He is still the principal of P.S. 20 today. As for the reverse busing arrangement, it dwindled away and at present it no longer exists.

Throughout District 13 there has been no discernible correlation between the amount of integration in a school and its reading scores. P.S. 7-8 has been the most integrated school in the district for the last ten years, with thirty percent or more white students at all times. Yet it did not lead the district in reading achievement from 1968 until this past year. P.S. 9 and P.S. 270 scored second and third in reading in 1973, yet they have only a handful of white students. In contrast, P.S. 20 and P.S. 307, which are between ten and fifteen percent white, scored ninth and fourteenth respectively. Such figures indicate that simply having a more integrated school is no guarantee that teachers will make more of an effort with the children or that the school will be any better. It is the *social* value of integration that is most important, and this is something that cannot be measured on tests.

One of the surprising things about the schools in Fort Greene is that until just a few years ago they had hardly any black principals, administrators, or teachers. Just about everyone running them was white, even though it is an overwhelmingly black and Puerto Rican school district. This is changing now, and in the past three or four years almost every white principal who has left has been replaced by a black principal. This happened in P.S. 307, P.S. 287, P.S. 67, Sands Junior High School, and Rothschild Junior High School, among others.

Argie Johnson, who works with all the schools in District 13 as science coordinator, pointed out some of the problems that can arise when a black principal takes over in a school that has an almost all-white administrative and teaching staff. "It's a whole big change for white teachers to have a black principal all of a sudden," she said. "It's a kind of resentment against taking orders, against having a black person at the top.

"This is not only in regard to the principals, either. Almost all the top people in the District 13 office are black now, too.

This has happened since decentralization. But since most of the staff in the elementary schools is still white, things get a little difficult sometimes. For example, when I became science coordinator for the district, I went around to all the schools and introduced myself to the principals and assistant principals. Some of them just looked at me and said, 'Who are you? Are you qualified for the job?' You see, they were skeptical and a little hostile, because first of all I'm black, I'm also a woman, and I'm in science. These were three things that bothered them right there. They were just not ready for this. But they're used to it by now.

"So when a black principal comes into a school, sometimes you get a kind of rebellion on the part of the staff, and it takes a while before they'll support him. There are really very few black teachers in the elementary schools around here. Do you know we have schools with just one or two black teachers? P.S. 133 just got its first black teacher last year. And in several schools the only black administrator is the principal. All the assistant principals are white.

"The way principals are picked now in this district is that the parents screen all the candidates first, then they recommend three in order of preference to the district superintendent. He interviews these three and makes the final choice. On occasion they have gotten in some principals who were picked solely on the basis of being black, but these people have not made the best principals. One or two whites were chosen this way, too, but the trend is toward more black principals.

"Lately we have also been getting in more black and Puerto Rican teachers. You see, because of the low reading scores in this district, we are able to hire teachers who have just passed the National Teachers Exam, not just those who have gone through the regular board of education exam. This has been going on for the past two years. Because of this we have gotten a large number of black and Puerto Rican teachers in, and white teachers, too. A lot of them take the NTE because you get the results back much faster than from the board of ed.

"There is a Title I program to recruit minority teachers that was started about three years ago with state and federal funds. They've been trying to get a representative number of black and Spanish-speaking teachers in the schools. Also, there are paraprofessionals who have gone to school and are now becoming teachers themselves. So they too are a pool from which to replace teachers who are leaving by attrition. Altogether there are a lot of ways that we've been able to get minority teachers lately.

"Sometimes getting in a new principal can make an enormous difference in a school. Take Sands Junior High School, for example. Before the new principal, Mr. Cox, came in about two years ago, everybody was ready to pull their kids out of Sands. It had an enrollment of less than one thousand students, and it was a horrid place. Anyone who worked there had a right to be terrified. The teachers had no control—none whatsoever—and the kids weren't in the classrooms. They were in the halls all the time. It was like Grand Central Station. But when you go into Sands now, you see there's learning going on. During class time you don't see any kids in the halls unless they have a pass and have someplace to go. They're not just running around anymore.

"In order to make all the changes, Mr. Cox had to get rid of quite a large number of teachers. Some of them left voluntarily, and some he had to rate unsatisfactory. Most of the time he gave them a chance to find another position before he let them go. He didn't just fire them on the spot. I think a lot of them wanted to leave anyhow. They were looking to transfer, and maybe he helped them get transferred. Right now he has a large number of young teachers who have only been in the system between one and three years, and they are doing a very good job. Sands is a well-run school now, but it still has its old reputation to live down. A lot of people still think it's a bad place because they don't know how it's changed. It's not the wild place it once was.

"The key thing in a school is the leadership, the administration. The principal's attitude is reflected in the teachers and the students, and Cox has a very good rapport with them. He runs the school very democratically and really consults with his staff. Although a lot of the teachers are new, the assistant principals are all the same as before. All of them are white and Cox is black, but he was able to reorganize them and set up a new system that seems to work very well.

"Both Sands and Rothschild Junior High are in Fort Greene, and it used to be that Rothschild was considered the better school, but I don't think that's true anymore. On the whole, the kids who go to Sands are poorer than the kids who go to Rothschild, because Rothschild draws from the middle-income buildings around here. Rothschild is also supposed to be for the kids in Brooklyn Heights, but not many of them go there. They're usually put into private schools instead.

"There's a whole design in the way these schools were zoned years ago by the central board of education, and it came about because of pressure from the people who built the middle-income developments around here. All the middle-income buildings were zoned into P.S. 20 and Rothschild, even though the kids from University Towers and the Kingsview cooperative have to walk all the way across Fort Greene Park to get there.

"Now that you have decentralization, I don't know if that kind of thing could happen so easily. Also, with decentralization the people in the district office began looking into things that had been neglected for years. For example, they've been checking back over the kids' health records to see if things have been kept up to date. This was something that had really been ignored before, mainly because there was just one person who worked as both health and science coordinator for the district. That's far too much for one person, and under decentralization it was broken down into two jobs. Just to be health coordinator in this district is a huge amount of work because there are so many health problems here.

"In general, I think decentralization is working, but like anything else it's going to take time. The last three years have been a learning experience for the administrators, the superintendent, the parents, and everyone else involved. Especially the parents. This is the first time that parents in this district have ever really had any say-so about their kids' education. As a result they're really using the power they have —and sometimes not in the best interests of the kids. There's a lot of politics in the educational system that just shouldn't be there. But I think in the next few years they will have gotten all this out of their systems and will really be down to dealing with the problems of education. I don't think the communities will ever let it go back to a centralized system.

"We certainly have enough basic problems to deal with, particularly with reading. There are a lot of reasons why the reading scores are so low in this neighborhood. One reason is that you have teachers who come in for three or four days or a few weeks and then decide that they can't deal with these kids, so they leave. I've even seen teachers walk into a school, stay one hour, and quit. So some kids end up having seven or eight teachers during the course of a year. There's no continuity, so the kids can't learn.

"Another thing you have in this district is a lot of absenteeism on the part of teachers. Last year there were people who were absent thirty-five or forty days without any major illness. The district is really cracking down on this now. A lot of the teachers who were out so much last year were rated unsatisfactory, and they were let go. This was with the consent of the parents and the community school board. The parents are interested in building up some stability as far as administrators and teachers are concerned, because they view this as one of the major problems. The policy now is that if teachers have a certain number of absences without being able to prove that they were really sick—especially on Mondays and Fridays—they have to answer to the superintendent.

"Another problem is that the kids are so transient. I don't mean the kids in the projects, because they're stable in regard to staying in the same school. But the kids in the rooming houses, and especially the kids from the welfare hotels. There is one school, P.S. 11, that gets a lot of welfare kids from the Mohawk Hotel. These kids are in transit almost all year, so it's very hard to follow them or keep track of them.

"P.S. 11 has a right-to-read program. This is a federally funded program where they set up a whole media center to teach kids reading. They use tape recorders and all kinds of gadgets. So far it seems to be working out very well. But because so many of the kids at P.S. 11 are on welfare and living in hotels, they're only in the school for two months or four months; then they're gone. So you can't do follow-up studies with them on the effects of the right-to-read techniques. This is something that's really hampering the program.

"The Granada Hotel also has a lot of welfare families. Supposedly the city is not putting welfare families into hotels anymore, but when you work in the schools, you know different. I see kids in the Granada every day. Just the other day I passed that hotel and there were a whole bunch of kids out in front of that building who lived there."

The problem of educating children from welfare hotels was far worse several years ago when it seemed as if every hotel in Brooklyn was overflowing with welfare families who wound up staying for as long as a year or more in many cases. These hotels are concentrated in the Brooklyn Heights–Fort Greene–downtown Brooklyn area, and they are all zoned into District 13 schools. Brooklyn Heights alone has seven hotels in the space of a few blocks, and each one housed many welfare families. If the children went to school at all, they were enrolled in P.S. 7-8.

Not only did the hotel children themselves suffer from their transient, unstable lives, but their effect on the schools was highly disruptive. A number of Brooklyn Heights parents were considering pulling their children out of P.S. 7-8 just because of the presence of the hotel children. As one mother put it, "It's not that we don't want our kids going to school with them simply because they're poor and black. After all, the Farragut kids are poor and black, too, and there hasn't been any problem. It's been a good relationship. But the hotel kids are totally different. They're just uncontrollable, and a lot of them have really severe emotional problems from the kind of lives they've led. They don't really have a home, and they're living in a neighborhood that's strange to them. They feel they don't belong anywhere, so they're very hostile and defensive. They need special help, but the school just isn't equipped to give it to them. The teachers can't handle them, and they disrupt the whole school. How can any of the kids learn anything in that atmosphere?"

The problem was resolved to a large degree—at least as far as the schools were concerned—when, after much public protest, the Department of Social Services finally made a concerted effort to find permanent homes for these welfare families. The hotels were emptied of most of the children at that time, but now that the public spotlight has been off for a while, the welfare hotels seem to have begun filling up with families again.

Another educational problem of a longer-lasting nature involves language difficulties. District 13 has a large number of Spanish-speaking children as well as a substantial number of Haitians who speak Creole, a form of French. According to Argie Johnson, District 13 is setting up a trilingual school in P.S. 9, where children will be taught either in Spanish-English or Creole-English. "This is something the parents want," she said, "because there are so many children who don't speak any English and they're not being educated. The trilingual school will start in the lower grades and move up progressively, adding a higher grade each year. We have one teacher who speaks Creole, and he's already working in P.S. 9. We'll have more coming in soon.

"One criticism we have of the reading tests is that most schools in this district have a lot of students who don't speak English fluently but who have to take the tests too. Of course the ones who don't speak *any* English are not included, but all the others are. Their scores are computed into the averages along with everyone else's, and this tends to bring the scores down. That's why you can't just look at these scores and take them at face value as far as deciding whether a school is good or bad. There are other factors involved.

"The fact that this district is a mixture of blacks, Puerto Ricans, and Haitians means that there are also some cultural differences to contend with in the schools. For example, the Puerto Ricans are very overprotective toward their children. Puerto Rican mothers will bring their kids to school every day, even in junior high school sometimes. In the elementary schools, the mothers will stay in the school all day long. There's usually a family room where they can go. They bring rubbers for the kids when it rains, and when the kids eat in the lunchroom, you can't move for the mothers. They'll hover over the kids while they eat, asking, 'Do you like this?'

"You see, this is part of Puerto Rican culture. In Puerto Rico the schools belong to the parents. They can actually sit in class with the kids. So when they come here it's hard for them to break tradition. They want to do the same thing here. In the elementary schools they're all over the place. The schools can't keep them away, so they try to utilize them by having them help out however they can.

"With the Haitian parents there's a different problem. They feel superior to American blacks because of their culture, and they hold themselves very high. They'll tell you in a minute, 'I'm not an American black.' They are very prejudiced because they think they're better than we are. I'm black and they're black, but they think they're better. So when these Haitian parents are dealing with American blacks in the schools, they can be very difficult.

"When you get into the junior highs and high schools around here, you start coming across a whole lot of other problems, like drugs, and pregnancies among the girls. As far as drugs go, it's mostly in the high schools. It hasn't hit the junior highs too much. The junior highs have had kids messing around with marijuana, sniffing glue and carbona and that kind of thing, but there's not much of a problem with the hard stuff. However, there are a lot of *potential* drug users in the junior highs, and the district has a drug education program to try to prevent these kids from becoming users.

"We also have a sex education program in the schools to try to cut pregnancies among teenagers. The health coordinator in District 13 has really made an effort to educate the people to the birth control methods that are available to them. I think the kids are really practicing birth control a lot more now than they used to.

"For example, I work in the District 13 office, and on the sixth floor of that building there's a family planning center. I see a lot of young kids in there all the time—kids I taught in junior high school just a few years ago. I meet them in the building and I ask them, 'Where are you going?' and sometimes they get bashful and don't want to say. So I say to them, 'You can tell me where you're going,' and finally they'll say. But bashful or not, they go. They do take advantage of that center.

"In the schools you need a certain type of person to handle sex education classes. Not everybody can do it because these kids are so aware. They really put teachers in turns. Like, there was this one young girl who was teaching a sex education class in a junior high and one of the kids asked her, 'What is the sixty-nine position?' And she didn't know what to say. She would have had to go into the whole oral-genital sex act, and she just didn't know how to handle it. These kids are very sophisticated, and you have to be ready to deal with that. This teacher just wasn't ready."

Once they leave junior high, the teenagers from Fort Greene are dispersed throughout a number of high schools in Brooklyn. Some go to Eastern District, others to Boys High or Fort Hamilton or Erasmus. They have a wide range of choices. The only academic high school that is actually located in Fort Greene is Brooklyn Tech—a school that specializes in math, science, and technology—and not too many students from the neighborhood go there. An entry examination is required, and as of 1970 Brooklyn Tech was still about eighty-eight percent white. However, this may be changing somewhat, for last year Rothschild Junior High School had nineteen students who made it into Brooklyn Tech, and three who got into Stuyvesant High School in Manhattan—another specialized school that requires an entry examination.

In 1970, City University began a major effort to gain more minority and low-income students by throwing open its door to anyone in the city who graduated from high school, no matter how low his or her grades. The city colleges had traditionally served as the pathway out of the slums for many New York City youngsters, but in the last few decades the student body as a whole had become much more middle class. Entry requirements had gotten so high and competition was so fierce that mainly the more advantaged students from the better high schools were getting in. Ghetto youngsters whose high schools were generally inferior couldn't compete, and they were virtually locked out of the city colleges.

It was hoped that the new open admissions policy at City University would have an effect all the way down the line—

that is, that many more low-income students would be motivated to finish high school because they knew in advance
that admission to one of the city colleges was guaranteed. The
university also instituted several scholarship programs designed to help low-income students get through college, such
as the College Discovery program at the two-year colleges and
the SEEK program at the four-year colleges.

It is still too early to gauge the success of open admissions
in regard to low-income students, but certainly many more
are now attending the various branches of City University.
At New York City Community College in the downtown
Brooklyn area, more than eight hundred students out of
about seven thousand are either receiving welfare themselves
or are from families that receive welfare money under the
Aid to Dependent Children program. Another forty-five
hundred students are from families where the income is low
enough so that they would normally be eligible for financial
aid—if there was enough aid money to go around. But with
all the cutbacks in education funds, only about three thousand of the poorest students are actually getting some sort of
financial help.

Most of the students at New York City Community would
probably not have been able to go to college at all if it were
not for open admissions, because their academic backgrounds are so weak. Less than half of those who enroll in
the school actually graduate. On a universitywide basis the
dropout rate among open admissions students is about forty
percent. Most of the city colleges are now involved in inten-
sive remedial reading programs for these students in an effort
to lower the dropout figures.

Nevertheless, many youngsters from low-income families
who never even considered going to college before are now
making an attempt at it—like Mario, the young Puerto Rican
who was working off his welfare check and is now enrolled
at Staten Island Community College. About twenty thou-

sand additional students are entering City University each year now, bringing the total freshman enrollment up to about forty thousand annually since open admissions began. The largest single ethnic group among incoming freshmen are Italians, most of whom come from blue-collar families. Italians had been very underrepresented at City University before open admissions, but they now comprise twenty-five percent of all entering freshmen. Black students have become the second largest group of freshmen, so the racial and ethnic composition of the university is changing, largely as a result of open admissions.

14

The War on Poverty

THERE was a time when you couldn't walk down Myrtle Avenue without tripping over an antipoverty agency. Within the space of just a few blocks there was the Fort Greene Rehabilitation League to combat drug addiction; NOC-YOC (Neighborhood Organizing Council–Youth Organizing Committee), a remedial educational and job counseling program for young people; the Buying Club and the Golden Key Society, two wholesale food cooperatives; Caballeros Hispaños, which helped Spanish-speaking people with a variety of legal, educational, housing, and welfare problems; and the Raymond V. Ingersoll Tenants Association, which dealt with housing problems.

Also nearby were Operation Intellect, which provided tutoring services and remedial courses for students and dropouts; the Progressive Youth Organization, which helped prepare young people for jobs; and the Faith Charity Fund, which provided consumer education and cultural-recreational sessions.

All these agencies and quite a few more were linked together under the auspices of the Fort Greene Community Corporation, the local arm of the federal antipoverty program.

The community corporation also supervised the funding of the Manpower job training and employment program and the Neighborhood Youth Corps programs.

All of these services were begun in the 1960s as part of the Johnson administration's "war on poverty." Antipoverty corporations staffed by community leaders and funded by the federal government were set up across the country to improve educational and job opportunities for the poor, and generally to help upgrade the quality of life in ghetto areas.

In Fort Greene, the local community corporation and all its delegate agencies started out with a flourish, and with the conviction that the evils of poverty could be eliminated now that they were being tackled by dedicated workers and sizeable federal funds. The staffs of the antipoverty agencies were drawn from the most dynamic and active community leaders of Fort Greene, many of whom were very poor themselves or on welfare. Some had been the leaders of local welfare rights organizations; others had organized rent strikes and fought for better housing; and others had been involved in the battle for community control of the schools. In short, they were the doers and organizers in the neighborhood, and they became the directors, administrators, and staff workers of the local antipoverty agencies.

The parent organization—the Fort Greene Community Corporation—was set up in an antiquated office building on Flatbush Avenue, while the delegate agencies were spread out in storefronts throughout the community.

At first these storefronts were gleaming new additions to the neighborhood, and their very presence seemed to indicate that the whole area would soon be uplifted. Posters, bulletins, and newspaper clippings announcing various social services or informing people of their rights were plastered in the windows, and enthusiasm ran high. It was a heady and exciting time for the poor.

But as the months and years passed, conditions in the

community did not really seem to improve as a result of the antipoverty operations, at least not in any significant way. People in the community were confused about what all the agencies were actually doing, for in most cases their specific functions were not very clear and they seemed to blur into one another, as if they did not really have distinct purposes.

Periodically, the community corporation issued reports on all that it had accomplished, but its claims seemed highly exaggerated. For example, the food-buying clubs supposedly serviced 28,320 people between 1970 and 1972—yet strangely enough the local supermarkets didn't notice any decline in sales; they barely knew that the buying clubs existed.

In the field of housing the agencies were supposed to have handled 25,409 individual cases in 1971–72, which would mean that about one-third of the entire population of Fort Greene sought help with housing problems that year through the poverty program alone!

Such apparently inflated figures probably stemmed from the fact that the funding for the antipoverty agencies depended on the number of people those agencies served. Zephaniah Nesbitt, who was assistant director of the Neighborhood Youth Corps for a time, acknowledged in a progress report that "the numbers game" is an "ever present aspect of our nation's antipoverty war. It was probably not preconceived that this be so. However, it is part and parcel of the program. Almost all funding is distributed on the basis of numbers (quantity). . . . Programs were evaluated on the basis of whether they serviced their quota or not. This was by no means the only criterion; but by and large it was the primary one. . . . Our program (as are all others in the city) is subject to numerical review every two months."

This would indicate that the agencies were forced to concentrate on how many people they served rather than on how well they served them, so that their emphasis was distorted from the outset.

In addition, there were instances when funds were apparently misappropriated or misused. Stories circulated that teenagers who worked for the Job Corps in the summer were still listed on the payroll in the fall or winter, even though they weren't working there anymore. In another instance, the community corporation was supposed to have sent ten busloads of people to Washington to protest cutbacks in federal spending. People paid twenty dollars apiece for the trip, although the buses were available at seven dollars a head. When it was over, people started saying that only six or seven buses actually made the trip, leaving about one thousand dollars unaccounted for.

One person who used to work for the poverty program said the attitude among a lot of the staff, especially in the last year or two, was "You make a killing, take what you can out of the program, and then leave it, because it's not going to be there for long anyhow." But others said it wasn't so much a matter of embezzlement, but rather that the administrators just didn't know how to handle funds. Whatever the reason, charges of fiscal irresponsibility and waste were hurled at almost all the community corporations, not just the one in Fort Greene (if anything, the Fort Greene Corporation was apparently *less* irresponsible than many of the others), and by 1972 it was becoming clear that the future of the poverty program as a whole was in doubt.

The enthusiasm and high hopes that people had for the program had begun to fade long before this. In Fort Greene, even the staffs of the various agencies seemed to lose faith, and many of the storefronts on Myrtle Avenue and elsewhere were allowed to deteriorate. Windows went unwashed for so long that people on the street could hardly see through them anymore, and faded, yellowing news clips were still being displayed long after they were outdated. It seemed that instead of uplifting the neighborhood, the antipoverty agencies themselves were reduced to the general level of dilapidation on Myrtle Avenue. Despite their efforts, they had hardly made a dent in the multitudinous problems of poverty and had accomplished little in proportion to the money that was spent.

In January 1973 President Nixon announced that he was dismantling the Office of Economic Opportunity in Washington and impounding funds for the antipoverty program because it simply hadn't worked. This meant that the local community corporations would be dissolved and all the people who staffed the neighborhood antipoverty agencies would be out of work. In Fort Greene this involved over a hundred people who had been full-time employees, plus countless others who had gotten part-time or summer jobs with the antipoverty program.

Aside from the loss of jobs, the main damage done by President Nixon's action was symbolic—it indicated very clearly that his administration did not give a damn about the poor and was far more eager to pull out of the "war on poverty" than it had been to pull out of the war in Vietnam. No significant new social welfare proposals were put forward to replace the poverty program, so the poor were left with nothing at all.

To make matters worse, the president announced across-the-board cutbacks in federal spending for education, health, housing, employment, and legal services for the poor, and the abolition of the urban renewal and model cities programs. These cutbacks may have hurt poor neighborhoods far more than the curtailment of the antipoverty program, for they struck a blow at vital institutions such as schools, hospitals, day-care centers, and mental health clinics.

In Fort Greene, as elsewhere, the few antipoverty agencies that had been successful were slated for elimination along with the others. Among them was Project Teen-Aid, the high school for pregnant adolescents. This too was a delegate agency of the Fort Greene Community Corporation. John Glover, executive director of the Willoughby House Settlement, echoed the sentiments of many people in Fort Greene when he said, "On the whole, a lot of the antipoverty programs were a waste, but Project Teen-Aid was an exception. That was really a very good place, and it shouldn't be disbanded."

There is a chance it won't be, because as with most of the other antipoverty agencies, the staff of Project Teen-Aid has been hunting around desperately for other sources of funding. Director Marie Swearer believes there is a good chance that the school will be picked up by the city's Human Resources Agency and will operate as part of the Department of Social Services. However, Ms. Swearer isn't totally happy about this.

"One good thing about the poverty program was that it was structured to meet the needs of what was going on at the moment," she said. "It was flexible. Like, when I had a problem I didn't have to go through any bureaucracy. I would just call up someone who could help and say, 'Here's the problem. . . .' But under HRA I probably won't have that kind of freedom, and if it becomes too structured it'll be just like the welfare centers—all red tape and forms. I think we'd have more freedom if we were sponsored by a foundation rather than HRA, but there aren't any in sight for this program.

"Overall, I think most people in poor neighborhoods like this won't really care about the elimination of the poverty program. They'll take it just like any other thing that's happened to them. It's not like ten years ago when there was really a surge of hope, with civil rights and the start of the war on poverty and even small things like the pairing of P.S. 7-8. Everybody thought it was a new day, and you had all this hope.

"But then it turned out that the poverty program didn't work. I don't care what anybody says, it just hasn't worked. The agencies haven't done anywhere near what they could have done. There were agencies that were supposed to handle

voter registration drives, but if you take a look at the registration in Fort Greene, you'll see it's still very low. These
agencies just haven't done their job.

"The food-buying clubs were supposed to do a lot of
consumer education, but they haven't. They got hung up in
just running the stores, and that's not good enough. You have
to get out and show people how to do comparative buying,
and convince them not to sign documents without reading
them when they're buying furniture. It's a shame that the
furniture stores around here are just so poor. The quality of
the furniture is disgusting. There's Mullins and Michael's and
two small furniture stores on Myrtle Avenue that work on
the same kind of installment plan. People get in debt and they
go to the loan sharks—a lot of people do that—and then they
spend the rest of their lives just paying off interest and never
even getting to the principal.

"If the poverty program was working like it should, they
could've taken kids in the Job Corps and trained them in
things like upholstery, furniture-making, carpentry, and so
on. They could have made sturdy, good-quality stuff, and
then people in the community would have been able to buy
this furniture right from the Job Corps and they wouldn't
have to go to places like Mullins.

"But a lot of opportunities went to waste, and the poverty
program wasn't effective. So you have all this frustration, and
people are at a point now where they just don't care.

"Like, I've gone to meetings at the Fort Greene Community Corporation, and they didn't even talk about services
to the people. All they were worried about was their jobs.

"Just look at how all our leaders have gotten co-opted. I
used to be involved with a lot of leaders in welfare rights. I
was younger then, and idealistic, and I loved demonstrations.
It was a lot of fun. But then the city just cropped off the whole
top of the welfare rights group and put them into private jobs.
Now, I call that a concerted effort. I think it was planned

that way. The last welfare rights handbook I got was about four years ago, and I don't think they've really done anything since. It's the same with a lot of the other local groups that used to be pretty militant. There's no one left now.

"I was thinking about getting together a neighborhood coalition, but then I realized, 'Who do we have to lead us?' I mean, I'm fine on an organizational basis. I can do a lot of junky things like making phone calls and talking to people, but I can't get up in front of a group and give them leadership. There's no one person in Fort Greene now who can lead everybody. We used to have Carlos Russell, but first he went into Human Resources and now he's head of an urban study program at Brooklyn College, so he's not active in the community anymore.

"It's happened all over. You don't hear anything from Milton Galamison now, or from Rhody McCoy—I guess he's just about destroyed. And look at the people who have been killed. Martin Luther King is dead; Malcolm X is dead; Robert Kennedy is dead—all the people who would have had a following and pulled us out of this and given us direction. There's no leadership on the national level, and none on the community level either."

Although the antipoverty groups went to court and got a reprieve until June 1974, clearly the end is at hand. What the federal government gave to poor neighborhoods in the 1960s it is now taking away. Nothing demonstrates more clearly how little control poor neighborhoods have over their own fortunes because the decision on the merits of the poverty program was not made by the communities that were directly affected, but by the Nixon administration far off in Washington. Local antipoverty leaders—ensconced in good jobs with generous salaries and impressive titles—had the trappings of power but not the reality of it. The big decisions were not in their hands.

People in poverty areas are heavily dependent on the government for a great many of their vital needs, and those on welfare are dependent even for the bread they eat. Yet they consistently fail to use one of the major weapons they have to influence government actions—the vote. In both national and local elections, the voting turnout in Fort Greene is pitifully low, perhaps because the people simply have no faith that anything they do will change things. As a result, the community has been represented in Congress (or rather, *not* represented) for more than twenty-five years by John Rooney, who is hardly sympathetic to their interests and has seldom set foot in Fort Greene in the last decade.

On the state level, Fort Greene at one time was gerrymandered into a Staten Island district and wound up being represented in the State Senate by the ultraconservative John Marchi. (Eventually a court edict put Fort Greene back into Brooklyn.)

As far as their city councilman is concerned, most people in the project area of Fort Greene have never even heard of him because he is so totally invisible. But one woman who moved from University Towers in Fort Greene to Brooklyn Heights —which is in the same councilmanic district—was amazed to discover that the councilman, Fred Richmond, was considered by the people there as very active and responsive to their needs. But of course Brooklyn Heights delivers both the votes and the campaign contributions, while the low-income population of Fort Greene delivers neither.

Right now, the mood of the country and of the Nixon administration is very antipoor, and the people in Fort Greene are really feeling it. The most vulnerable are those on welfare, who make up about twenty-five percent of the population in the project area, and those who are living below the poverty level but are not on welfare.

As political pressures demand greater cuts in the welfare

rolls, many poor people in Fort Greene are discouraged from getting the help they need by such means as lengthy and difficult application forms and the need to produce the type of detailed documentation that many poor people simply do not have and don't know how to get. In short, they are being intimidated.

In the matter of finding jobs for welfare recipients, the various "workfare" programs have not been a notable success so far. The percentage of job placements is low, and many of the jobs that welfare recipients do get last only a short time, either because they quit or because they get laid off. The main problem with most of these jobs is that they pay so little that people are really better off on welfare—with all its extra benefits—than they are if they work.

The job-training programs that are supposed to give poor people and welfare recipients skills with which to obtain better paying jobs are also not very successful. Practically every other person you meet in Fort Greene has been through some sort of job-training program at one time or another, yet their earning power remains very low because they often can't get jobs in the occupation for which they were trained. Maybe not enough jobs exist in these fields to begin with, or maybe employers would rather not hire them because they lack a stable work history. Whatever the reason, the result is that job-training programs raise people's hopes and expectations, and then often leave them doubly frustrated when they still can't get decent paying jobs. All of these training programs should be tied in much more closely with the specific needs of businesses and industries, and an all-out effort should be made to line up a pool of employers who would agree in advance to hire a certain number of trainees. In this way the training programs could feed directly into jobs.

Perhaps it is also time to approach the problem of welfare from a different angle, and to take a good look at the kinds of jobs that *are* readily available right now and that welfare recipients *can* get—that is, the lowest paying jobs in the city. These are the jobs that pay the minimum wage or slightly more (sometimes less) and may bring in an income of under four thousand dollars annually for full-time work—substantially below the poverty level for a family of four in New York City. Most often these are the only kinds of jobs that welfare mothers, in particular, are able to get.

If these jobs were subsidized by the government—if a floor were put under the salary of every full-time job in the city— then even the most unskilled and undereducated man or woman could at least earn a living wage in exchange for his labor and would have a very real incentive for getting off welfare. As it is now, the working poor are no better off than the welfare poor, and this very fact demeans the dignity of labor in a country as wealthy as ours. A subsidy to the working poor, somewhat on the order of a guaranteed annual income, could help revive this dignity by bringing people's earnings above the poverty level and genuinely improving their standard of living. (This assumes, of course, that the wage floor would be set high enough to make a real difference.)

The cash subsidy, or wage floor, might vary according to the number of dependents an employee had, so that it would enable men with low earning power who cannot make more than eighty or ninety dollars a week on their own to earn enough to support a family. On the assumption that a man is more likely to desert his family if he can't support them and that his living with them in poverty only reinforces his sense of failure, a wage floor might very well help reduce the large number of one-parent, female-headed families that now comprise the bulk of the welfare population.

Although the costs of such a program might be staggering at first, they would be offset eventually if the wage subsidy succeeded in drawing significant numbers of people off the welfare rolls. After all, it is much cheaper for the government to subsidize a working family than to support that family entirely. Also, it is better to put money directly into poor people's hands than to set up costly and ultimately ineffective operations such as the antipoverty program.

The subsidy need not be all in cash. The working poor should be able to retain a lot of benefits they would receive if they were on welfare—such as Medicaid—by paying a small percentage of their earnings. As their earnings went up, the amount they pay could increase. This would be better than the way the system works now, because at present someone whose income jumps from forty-five hundred dollars a year gross to sixty-five hundred, for example, immediately loses Medicaid, food stamps, day-care services (under the new regulations), and just about every other welfare benefit, leaving him at about the same level as before he got the large raise.

The combination of a wage floor plus benefits could make even the lowliest work worthwhile in terms of a higher living standard, and would give people more of a reason to stick with a job and try to perform well on it so as not to be fired. This in turn might benefit the many small, marginal businesses and factories that provide the bulk of the unskilled and low-paying jobs in New York City. A lot of these small operations are in trouble because they can't get steady, reliable help at the wages they can afford to pay. A study by the State Labor Department predicts a decline of about 22,200 jobs in the city by mid-1975 as more apparel manufacturing firms and other small businesses shut down because they can't compete. A subsidy to the underpaid employees of these businesses would be, in effect, a subsidy to the businesses themselves and might help them remain alive and well in New York City.

Epilogue: Fort Greene, U.S.A.

IN LOOKING at a poverty area such as Fort Greene in New York City, it would appear from the outside that very few changes have taken place over the last ten years, and that living conditions are about the same as they were before the civil rights campaigns and militant demonstrations of the sixties began. But if you look a little deeper, you see that this is really not so. There are a number of positive forces at work in these areas that are having an important effect on the economic and social structure of the communities.

For example, if you walk into a store in Fort Greene or Bedford-Stuyvesant today, the black man behind the counter may very well be the owner rather than the clerk. This alone is a significant change from ten years ago.

With the advent of school decentralization, there are many more black and Puerto Rican supervisors and administrators on a districtwide level than there were before. Black school principals are no longer such a rarity, and in Fort Greene almost all the newly appointed principals are black. There are somewhat more black teachers now, too, although the changeover has been very slow on this front. All in all, there has been a steadily increasing amount of black and Puerto

Rican control over schools in predominantly black and Puerto Rican neighborhoods.

Minority groups have become more prominent in other fields, too. In Brooklyn Hospital black nurses are being elevated to higher positions than they ever held before, and many black social workers are on the hospital staff. The director of the Fort Greene Senior Citizens Center is a young black woman; her assistant is a white man. The director of the Fort Greene Day-Care Center is a black woman; the executive director of the Willoughby House Settlement is also black; and so it goes. Increasingly the positions of authority in the neighborhood are being filled by black people.

The same is true regarding the staff and supervisors in the welfare centers in and around Fort Greene. In fact, one black welfare supervisor recalled an incident a short time ago when a white man came storming up to her desk demanding to get on public assistance immediately. "I told him he would have to go through the regular procedure just like everybody else," she said. "But he wasn't satisfied with that and he kept screaming at me. Finally he said, 'I don't want to deal with you! I don't want to deal with no blacks and no Jews! Get me someone else!' Well, I wouldn't have minded getting him someone else—anything just to get rid of him—but in our center there's hardly anybody except blacks and Jews. Finally I got hold of this one worker, our only Wasp, and I asked him to help me out with that loudmouth character."

Further evidence of the growth of the black middle class can be seen in the brownstone area of Fort Greene, where black teachers, accountants, businessmen, engineers, and architects are buying and renovating their own townhouses, along with white middle-class homeowners. It is a "changing" neighborhood in the sense that it is changing from poor to middle class, and as it changes it is becoming more effective politically. The new brownstoners were able to induce the city to restore Fort Greene Park to its former loveliness and have also been waging a well-publicized battle to reduce the number and size of the methadone centers in the area. However, many of the poor people who used to live in the brownstones in Fort Greene are not benefiting from the changes at all, since they have been pushed out of the neighborhood entirely, often into worse housing in Bedford-Stuyvesant and elsewhere.

Another positive force at work in Fort Greene is the fact that abortions are now legal and birth control devices are much more readily available. Indications are that more and more women are taking advantage of these developments to keep their family size down, and in the long run this may have a strong impact in reducing the welfare rolls and raising the standard of living in poverty areas. One immediate effect has been that far fewer unwanted babies are being left in the hospitals now.

Medicaid—another positive force—has already done much to improve health care in communities like Fort Greene, and its potential is even greater. The trouble is, many poor people regard Medicaid as so vital to their well-being that they are afraid to get off welfare for fear of losing their Medicaid benefits. This is another reason why Medicaid should be extended to far more working people than are currently eligible.

The three-year-old open admissions policy of City University is another factor that may ultimately benefit poverty areas insofar as it induces youngsters to finish high school by guaranteeing them automatic admission to a free college. But with the colleges—just as with the job-training programs—much more effort should be made to guide students into fields where there is a demand for their services. Otherwise, despite their extra years of education and training, they may still wind up as a glut on the job market. This is something that is happening right now to education majors who cannot find jobs because there is a surplus of teachers.

All of the above are positive forces that may in the long run improve the quality of life in ghetto areas, and many of these forces were set in motion as a direct or indirect result of the black militancy of the sixties. But there are also negative forces at work, the most obvious of which right now is the Nixon administration. The president has openly demonstrated his disdain for the poor by impounding funds that Congress had specifically allocated to improve the health, education, and general well-being of poor Americans. Such actions on the part of the president not only deprive the poor of badly needed services; they also affect the intangibles, such as people's dreams for a better life. After five years of Mr. Nixon's indifference, the people in Fort Greene seem apathetic and apolitical. The revolutionary fervor of the sixties has passed, and a sense of resignation has set in. Considering the broad scope of the federal cutbacks and the sudden, total elimination of the poverty program, there has been relatively little protest in Fort Greene or any other poor community in New York City. In commenting on the current apathy, Marie Swearer said, "If you remember the book *1984,* they had this group of people who lived in the slums and they just didn't care. They just weren't involved in trying to change things. Well, this is what I think is happening now, and it's really horrible when you think about it."

Such apathy is not confined to Fort Greene alone, or even just to the New York area. It appears to be nationwide, for in the last year or two there has been very little turmoil in poor communities anywhere across the country. The abandonment of the antipoverty program—a federal undertaking that was nationwide in scope—plus all the other damaging cutbacks in federal funding affected thousands of poor communities from the East Coast to the West Coast, yet nowhere did the poor band together for any sort of dynamic or militant action. In this respect, the prevailing mood of apathy in Fort Greene has been typical of the mood in poor neighborhoods everywhere.

On the other hand, the advances that have been made by blacks and Puerto Ricans in Fort Greene are also fairly typical of what has been happening in other poor urban communities. Neighborhoods are not isolated islands that evolve all by themselves; they are interdependent, and they simply reflect the changes that are taking place in society as a whole. Thus, by taking a close look at one particular poor urban neighborhood, we are really getting a glimpse of how the poor are faring in cities all over America. In short, Brooklyn's Fort Greene could just as well be anyplace in the nation where the urban poor are clustered.